amer. Int
Phillip

478
Date Loaned

Traditions in American Literature

TRADITIONS IN

AMERICAN LITERATURE

A STUDY OF JEWISH CHARACTERS AND AUTHORS

BY JOSEPH MERSAND

THE MODERN CHAPBOOKS, NEW YORK, 1939

Copyright 1939, by Joseph Mersand. Composed and printed in the United States of America by union labor at The Comet Press, Brooklyn, New York. First printing, June 1939 65 JJB

To My Parents

CONTENTS

PART ONE: JEWISH AUTHORS

1.	Jewish Dramatists and the Contemporary Drama	1
2.	George S. Kaufman: Master of the Technique of of Good Theatre	14
3.	Elmer Rice: Realist of the Drama	25
4.	Clifford Odets: Anatomist of Frustration	32
5.	S. N. Behrman and the American Comedy of Manners	51
6.	Irwin Shaw	68
7.	Bella and Samuel Spewack	73
8.	Jewish Novelists and the Contemporary American Novel	78
9.	Jewish Novelists Portray the Jew, 1867-1939	83
10.	Robert Nathan: Master of Style and Mood	93
11.	Ben Hecht: The Re-Discovery of the Artist	112
12.	Jewish Poets in America in the Nineteenth Century	118
13.	Contemporary Jewish Poets in America	128

CONTENTS

PART TWO: THE JEW AS PORTRAYED IN AMERICAN LITERATURE

14.	A Survey of Three Centuries	149
15.	The American Drama Presents the Jew	164
16.	Farewell to Shylocks and Fagins	175
17.	Righteousness above Compromise: Noble Jewish Literary Types	181
18.	The Jew in War and Peace	186
19.	Victims of Nazism as Portrayed in American Drama	192

BIBLIOGRAPHIES

1.	A List of Novels and Short Stories of Interest to Students of Jewish Life in America	201
2.	A List of Plays of Interests to Students of Jewish Life in America	209
3.	Volumes of Poetry by Contemporary Jewish Poets in America	213
4.	Autobiographies of American Jews	221
5.	Biographies Written by American Jews	224
6.	Books of Criticism and Belles-Lettres	227
7.	General Bibliography	230
	Footnotes	237
	Index	239

viii

PREFACE

Literature by Jewish writers in America appeared as early as 1636, four years before the printing of the first book in English in the American colonies. In the three centuries since then Jewish authors have made significant contributions to the American literary tradition. Although isolated studies have appeared of certain authors, such as Isaac Goldberg's *Major Noah* and Lucius Moise's *Isaac Harby,* no complete historical and critical survey of all the American writers of Jewish origin exists. One volume of convenient size could not do justice to even a fraction of the literature which has already appeared.

The misfortunes which have overtaken the Jews of Germany, Austria, Czechoslovakia, Poland, and Roumania, and the many misrepresentations which have precipitated the cultural and economic impoverishment of almost a third of the world's Jews must be taken as a warning to those who are more fortunate to be on their guard. Slanders and falsifications must be met with objective truth. For example, critics should not be able to state unchallenged of the contemporary American drama that it is *verjudet* as it was said of the German drama in its renaissance after the Great War. Jewish talents should not be minimized, and falsehoods about Jewish writers' attitudes toward our political and economic problems must be exposed.

Many malicious libels have gone unanswered because the mate-

PREFACE

rial with which to deny them was not at hand. Here and there a novel of Jewish life in America, like Abraham Cahan's *The Rise of David Levinsky* or Ludwig Lewisohn's *The Island Within,* becomes nationally known. Yet there have been scores of novels and plays of Jewish interest with which the general reading and theatre-going publics are hardly acquainted. One aim of this book is to indicate such works for those who wish to read more intensively in this rich field of literature. In the appreciation of the contemporary drama, particularly, those who live away from the play-producing centres like New York, Chicago, and Boston, are at a great disadvantage. Do the Jews of Texas, Oregon, or any state far from New York know such plays as Elmer Rice's *Counsellor-at-Law,* Irwin Shaw's *The Gentle People,* and Clifford Odets' *Awake and Sing*? These are studies of Jewish life in America by Jewish playwrights, which aroused considerable discussion in New York. It is not unreasonable to assume that they will prove equally interesting to students of Jewish problems who are living in other sections of America. Hence a detailed study has been made in this volume of both the portrayal of Jews in contemporary drama and of the significant plays by American dramatists of Jewish origin.

Even a casual glance at some of the criticisms of novels of Jewish life will reveal the necessity for such an extensive analysis of this type of American fiction as is presented in the following pages. Hundreds of these novels have been written in America. To date no organized study has been made of them, although it is desirable. In this book only an initial attempt can be made to distinguish the various types of characters, authors' points of view, locales and styles of writing.

Finality would obviously be impossible in a branch of literature which is growing constantly. An encyclopedia of many volumes, rather than a single book, could do justice to the topic. A great service would be accomplished for American culture and the Jewish contributions thereto if a corps of American scholars would cooperate in writing such an encyclopedia. Americans,

PREFACE

both Jews and Christians, have been made more conscious of Jewish problems in the last few years than ever before. Hence a frank exposition of the Jewish participation in America's cultural growth may be of some benefit to the cause of mutual understanding and appreciation.

A few words of explanation are required in order to account for the treatment of certain phases of the subject. Since the book has not been written primarily for scholars, it does not pretend to be a complete history of the literature about and by Jews in America. Only some of the more interesting personalities of the nineteenth and twentieth centuries have been discussed. The bibliography, however, will guide any student who chooses to perfect his knowledge in any particular literary personality or movement. The author has not written a book of final authority, but a collection of essays for the general reader who may be interested and stimulated to acquaint himself with this abundant literature. The bibliography of books and articles contains the most readily available material, and does not pretend to be complete. The vast Yiddish and Hebrew literatures which have appeared in America have been excluded because they deserve individual volumes. Only the writings in English come within the scope of this study.

Since we are all more aware of, and interested in, the present than in the past, the contemporary contributions of Jewish authors have been emphasized. The essay on Robert Nathan discusses for the first time the complete literary output of one of the most gifted of all American novelists, who in the last five years has become more and more conscious of his Jewish heritage. S. N. Behrman and George S. Kaufman are represented because they are outstanding artists in their respective fields of drama; the former in the comedy of manners, the latter in the more popular comedy of character. Elmer Rice, Clifford Odets, Irwin Shaw, the Spewacks, and Ben Hecht have written primarily about the entire American scene and only occasionally, although provocatively, about Jewish life in America. Their entire creative output is

PREFACE

evaluated because they have entered the front rank in their own special spheres.

The division of the book into *The Jew as Author* and *The Jew as Subject* is a natural one, since the American literary tradition includes both phases.

The remaining essays are self-explanatory. They indicate the many ramifications of the subject. The studies of the Jewish writers on war, and the Jewish writers on nazism are only two of a number of similar investigations which might well suggest research in other fields. The Jewish physician, teacher, social worker, civil servant, diplomat, philanthropist, spiritual leader, and farmer are only a few of the personalities who might be suitable subjects for special essays. When the average critic speaks of them he always has a certain stereotyped representative in mind and all his criticisms are limited by his preconceptions. It is time that these vague generalizations gave way to scientific studies based on all the material at hand.

To summarize, the aims of the writer are: first, to inform; second, to stimulate to further reading; third, to provide ideas for discussion and debate; and finally, to introduce conclusions based on an actual acquaintance with the people and the literature about them.

The author is indebted to many friends and advisers for any merits the book may contain. For all its faults he assumes complete responsibility. To the editors of *Opinion, The Advocate,* and *The Jewish Spectator,* he extends his thanks for their kind permission to reprint certain essays which originally appeared in their periodicals. To Dr. Trude Weiss Rosmarin, Director of the School of the Jewish Woman, and Dr. Sidney B. Hoenig, Educational Director of the Young Israel Extension Courses of Yeshiva College, he wishes to express his gratitude for the opportunity to present many of the ideas of this book in the classes of these institutions of adult learning. He is grateful to his many students in these classes and to his listeners of many cultural organizations who have inspired and encouraged him to pursue

PREFACE

studies in this field. It was their interest which prompted the writing of a book which they might consult at their convenience.

To the publishers of copyrighted material he is grateful for permission to use quotations the absence of which would have made the book less valuable. These are indicated in their proper place in the text.

It is perhaps unfair to single out individuals for special mention when a book is really the result of the inspiration and suggestion of hundreds, but the writer cannot forego the privilege of thanking Rabbi Isaac Landman, of the Congregation Beth Elohim of Brooklyn, for reading the manuscript, for his many valuable suggestions and criticisms, for the privilege of contributing to the *Standard Jewish Encyclopedia,* and for his readiness to place at my disposal his rich resources as rabbi, scholar, and editor. Miss Delsy M. Jablow has prepared the copious index and has been unsparing in her encouragement in many moments of doubt, her generous advice, and her genuine interest. He is deeply indebted also to Mr. Allen Lesser for many comments and corrections and his sincere criticism; Rabbi Abraham A. Burstein for his assistance; Mr. Edward D. Coleman, Secretary of the American Jewish Historical Society, for material placed at the author's disposal; Mr. Henry Hurwitz, Editor of *The Menorah Journal,* for helpful comments; and Miss Claire H. Danchig, Dr. Abraham B. Berman, and Mr. Jacob Rapoport who have assisted in correcting the proofs.

The author's tasks in seeing the book through the press have been considerably lightened by the cooperation of Mr. Samuel Chernoble and his associates of the Comet Press.

J. M.

Brooklyn, New York
June 1, 1939

PART ONE

Jewish Authors

1. JEWISH DRAMATISTS

AND THE CONTEMPORARY DRAMA

The evaluation of the contributions of Jewish creative artists to the pre-eminence of American drama in the world today is a hazardous undertaking. Those professional anti-Semites who will not endure the participation of Jews in any activity denied to them in the Dark Ages will find more material for their prejudices in the statements about outstanding Jews of the American theatre. Those who are less violent in their attitude toward Jews, but who suffer from excessive xenophobia, will find much cause for regrets and laments in the fact that significant figures in the American theatre today should be Rice, Kaufman, Odets, Behrman, Kingsley, Sklar, Wexley, Maltz, Bein and Lawson.

The future historian of the American theatre of the last fifteen years cannot ignore the rôle of American Jews in making American drama the most vital in the world today, as it is conceded to be by most authorities. It is as an objective student of the drama in America that one comes to the conclusion that American Jews have played a most important part in bringing to this country the banner of supreme excellence in the field of dramatic arts.

Such a conclusion may result in no lasting benefit to American Jews and may make even more intense the feeling of antagonism to Jewish influence of any kind. There have been precedents in other countries in which Jewish artists have assumed nation-wide importance. One cannot easily forget the statement in an essay on French civilization printed in the *Atlantic Monthly* of August, 1918:

Does anybody who knows the real state of affairs imagine that the French stage is French? It has long ceased to be. All the prominent managers, actors, and actresses are Jews; and while I am aware that many Jews living in France have done remarkably well during the war, and while I think that a book which was written about them ought to have had more success, I cannot help feeling that the Jewish influence is not good. Greed and vanity are its mainsprings, materialism invariably goes with it, and the sentimentalism, attitudinizing, and meretriciousness generally, which I deplore, have been created by the unusual admiration of the Romanticist of low degree and the Jewish actress of whatever degree, including Rachel herself. There was no trace of it in French literature before the nineteenth century, and any visitor who has a chance to meet enough specimens of undoubted origin becomes convinced that it is not indigenous.[1]

Notice, if you will, all the old clichés of denunciation which so frequently confront the Jewish artist: greed, vanity, materialism. John Wexley, pleading the cause of justice in *The Last Mile;* Elmer Rice, showing how innocent men may be railroaded to death in a dictatorship in *Judgment Day;* Sidney Kingsley, demonstrating the appalling influence of wrong environment on youngsters at the impressionable age in his *Dead End*—all these sincere artists, burning with their desire to tell the truth as they see it would be accused of "sentimentalism, attitudinizing, and meretriciousness" by followers of the school of critics represented by the author of the aforementioned essay.

Pre-Hitlerite Germany was by no means fair in its appraisal of the merits of its Jewish dramatists. It was after the World War that the term *Verjudung* was coined to express the contempt of the Jew-baiters for the efforts of Jewish men of the theatre like Max Reinhardt, Ernst Toller, Franz Werfel and Stefan Zweig, who were helping to make the drama of Germany the most original in all of Europe.

---

1. All references are given in a special section at the end of the book.

JEWISH DRAMATISTS

Ludwig Lewisohn, and Alfred Kerr.

The anti-Semites are quite right: modern German literature is 'verjudet.' From the days of Heine and Börne on, German literature and art have been under a critical and creative Jewish influence which is out of all proportion to the Jewish population . . . .

Writing in the *Menorah Journal* in the August-September, 1926, issue, the famous German critic, J. E. Poritzky, stated:

But all that I have said gives no clear picture of the greatness, the extent, and the significance of Jewish influence and Jewish activity in German literature. To finish the picture we should tell how many stage directors, stage managers, actors, critics, editors are Jews. The percentage is so great that at first one is inclined to be incredulous.

All this has been destroyed. Who knows what part this great Jewish influence played in serving as campaign material for Hitler and his cohorts? In America the cry against Jewish influence on the stage has already been raised, now indirectly, now blatantly and unmistakably. It is surprising, however, that such opinions should come from a former member of the dramatic staff of the *New York Times*. Writing in *Scribner's* of May, 1933, John Corbin declared:

When a people comprise only a small fraction of a nation's population, and who hold themselves aloof from the main currents of its life, find themselves a major influence in its drama, the situation is fraught with difficulty and danger

Mr. Corbin was particularly concerned with the "Jewish domination" of the Theatre Guild, as he termed it, which was responsible, in his opinion, for the preponderance of plays of satirical or ironical content. It was impossible, he declared, for the directorate to see anything praiseworthy in American life. Hence the preference for the plays of Bernard Shaw, grand old American-baiter, and for Eugene O'Neill, who was a corrupting influence because of his pictures of degenerate native American stock in *Strange Interlude, Beyond the Horizon,* and *Mourning*

Becomes Electra. Such a claim is preposterous, of course, to anyone who has attended the performances of all of the plays produced by the Theatre Guild. Certainly no plays could be more respectful of American history and ideals than Anderson's *Valley Forge* and O'Neill's *Ah, Wilderness* and *Days Without End.* If the Theatre Guild has produced no plays glorifying the Battle of Bunker Hill or the victory of the *Monitor,* it is because America is still a country where plays must be plays and not chauvinistic rantings.

A true evaluation of the part dramatists of Jewish origin are playing in the enrichment of the American theatre can be obtained from a contemplation of recent dramatic seasons. There is Clifford Odets whose four plays in one year represent the richest output of any American dramatist of 1935. Even Eugene O'Neill could not approach in creative composition in one year the combined merit of *Waiting for Lefty, Till the Day I Die, Awake and Sing,* and *Paradise Lost.* New York's critical confraternity has treated the Group Theatre's outstanding dramatist with extreme consideration. He has been considered the great white hope of the American theatre now that O'Neill seems interested in mysticism in *Days Without End,* or reminiscing of the joys of yesteryear in *Ah, Wilderness.* The critics have done much for Odets. They gave him encouragement when he faltered, adulation rarely granted to contemporary dramatists when he succeeded, and they expressed a sincere faith in his artistic future. His play, *Golden Boy,* won new laurels in America and in London.

Rocket to the Moon, which opened in New York in November, 1938, revealed a deep interest in psychology, indicating a new departure for the dramatist. Odets is still developing his talents as a craftsman of the technique of the theatre and his insight into the emotions of human beings. John Masefield, poet laureate of England, told reporters when he arrived in America in 1936, "You can only have great art when you give great encouragement." The critics have done their full share in encouraging Odets to finer efforts.

Alfred Bein and Leopold Atlas were named by Barrett H. Clark, director of the play service for the Dramatists Guild, in a speech at the Mohawk Drama Festival on July 26, 1936 as among the most promising of the newer writers.

It would be neither interesting nor valuable to list the number of plays of Jewish authors produced each year; lists of stage designers, progressive producers, and directors would likewise be of little value. The question to be answered is not "Are many plays of Jewish dramatists produced?", but "Are plays of Jewish dramatists enriching American drama, art, and culture?"

Perhaps psychologists and sociologists could find acceptable explanations for the preoccupation of Jewish dramatists with the evils of our time. It may be the indignities and suppressions of the Jews carried in the blood-stream—erythrocytes of suffering for centuries—that make of such writers as Odets, Rice, Irwin Shaw, Sklar, Maltz, and Kingsley the spokesmen in the terms of dramatic art for the oppressed and the downtrodden. The story is told of the late Jakob Wassermann that he once described an oriental scene without ever having visited the country. When told by one who had lived in that region that his realistic description was marvellous in its verisimilitude, the novelist replied that he had never seen or read about the place. He explained it as some subconscious recollection of scenes in the home of his ancestors centuries ago.

Arthur Hopkins gave a somewhat similar explanation in an address delivered in 1935, "Is Amusement All?" Believing with the psychologist Jung that there exists within a man a complete record of whatever has happened emotionally to the species man, he contends that the dramatic genius has found access to this region of recollection and that true inspiration is but a sudden unaccountable revelation of this domain. Such a theory might explain the preoccupation with social improvement of the young Jewish playwrights of America.

It is strange that this very capacity of Odets and his contemporaries to magnify the potentialities of the stage for the projection of a more intense view of life has been considered a fault. Thus Samuel Barron, in *Harpers* of December, 1935, expressed his dislike for *Till the Day I Die* because it was burdened with "too heavy a load for the creaking proscenium arch to carry." That a dramatist should be criticized for extending the limits of his artistic medium seems faintly amusing to the student of the history of the theatre. This most inclusive of all the arts has ever been expanded by its outstanding practitioners. Euripides added a third character to the maximum of two that were permitted on the Athenian stage, and has always been praised for his innovation. No one knows how many cries of woe went up when the plays in the medieval churchyard developed into the miracle plays performed on large wagons. An unknown genius was responsible for fashioning *Everyman* out of the morality plays of his time. Shakespeare revised the tragedies of blood of Kyd and fashioned his great tragic masterpieces. Can one not hear the protagonists of the three unities bewailing the Bard's scenic peregrinations from Venice to Cyprus in *Othello,* through various parts of Scotland and England in *Macbeth,* through several Italian cities in *Romeo and Juliet?*

Molière fashioned the crude though lusty Commedia dell' Arte into a new and glittering variety of comedy. Ibsen took the well-made play of Scribe and transformed it into a vehicle of compactness in which each sentence had some intrinsic connection with the exposition of the past, development of character, or evaluation of the plot. Bernard Shaw transformed the stage into a lecture hall. O'Neill broke all dramatic rules, defied his teacher, George Pierce Baker, who denied that *The Moon of the Caribbees* was a play, and for a time was the most fruitful of all dramatists living. Now it is Clifford Odets and Marc Blitzstein and John Howard Lawson who push on to new frontiers in stageland.

Other members of the young Jewish craftsmen of the stage have enriched it in different directions. Mielziner created a *mise-*

en-scène in Maxwell Anderson's *Winterset* that was a drama in itself. Kingsley took a group of undernourished boys and gave them a reality so intense that the barrier between life and the stage was forgotten. Odets expressed in *Awake and Sing* the decline of a whole class from grandfather to grandson, with an economy of effort, a vividness of characterization, and a crushing power of conviction truly remarkable in a writer so young. More emotion about war and munition makers was conveyed in one evening with *Peace on Earth* by Sklar and Maltz, than by the Nye investigation for months. When have the sufferings of the Negro race in America been portrayed with such power as in Sklar and Peters' *Stevedore?* To compare it with *Uncle Tom's Cabin* is to realize how much the American theatre has advanced in the last seventy-five years. One calls to mind the speech Otis Skinner made after the Players' revival of the old classic in 1933. "It was grand theatre," said one of the grand old men of our theatre. Precisely! *Uncle Tom's Cabin* was good theatre. *Stevedore* was not theatrical, but true to life.

The young Jewish dramatists have told the truth about American life—truth as it was never told before. The South of magnolias and mint-juleps may still be the South of romantic novels, but it is not the South as pictured by Alfred Bein in *Let Freedom Ring.* When was the misery, the heartlessness, and the cruelty of mining life portrayed as faithfully as in *The Black Pit* by Albert Maltz? Certain people may object that "foreigners" are drawing false pictures of American life in such plays. But they are pictures of the real America. What Gerhart Hauptmann did forty years ago in his *Weavers,* these young Jewish dramatists have done for American industrial life.

Naturally there have been cries of complaint and indignation from those who look upon the theatre only as a place in which to rest from the labors of the day. In all certainty such true revelations of American life are not conducive to relaxation. Rather are they stimulants of the kind Aristotle had in mind when he ascribed to great tragedy the effects of pity and terror.

JEWISH DRAMATISTS

The authors of plays like *Stevedore, The Black Pit,* and *Awake and Sing,* are writers of tragedy in the noblest sense. They differ from the Greek tragedians and from great individualists like Shakespeare in the respect that they do not contemplate the tragic significance of a *single* character. Shakespeare could build a play about Hamlet, Othello or Macbeth, and could stir audiences to pity and terror over the base emotions of otherwise eminent personalities. In his age of individualism, when so many great personalities lived, his plays were of great significance. But in an age like ours, when one dictator may compel millions upon millions to live and think in precisely the same manner or pay for individuality with torture and loss of life, can the tragedy of the individual compare with the tragedy of the masses of human beings?

Kingsley's *Dead End* is not concerned with one youngster who must go to the reformatory. It cries out against all slums from Warsaw to Liverpool, from New York to Los Angeles, where environment breeds crime, disease, and death. The development of Sidney Kingsley from his interest in the individual physician in *Men in White* to the undernourished, misinformed children is paralleled by the development of the modern social American drama.

The Jewish dramatists may in some instances be the children of immigrants, but in certain respects they have seen most clearly the America of today and have presented their vision with great clarity, with a sincerity that is not the "hard, gem-like flame" of the aesthete Walter Pater, but that flaming zeal of the reformer of mankind.

Some of the most convincing realistic dramas of recent years have come from Jewish playwrights. It is fruitless to argue over the relative merits of realism and romanticism, naturalism and expressionism. Each is a way of contemplating human existence and it is puerile to contend that only one way is the right way. That is intellectual myopia or color-blindness, or both. The richly-cultured individual can appreciate a photograph because it has caught life in its reality and a landscape of Van Gogh because it has not attempted to do anything of the kind. To the realistic drama, Elmer Rice has contributed two plays that can scarcely be matched: *Street Scene,* which was awarded the Pulitzer Prize of 1928, and *Counsellor-at-Law* (1931). His succeeding plays have been more colored by his social consciousness. *We, the People,* coming in 1932 when the American theatre-goers were apparently not ready for the social drama, was financially unsuccessful, but indicative of the dramatist's courage in daring to assault the money-changers in their own temple. The disapproval of the ermine-wrapped and the mink-coated was similar to the disapproval that greeted Ibsen's plays when the present century was in its infancy. Today Nazimova, Ruth Gordon, and Eva Le Gallienne can tour the country in *Ghosts, A Doll's House,* and *Hedda Gabler* and score great personal triumphs. One never heard of a city banning the plays because they discussed controversial issues. Our American audiences have grown up. Some commissioners of police and city censors may ban a performance of *Waiting for Lefty* or *Let Freedom Ring,* but they are exceptional.

Other portraits of American life as viewed by Jewish eyes include Rose Franken's *Another Language,* one of the most significant plays of 1932. The struggle of the intellectually superior stranger against a family of intellectually stagnant men and women has achieved in this play unusually lucid expression.

Ben Hecht in collaboration with Charles MacArthur has attained a marvelous verisimilitude in *The Front Page.* Bella and Samuel Spewack have contributed some convincing portraits in *Boy Meets Girl, Spring Song,* and *Clear All Wires.* They represent also the Jewish writers of comedy who have been very successful.

The historian of the contemporary stage cannot help acknowledging the supremacy of S. N. Behrman in the comedy of manners, and of George S. Kaufman in theatrical technique. Behrman has progressed from his excessive preoccupation with the subconscious in his *Second Man,* his interest in the tycoon in *Meteor,* in the slut transformed in *Brief Moment* to his realization of the powerful forces attacking our civilization, in his *Rain from Heaven, End of Summer,* and *Wine of Choice.* His plays have dialogue that is matchless today for its crispness, pungency, and polish. He is still managing to present an objective, liberal point of view, but one wonders how long he will rely on mere objectivity to solve our problems. His mind is an embodiment of that cold impartial attitude of the Jew as man of science. He is the dramatic surgeon who can cut away the rationalizations and prejudices of his characters and reveal them to us naked in their insipidity. In his class belong such Jewish writers as Heine, Robert Nathan, Joseph Auslander, philosophers like Morris Raphael Cohen and Sidney Hook, critics like Georg Brandes, Ludwig Lewisohn, and Alfred Kerr.

Mr. Corbin in the article quoted above speaks of the satire of George S. Kaufman, our most distinguished man of letters in that field. He admits that Kaufman's satire is truthful, though the derision is aimed at the low intelligence quotient of certain representatives of Anglo-Saxondom. In *Dulcy* we have a moronic young wife. In *To the Ladies* there is expressed a contempt for the foolish pretense on the part of the men that they supremely honor American womanhood. In *Beggar on Horseback* Kaufman ridiculed the Rotarian; in *Once in a Lifetime,* the absurdities of Hollywood; in *June Moon,* the vagaries of the popular song racket.

In *Dinner at Eight, Merrily We Roll Along, You Can't Take It With You* and *The American Way,* Kaufman has stopped poking fun. Life is not so funny when it can produce such a group of tragic misfits as is found in *Dinner at Eight.* In *Merrily We Roll Along* the tragedy of the writer who has sacrificed his personal integrity to his lust for gold has been given a poignancy that almost approaches great dramatic art. Discounting the technique of playing in reverse, the drama remains significant as a sincere study of the artist in America. Kaufman's achievement in his Pulitzer prize play, *Of Thee I Sing,* must not be discounted by the historian of the American theatre. Despite its own limitations as an art form, it was the nearest approach to W. S. Gilbert's immortal operettas. Kaufman may not be accorded a place among the greatest contemporary talents, but he is easily the greatest technician of good theatre, whose plays invariably become successes because their author knows what delights his public.

The daughters of Israel have not been slow to express themselves through the medium of the drama. In this one respect they are superior to their fellow-artists in Continental countries. Few Jewesses in England or France specialize in drama, although in the novel, G. B. Stern, Naomi Jacob, and Sarah Gertrude Millin have won great distinction. One of the best tragedies in recent years, *The Children's Hour,* was written by Lillian Hellman. Most critics felt certain that the Pulitzer Prize of 1934 would be granted to *The Children's Hour* rather than to the *Old Maid* of Zoe Akins. Miss Hellman's *The Little Foxes* was hailed as one of the best plays of 1939. Rose Franken's *Another Language* was welcomed by a depressed and discouraged theatre public in the spring of 1932. Her play was significant because it was a true picture of American life that was at the same time free from sentimentalism and falsity. Gertrude Tonkonogy in her *Three-Cornered Moon* presented a more hilarious picture of an American family, that was surprisingly vivid for a first play. Bella Spewack has been collaborating with her husband for several years and the pair have developed their skill in comic presentation to the high level of *Boy Meets Girl* (1935) and the musical comedy *Leave It to Me* (1938).

Now and then the Jewish dramatist remembers his heritage and attempts to present his own people on the stage. The Spewacks wrote *Spring Song* (1934) and, with Francine Larrimore and Helen Zelinskaya to lend their almost perfect art to the performance, the picture of Jewish life on the East Side was charged with an unforgettable sympathy and truth.

Writing in *Current History* of April 1936, John K. Hutchens admitted that the outstanding theatrical development since 1929 was the drama of social doctrine (called by its critics "propaganda") as produced by the Group Theatre and Theatre Union. Most of the personnel of these groups is Jewish. Thanks to the New Theatre League, this dramatic tendency was encouraged throughout the country. *Waiting for Lefty* was inspired by the New York taxi strike of 1934, but it has been played in hundreds of American cities. The exposé of union racketeering and the call to honest labor solidarity have been heard on stages from Maine to California. The Jewish playwrights have written in an idiom that is understandable not only to the sophisticated New Yorker, but to every person throughout the land who has eyes to see and an unprejudiced mind to understand. Corruption and oppression in all walks of American life have been exposed mercilessly through the medium of the drama. Correct indeed is Mr. Hutchens who called John Wexley's *They Shall Not Die* the most effective full-length propaganda play. Wexley's earlier plays, *The Criminal Code* and *Steel,* were produced in Russia as true representations of phases of American life.

In searching for comparisons between Wexley and other dramatists, one must stop at no less a master than Ibsen. The courage of Rubin, attorney for the Negroes, and the courage of his author in writing on such a controversial topic are like that of Dr. Stockman in *An Enemy of the People* and of its author, Henrik Ibsen.

Jewish dramatists have demonstrated an astounding intrepidity in their portrayal of corrupting influences in American life. Sklar and Maltz in *Merry-Go-Round* (1932) turned the dramatic spotlight on municipal politics. John Howard Lawson in *Success Story* (1933) "lashed the moral decadence of competitive commercial struggle." Albert Maltz in his one-act play, *Private Hicks,* castigated the National Guard for shooting at pickets in order to break their strike. The clear-seeing eye of the Jewish dramatist penetrates the forces corrupting America. But he is not concerned merely with assailing institutions. He wants America to be the realization of the dream of all who have sought on American soil their haven of refuge. Pilgrim of 1620 or German refugee of 1939 have all hoped to find here the peace, the nobility, the honesty, and the true culture which were denied them in the lands they left. The young dramatists of today are burning with eagerness to help in the building of this America of their ideals. But before they can build firmly they must remove the cancers of our civic and industrial life. Dramatic surgery is their specialty. They scoff at mere "good theatre." They may be lured to Hollywood by fabulous salaries, but the enslavement is temporary. When they have acquired enough to insure them the quiet and freedom from worry that is necessary for the best artistic achievements, they will come back to do their part in battling the forces of darkness and reaction which have made of Italian and German art mere shadows of their former greatness. When their victory is assured they will work with all other American artists toward the creation of an American art that should and inevitably will rival the great art of the Renaissance and the Golden Age of Pericles.

Speaking at the Tercentenary Celebration at Harvard on September 13, 1936 Etienne Gilson, of the Collège de France, said:

> The future of European culture and of Western civilization ultimately rests with what the United States will make it to be during the next one hundred years. Europe has received it from Greece and Rome; we have done our best to keep it alive and to enlarge it; but the time has now come for us to pass it on to others.

The torch has been brought to our shores. It shall be kept alive, burning ever more brightly. Jewish artists in all fields of endeavor, but especially in the drama, will play a great part in strengthening the flame of culture and civilization. If they are only granted the right to work unhampered by censorship, they will help to make of American drama a thing of power, strength, and beauty which can be compared only with the drama of the Age of Shakespeare.

2. GEORGE S. KAUFMAN: MASTER OF

THE TECHNIQUE OF GOOD THEATRE

George S. Kaufman's *The American Way* (1939) is his thirty-second play written in collaboration. Though critics may argue as to the ultimate value of his plays in the history of American drama, they almost unanimously agree that he is the most successful collaborator working in our theatre. His associates have included Irving Pichel, Larry Evans, Marc Connelly, Edna Ferber, Katherine Dayton, Alexander Woollcott, Moss Hart, Ring Lardner and Morrie Ryskind. The only play he wrote alone was *The Butter and Egg Man* (1925). Superlatives of various kinds have been used with Kaufman. He is generally recognized as the most successful master of stage technique in our contemporary theatre. He is acknowledged as our outstanding satirist, one of our best directors, one of the best writers of dramatic dialogue, and as our most capable "play-doctor."

The surprising thing about his wizardry on the stage is that he had already been credited with it in 1927 when he wrote *The Royal Family* with Edna Ferber. Since that time, when critics thought that he reached his peak, he has developed in the versatility of his technique, in the depth of his social consciousness, in the sparkle and wit of his satire, and in his understanding of human nature. Basing his plays on the occurrences in his immediate environment, he has been compelled to change his technique, his subject-matter, and his point of view with each new production. Consequently he has become unpredictable. His many admirers have come to expect a good and even exceptional evening in the theatre, but their expectations are never as delightful as their experiences with the realities. Kaufman's play, *I'd Rather Be Right,* marked his twentieth anniversary as a dramatist, and his two decades of labor merit a new evaluation.

Kaufman's personal development has run parallel to that of the American drama in general. Twenty years ago, we had plays which were either diluted imitations of Continental and British successes or feeble attempts at portraying the American scene. Louis Anspacher's *The Unchastened Woman* (1915) was considered a significant study of the modern woman and Eugene Walter's *The Easiest Way* (1909) was a bold venture in the study of morals. It is doubtful whether either play could endure a successful revival.

Today our drama is watched by alert playgoers everywhere. Eugene O'Neill, Maxwell Anderson, S. N. Behrman, George S. Kaufman, Elmer Rice, John Wexley, Clifford Odets and dozens of other American playwrights have seen their plays produced on the stages from Stockholm to Vienna. Maxwell Anderson's *Elizabeth the Queen* won over the critical audience of Vienna, Eugene O'Neill's *Strange Interlude* was acclaimed in Stockholm, John Wexley's *Steel* was successful in Moscow, and Elmer Rice's *Judgment Day* was a hit in several countries.

Even though Kaufman's *You Can't Take It With You* was a failure in London, the circumstance was the occasion of lengthy comment by critics here and abroad. Kaufman's success has been so remarkable in New York that his failure in London seemed inexplicable. All sorts of explanations were made. Charles Morgan, the critic and novelist, writing from London, the novelist J. B. Priestley, writing in New York, and Brooks Atkinson, drama critic of the *New York Times,* covered almost the entire front page of the Sunday drama section of one issue of the *New York Times* in discussing the London debacle.

GEORGE S. KAUFMAN

The career of Kaufman is similar to that of many dramatists of today: journalist, columnist, dramatic critic, dramatist. Such has been the experience of George Ade, Ring Lardner, and S. N. Behrman, all of whom came to the stage after a career in journalism.

Kaufman was born in Pittsburgh in 1889. After graduating from the public high school, he studied law for a few months and finally gave it up because he found it too difficult. His occupations were numerous and various and brought him into contact with all sorts of human beings who undoubtedly enriched his understanding of human nature. He worked as a chainman and a transit man on a surveying corps, a window clerk in the Allegheny County tax office, a stenographer, and a traveling salesman.

In 1908 he came to New York and began his literary career as a volunteer contributor to Franklin P. Adams' column in the *Evening Mail*. Through Adams' help he secured the position as columnist on Frank Munsey's *Washington Times* (1912-1913). Although Kaufman thought the column humorous, his employer seems to have disagreed with him. A year later Kaufman succeeded to Adams' column when his mentor joined the staff of the *Herald*.

From writing for a humorous column to reporting on the new plays was an easy step. Kaufman eventually became dramatic editor of the *New York Times*. Every dramatic critic, as some disappointed playwright has said, is either an unsuccessful or an expectant dramatist. Kaufman's interest in the practical side of the theatre was not long in developing.

About this time, Henry R. Stern of the Joseph W. Stern Music Company formed an organization for the encouragement of young playwrights. Kaufman, who was recommended for his promising talent, submitted a check-raising farce called *Going Up*. The play was never produced, but among those who read it and admired its snappy dialogue and comic situations was John Peter Toohey, at that time an associate of George C. Tyler, the producer. Toohey

GEORGE S. KAUFMAN

suggested Kaufman's possibilities to Tyler, and Kaufman was soon working on *Dulcy*. It seems inevitable that John Peter Toohey is the press representative of Kaufman's new plays, for he is the dramaturgic godfather to Kaufman.

Before writing *Dulcy* (1921) Kaufman had collaborated with Irving Pichel on *The Failure*, which never reached production. With the late Larry Evans he wrote *Someone in the House* (1918), which was unsuccessful. The writing of *Dulcy* deserves detailed treatment, because it is one of those plays whose genesis is well known and is an illuminating insight to dramatic creation.

George C. Tyler needed a comedy for Lynn Fontanne, Ellen Terry's brilliant protégée. Kaufman and Marc Connelly were invited to write a play using material which had appeared in Franklin P. Adams' column in the *Herald* in 1914. Kaufman has described its composition thus: "We had a great break of luck with it—the various parts fell into place all in one Sunday afternoon." It was fairly successful in New York, which was in a receptive frame of mind in the early twenties to plays deriding low I.Q.'s. Only a year later Sinclair Lewis' *Babbitt* appeared. Outside of New York the audiences were colder. Sophistication had barely reached the peripheries of the large cities. Not until another decade could satire and social criticism in plays succeed in such preliminary testing-grounds as Boston and Baltimore. Now Kaufman prefers to have his latest plays open out of town. *I'd Rather Be Right* put the Bostonians in quite a turmoil and then Kaufman knew he had nothing to fear. When *Bring on the Girls* appeared to be sending them homewards in Baltimore and in Washington, the play folded up and never reached Broadway.

Babbitt is perhaps the most enduring of the literary works of the early twenties which ridiculed rotarianism, hypocritical woman-worship, and frequent banqueting. For students of human nature who wish to compare the characters in a play written during the depression of 1921 with those of the Great Depression of 1929—the following two bits of dialogue are illuminating. They reveal that Kaufman often says the same clever things in different plays.

Gordon (in *Dulcy*) is a pompous business man, greeting Bill, who is more flippant and serves as the mouthpiece of the author:

GORDON: I say, how's business?
BILL: Haven't you heard?
GORDON (*a bit cheery*): Oh, I don't know. I have an idea it may pick up presently.
BILL: You've been reading Mr. Schwab. "Steel Man Sees Era of Profits."
GORDON: Well—I think he's right at that.
BILL: Yes . . . Rockefeller expects to break even this year, too.
GORDON: Just the same I look for improvement. (*Earnestly*) Bill, if it could just be arranged that all the outstanding accounts could be absorbed by the banks, and then these accounts into payable—
BILL: I know. You mean—things would be better if we weren't all broke.[1]

In 1933 in what was known as the depth of the depression Kaufman again discussed business, this time with Morrie Ryskind, collaborator in *Of Thee I Sing*. For those students of contemporary drama who are curious to distinguish the contributions of Kaufman from those of his associates, the following Socratic dialogue is helpful:

SOCRATIC DIALOGUE
By George S. Kaufman and Morrie Ryskind

(*The scene is Mr. Ryskind's favorite speakeasy—the one where Mr. Kaufman signs the checks.*)

MR. K.: Another glass of beer, Mr. Ryskind?
MR. R.: Don't care if I do. And thank you very much.
MR. K.: Don't thank *me*. Thank Mr. Roosevelt.
MR. R.: Say, that's right. If it wasn't for the President we'd still be drinking that 6 per cent stuff, instead of this 3.2.
MR. K.: What's the matter with 3.2? That's not a bad percentage. Those Harriman depositors would settle for that in a minute.

GEORGE S. KAUFMAN

MR. R.: Yes, but will Harriman?

MR. K.: Well, he hasn't decided yet. As I understand it, Harriman is going to get together with France, and they'll make us a combined offer.

MR. R.: That means Harriman won't pay unless Germany disarms?

MR. K.: No, it just means Harriman won't pay.

MR. R.: There's just one sure way to keep the banks open. Pass a law against them, the way they did with the speakeasies.

MR. K.: That wouldn't do. You'd have too many banks in one block.

MR. R.: I guess you're right. With as many banks as that, the prisons would get too overcrowded.

MR. K.: Tell me—with all the bankers going to jail, what do you think will happen?

MR. R.: Well, the first thing they'll do is float a series of Mutual Welfare Gold Debentures, guaranteed by Singer and Marcus and S. W. Straus and Company, and payable in 1962, with time off for good behavior.

MR. K.: That's all right for 1962. But what happens in 1934, when the bonds drop to three and a sixteenth asked, and one-sixteenth offered?

MR. R.: What do you think'll happen? They'll close the jails.

MR. K.: Then what? You mean we have prison reform?

MR. R.: Sure. A bill is rushed through Congress giving the President dictatorial powers over the jails. So he opens the good jails and the rest of them stay closed. Maybe some of the Detroit jails will never open.

MR. K.: But what about the Reconstruction Finance Corporation? Aren't they supposed to help out?

MR. R.: Oh, sure. They keep right on lending money—good jails and bad. No matter what happens.

MR. K.: Let me get this straight. The Reconstruction Finance Corporation just keeps on lending money?

MR. R.: That's right. On condition that there's no security.

MR. K.: Well, whose money is it? Whose money are they lending?

MR. R.: It's very simple. You see, they take the money that the depositors put into the good banks.

MR. K.: And lend it to the bad banks.

MR. R.: Now you've got it!

MR. K.: But if they're going to do that, why don't they let Harriman keep it in the first place?

MR. R.: Don't worry—he's going to. Waiter! Two beers!

MR. K.: Make mine the same!

MR. R.: Two times 3.2—that's 6.4, isn't it? That's not bad beer, Mr. K.

MR. K.: That's what it isn't. But tell me—have you tried any of this 3.2 wine?

MR. R.: No, I haven't. Tell me about that.

MR. K.: I've been making some at home. You take two parts of hydrogen and one part oxygen, and mix them together. That gives you H_2O, or 3.2 wine.

MR. R.: H_2O? That's water isn't it?

MR. K.: Well, what do you think 3.2 wine is? Wine?

MR. R.: That depends on the Supreme Court. If they say it's wine, it's wine—with Brandeis dissenting.

MR. K.: Just the same, Mr. Roosevelt is doing a pretty good job. He's got the whole country behind him, and we Democrats have got a right to be proud.

MR. R.: We Democrats? I thought you voted for Thomas?

MR. K.: I did. But that was in New York City, and it wasn't counted.

MR. R.: Then I'm a Democrat, too?

MR. K.: Sure you are. If you voted for Thomas.

MR. R.: Well, I'll be darned! We've got to celebrate that! Waiter! Four beers!

MR. K.: Make mine the same!

MR. R.: Yes, sir, he's doing a great job—Roosevelt. A great job. Tell me—is Roosevelt married?

MR. K.: Sure he's married. Been married for years.

MR. R.: Funny. You never read anything about his wife.

MR. K.: Waiter! One rotogravure section![2]

Comparing the two dialogues written twelve years apart, one notices certain elements which might well characterize the dramatist. There is a contemporaneity, first of all, which ties the play closely to its environment and which may work to its disadvantage in the final reckoning of the playwright's contributions. Ibsen's *A Doll's House* could be revived in 1937 as a moving, provoking drama, because of its timelessness. There is no need to summon the platitudes concerning Shakespeare's revivability. The season of 1937 saw the Mercury's *Julius Caesar*, Talullah Bankhead's *Antony and Cleopatra*, the Surrey Players' *As You Like It*, and Charles Hopkins' *Coriolanus*. In 1938-1939 Maurice Evans produced *Hamlet* and *Henry IV*.

Since Kaufman's wit is essentially the kind which takes one by surprise because of its appropriateness and its felicity of phrase, will the same wit amuse an audience the second time? Nothing is so boring as a wise-crack endlessly repeated. Kaufman is perfectly aware of the immediacy of appeal of his plays as his well-known remark about his opinion of satire indicates. When questioned why he did not write satire more consistently instead of his popular plays with a touch of satire, he is said to have answered: "Satire is what closes Saturday night."

There is no doubt of his popular success. After his happy experience with Marc Connelly in 1921, he lost no time in writing *To the Ladies* and *Merton of the Movies* in 1922. The following year they wrote in collaboration *The Deep Tangled Wildwood*, an exposé of New York's sophistication, which was a failure. Ten years later, with Edna Ferber, Kaufman tried again with the same theme in *Dinner at Eight*, a mordant criticism of Park Avenue society folk. In 1923 Kaufman wrote his first book for a musical comedy, *Helen of Troy, New York*. *Be Yourself* (1924), *The Cocoanuts* (1925), *Strike Up the Band* (1927), *Animal Crackers* (1928), *The Band Wagon* (1931), *Of Thee I Sing* (1931), *Let 'em Eat Cake* (1933), and *I'd Rather Be Right* (1937) are other musical comedies for which he has fashioned the plots.

A dramatist deserves more than passing mention when his works achieve not merely a success of the moment but also enrich the art-form, remove its limitations, and open new fields in which it may flourish. Has Kaufman been more than a wizard of stage-technique? Are his many popular successes readable and revivable? The two Pulitzer prizes for *Of Thee I Sing* (1932) and *You Can't Take It With You* (1937) indicate at least a certain committee's testimony to his merit. To the historian of the drama, perhaps his two outstanding achievements have been *Of Thee I Sing* and *I'd Rather Be Right*.

Of the first it might truly be said that it was a pioneer effort. Critics thought that they had touched the zenith of adulation when they spoke of it as the nearest American counterpart to the Gilbert and Sullivan operettas. Yet *Of Thee I Sing* was even superior to the immortal Savoy operettas in certain respects. There is about such productions as *Pinafore, Iolanthe* and *Ruddigore* a feeling of gayety, yes, but also a childish kind of gayety. To make sophisticates laugh, to have tickled the mind, not the ribs, that was Kaufman's feat. To wring a laugh out of the war debt tangle, to have made a Presidential campaign exciting before the 1932 and 1936 battles; to have dared to present the Nine Old Men on the stage in an attitude more prejudicial than judicial; to have taken the dullness out of politics and to have substituted laughter—that was something new in American drama.

Although John Corbin in an article in the May, 1933, *Scribner's* was displeased with the influence which dramatists like Kaufman exercised in American drama, he admitted that Kaufman's spirit of satire was not wholly worthless. Kaufman found so much in American life to ridicule, because there are so many foibles and follies that deserve only ridicule. Tin Pan Alley was the subject for his satire in *June Moon* (1929); the stupidities of the moguls of Hollywood were ridiculed in *Once in a Lifetime* (1930); joiners were told some unpleasant things in *The Good Fellow;* and the Republicans surely were satisfied with the criticism of the New Deal in *I'd Rather Be Right*.

As a satirist of the more obvious inanities and crudities of American life, Kaufman is easily the master. His training as a columnist twenty-five years ago has made him a kind of dramatic column-writer, writing ironically about things that have amused him. No one expects a unique philosophy of life from such a writer, any more than one expects gossip columnists to be included in a revision of Will Durant's *Story of Philosophy*. Yet no man of intelligence, living in such times as these, can have failed to adopt certain definite ideas about artistic, economic and social problems.

Kaufman's artistic philosophy is perhaps most clearly stated in *Merrily We Roll Along*, written with Moss Hart in 1934. The dramatic device of beginning a play with the present and then retreating into the past was effective, to be sure, but after all, only a dramaturgic trick. To many observers this story of the commercialization of the ideals of a young playwright seemed something in the nature of a confession on Kaufman's part. Certainly no American dramatist would understand better the emotions of a successful dramatist whose millions do not satisfy his artistic cravings. The conquest of dollars over idealism has often been treated by our dramatists, but seldom with the poignancy and irony which Kaufman gave to his play. The times may have influenced the dramatist, for a few years later he was back to character comedy. His excursion into the field of literary art and its difficulties is one of the truly revealing contributions to this difficult subject.

What is Kaufman's general philosophy of life? Will he eventually join the immortals or is he just another successful dramatist, another Kotzebue, a Scribe, a Boucicault? Mere technical proficiency never produced an enduring playwright. Is Kaufman satisfied with his financial returns and content to leave dramatic art to his younger contemporaries?

In the opinion of Joseph Wood Krutch, drama critic of the *Nation*, Kaufman has not a consistent point of view. "He has said a hundred witty things; he is certainly on the side of good sense; yet it would be very difficult after reading his twenty-odd plays to say that they tend in any direction."[3] Since this statement was made in 1933, certain plays have appeared in which ideas play an important part. These are *Merrily We Roll Along* (1934), *First Lady* (1935), *Stage Door* (1936), *You Can't Take It With You* (1936), *I'd Rather Be Right* (1937), *The Fabulous Invalid* (1938), and *The American Way* (1939). Sometimes Kaufman's point of view is one of good common sense, such as expressed by Grandpa Vanderhof in *You Can't Take It With You*. Briefly, his philosophy of life is one of enjoying it while one can. Perhaps Kaufman, who knows what audiences want, gave them their own land of heart's desire. In our nerve-wracking civilization we all crave a Shangri-La, a haven of refuge.

Kaufman's philosophy of life may not be consistent, not even positive, but it is quite evident and animates his plays. In all his satires and comedies with satirical flavors he shows his refusal to be fooled by the things which befuddle most people. His superiority to other writers like Sinclair Lewis and H. L. Mencken, who likewise have capitalized on their clarity of vision, lies in his ability to preserve that attitude when the others have succumbed to illusions.

Kaufman has shown Americans how ridiculous some of their most cherished institutions are: their Rotary clubs, their hypocritical adoration of women, their thirst for the dollar, their worship of material success. To have become successful by condemning the pet notions of one's audiences is an unusual accomplishment. It was said of a certain performance of *You Can't Take It With You* that one of the spectators laughed so heartily that he fell off a balcony and yet was unharmed. There is something symbolic in that. Kaufman has turned some of America's most sacred prejudices upside down, but their possessors have survived the experience. Perhaps it does us much good to see the world sometimes standing on our head. Kaufman may be able to stand on his feet and see what a crazy, silly, yet happy world this is. Our age demands more people with eyes that cannot be fooled by superficialities, with minds which can sum up the absurdities of a situation in an epigram, with courage to laugh at the weaknesses of men, be they movie moguls or Presidents.

3. ELMER RICE:

REALIST OF THE DRAMA

Certain writers have become associated with definite areas, rural and urban, which always influence their books: Thomas Hardy and Wessex, Arnold Bennett and the English Pottery District, Ben Hecht and Chicago, Mary E. W. Freeman and New England, Schnitzler and pre-War Vienna, Maupassant and Paris. Elmer Rice has been the interpreter of New York. His novel, *Imperial City* (1937), is the most complete picture of the metropolis ever attempted; and many have been the attempts. By 1900 enough novels had been written about New York to warrant the publication of *New York in Fiction* by Arthur Bartlett Maurice.

Of all the numerous plays about poor New York, Rice's *Street Scene* (1929) is probably the most convincing. Rice has not confined the scenes of his plays to Manhattan, although his best work was done when he was concerned with it. His play, *Between Two Worlds* (1934), took place on an Atlantic liner going to Europe. *Judgment Day* (1934) was a story of some central European country, though it was obviously a dramatization of the trial of Dimitroff for the alleged burning of the Reichstag. *The Left Bank* (1931) had Paris as its setting. *American Landscape* (1938) dealt with Connecticut. Yet critics will agree that he has been most successful when he described New York and its inhabitants, in *Street Scene* (1929), in *Counsellor-at-Law* (1931), in his various other plays concerned with legal problems.

Rice's study of law may explain his qualities as a playwright. Almost from his first play to the last he has exhibited a passionate hatred for injustice, which at times worked to the detriment of his dramaturgy. He has always been admired for the marvelous accuracy of his observation of little, though vitally characteristic, details. New Yorkers experienced many pleasures in *Street Scene* and in *Counsellor-at-Law* which were denied to a visitor. These were due to his power to recognize characters by the appropriateness of their speech, their dress, their mannerisms of deportment.

Elmer Rice's plays abound in many cameos of portraiture. *Street Scene* had forty-five characters, most of them sharply delineated and clearly differentiated. *Counsellor-at-Law* and *We, the People* also had large casts.

Equally apparent throughout his plays, in addition to his love for justice and his accuracy of observation, is his sensitivity to and dislike for the more material aspects of contemporary American civilization. In his first play, *The Subway*, which was not produced until *Street Scene* became a hit, he describes the wearying effects of the daily office routine upon a sensitive young girl. In this respect it antedated Sophie Treadwell's *Machinal*, which was considered by Burns Mantle, critic of the *Daily News*, one of the best plays of 1928. *The Adding Machine* (1923), which was produced by the Theatre Guild, was an allegory of a man's travail in a business civilization which had little respect for individual personalities.

As long as Rice confined himself to demonstrating the tragic implications of industrialization and commercialization, critics were willing to accept him. They had the precedents of Galsworthy's *Justice*, of the plays of Shaw and his imitators, of the young dramatists of the Twenties and the O'Neill of *Beyond the Horizon*. When Rice, after his great success with *Counsellor-at-Law*, which contained an assortment of portraits in a metropolitan law office, tried to present his vision of the disintegrating effect of the depression, critics abandoned him. They had expected another series of portraits and not a passionate outburst against prejudiced judges, company-unions, unscrupulous employers, and other unpleasant features of Big Business. The following year Rice's anger at the persecutions in Nazi Germany led him to portray the Reichstag fire trial in which such characters as Goering, Hitler, and Van der Lubbe appeared. The New York critics were even more dissatisfied. Granting that Rice was within his rights as a dramatist to be angry with the Nazis, they denied him the privilege of using the stage as a soap-box against Nazism.

Here, they said, was a melodramatic harangue, not a play. Rice was accustomed to unfavorable criticism, and went ahead with the presentation of another play that same year. This time the critics' disapproval was too much and *Between Two Worlds* marks his last venture in drama up to 1938.

His refusal to compromise with his principles caused trouble in 1935 when he resigned from his position as New York City Director of the Federal Theatre Project because the Federal Government refused to permit the first edition of the Living Newspaper to include impersonations of Mussolini and Haile Selassie. One may admire a man's courage in facing his adversaries undaunted and yet admit that he is an inefficient dramatist. That seems to explain the critics' attitude. It does not explain Elmer Rice's respect for the power of the critics, for his last three plays failed not because the critics disliked them but because the public was disappointed. Rice knew as well as any man in the theatre that any number of plays have become pronounced successes after universal condemnation by the reviewers. One always likes to mention *Abie's Irish Rose* and its closest competitor for the long-run record, *Tobacco Road*, as examples of hits which were left unsung by the critics.

One explanation for the lukewarm reception to his last three plays is found in the unpreparedness of the New York audiences. Only two years after *We, the People,* Clifford Odets' *Waiting for Lefty* made its appearance. Plays of socal significance were wanted. The Theatre Union was born in 1933 and could offer such tendentious dramas as *Peace on Earth, Stevedore, The Black Pit,* and *Sailors of Cattaro.* Could *Pins and Needles* and *The Cradle Will Rock* have been successful in 1932? It is extremely unlikely. Rice's was that pioneering effort which seems always destined to fail because of its strangeness.

Today in reading this early dramatic study of the American depression, one cannot help admiring the courage of its author. Rice in 1931 had written a great popular and critical success. Perhaps only the appearance of *Of Thee I Sing* in the same season took the Pulitzer Prize out of his hands. He knew enough of New York (his novel *Imperial City* has enough plots for ten plays) to have produced another colorful *genre* painting. Yet he chose to do something entirely different. Time will tell whether Rice lost himself as a dramatist while he found himself as a campaigner for social justice. Perhaps Rice should have written a satire and thus have won the audiences which later thronged to *The Cradle Will Rock* and *Pins and Needles.* It is not characteristic of him to descend to comedy simply because it is easier to accept than drama. When comedy appears in his plays it usually derives from the characters. The mother of Mr. Simon, the district leader, the gum-chewing stenographer, all of *Counsellor-at-Law;* the Italian janitor and the Russian socialist of *Street Scene*—these are comic characters because they are human and the verisimilitude of their portraits provokes one to the laughter of recognition, a frequent experience in the theatre.

Has Elmer Rice made any distinguished contributions to American drama, or is he another successful dramatist popular for the moment, meriting but a paragraph in the history of American drama of the twentieth century? Out of an average season in New York when about two hundred plays are produced, Burns Mantle selects ten for his annual collection. Most often these are the most significant plays of the season. Have Rice's plays fared well with Mr. Mantle? A test of excellence of some value is the inclusion in the annual volume. *Street Scene* was included in the 1928 volume and *The Left Bank* in 1931. It must be admitted

ELMER RICE

that Rice is no George S. Kaufman, whose latest hit almost invariably meets Mr. Mantle's requirements.

Certain gifts of characterization have been revealed by Rice, which incline one to the belief that on the permanence of these characters will depend his reputation. In the theatre one easily comes under their spell and is quite willing to believe in their existence. Rice knows the souls of several people and can describe many more. Thus his portrait of Simon, counsellor-at-law, is probably his masterpiece. Having worked in law offices, knowing the personality of the Jewish professional, whose parents were humble immigrants, as well as any practicing dramatist, Rice naturally excels in such portraits. The mother of Simon, with her pardonable pride in her son's prominence, with her constant expression "I've got plenty time," is a living portrait. Not many dramatists have succeeded in creating such characters. A few, however, notably Bella and Samuel Spewack, in their *Spring Song*, have painted convincing portraits.

With the dramatist's keen eye for the revealing detail, Rice can create a character by giving her a distinctive walk, as he did in *Counsellor-at-Law*. One of the secretaries walked as if all the sense of weariness and of her unappreciated excellence were locked up in her heart. Whenever she appeared the audience was moved. It may have been merely a dramatic trick, but it was effective.

Next in importance among his significant contributions is his skill in interpreting sections of New York life. Among the favorite topics of discussion among play-goers when *Street Scene* was the hit of the town, was the exact location of the street described. Some observers went so far as to photograph three-storied houses which they were certain were the originals of the one in the play. Only Rice's statement that his picture was a generalization of the many brownstone houses in Manhattan put an end to the discussion. The eagerness of the debaters was an indication of that "willing suspension of disbelief" which Coleridge said was so necessary for complete enjoyment in the theatre. Very few stage pictures of the ordinary daily life in New York City can compare with *Street Scene.*

It is as a dramatist of social justice, however, that Elmer Rice probably prefers to be judged. To be sure, he is in a great company that includes Bernard Shaw, John Galsworthy, Gerhart Hauptmann, Sean O'Casey, to mention but a few. Alexandre Dumas *fils'* doctrine that art should be for man's sake motivates these writers. These authors do not weigh out their emotions, being careful that their indignation does not overbalance their sense of the dramatic. Sometimes, as was the case of Galsworthy, whose temperament was more under control, the indignation will be perceived by the sensitive speculator rather than smeared all over the play. It is ridiculous, of course, to chastise Rice because his temperament is unlike Galsworthy's and hence causes him to shout where the more restrained Englishman used understatement.

It is to Rice's credit that he refused to curry popular approval merely by turning out acceptable realistic portraits simply because these had proven successful. What places Rice in the higher category of American dramatists is his refusal to confine himself to one successful type of play. Like O'Neill, who has been constantly experimenting with new forms, Rice used different techniques. In *The Adding Machine* he tried expressionism at a time when it was the "last word" in Continental drama. In *We, the People,* particularly in the last act, Rice took the audience into his confidence as he made it the jury before whom the hero was tried.

Finally, Rice is one of the brave fighters using the vehicle of the stage. He is not a propagandist preaching universal unionization as a solution of the economic ills of our time, or a revolution from the right or left. He preaches *against* rather than *for*. He is against oppression, whether he finds it in Germany or in a mid-Western American town, or in Czarist Russia. He is alive to the beauties of the world, one of which, young love, is tenderly portrayed in several plays. He has written about the ugliness of our impersonal business civilization which makes possible such tragedies as he described in *The Adding Machine, Street Scene* and *We, the People.*

His novel *Imperial City* is an enlarged play, such as he might have written if he had a week of nights in which to present it. His talent in revealing character by significant details enables him to include a vast array of personalities, most of whom are convincing in their verisimilitude. It represents in some respect the climax of his achievement as the portrayer of New York. His social consciousness, his clear eye which enables him to see corruption in politics as well as in family life, his sympathy for the man of good taste, Professor Coleman, his awareness of the thousand and one sights and sounds of the city, they are all characteristic of the Elmer Rice who began his remarkable literary career with *On Trial* (1914).

What direction will Rice take now? The grievances which inspired him to significant dramas are still existent and many new ills have arisen since 1914. An artist who has been stimulated once must create or lose the name of artist. Whether Rice will use the novel or the play we can be certain that his work will result from careful observation, from intellectual honesty which cannot be bribed by popular acclaim or browbeaten by governmental edict, from a passionate indignation aroused by brutality, stupidity, and ugliness, and from an unflinching desire to portray the truth that ought to set slaves free.

4. CLIFFORD ODETS:

ANATOMIST OF FRUSTRATION

Reviewers of the drama have extolled the virtues of so many mediocrities that one may be pardoned a healthy skepticism regarding their latest discovery. Clifford Odets, and his drama, *Golden Boy* (1937), called forth a new set of superlatives. "Just about the most exciting stuff being written for the American theatre," says one critic, while another terms the playwright "a master of characterization." Yet, for every Eugene O'Neill who lives up to the expectations of his early writings, how many scores of young writers degenerate into nonentities?

It is difficult, however, to disagree with such esteemed critics as Joseph Wood Krutch, George Jean Nathan, Stark Young and all the New York newspaper critics who have encouraged, praised, and defended Odets. Such encomia heaped on a writer just turned thirty, with only four long plays and three one-act plays to his credit, call for an explanation. Have we here another shooting star searing the literary firmament for a moment, then vanishing into oblivion? Or are we in the presence of a genuine dramatic genius?

What has Odets contributed to American drama that has earned him such extraordinary praise? Criticism has so far failed to determine the extent of his accomplishments. His plays merit a more extensive critical treatment than the daily reviewer has time

CLIFFORD ODETS

or space for. His contributions to the drama of the depression need evaluation and classification. An intensive study of his plays, moreover, will prove fruitful to the student of literary inspiration and dramatic technique. For Clifford Odets has granted us the privilege of living through his own creative experiences from the original impulse to the completed work.

Such a revelation is rare in the history of the literature of the drama. Grillparzer, Hebbel, Schiller, Goethe, Shaw, and Ibsen, to mention but a few, have left us many note-books of preliminary sketches, snatches of dialogue, outlines of plots and other indications of their struggles for articulate expression. Odets, too, has told us how he wrote his plays, but he has gone one step further: he has told us why he wrote them. In several interviews and articles, he has expressed clearly and vividly his philosophy of life as well as his theories of drama. Asked to discuss the origin and purpose of *Awake and Sing,* he replied:

Understand that I'm supposed to confess how I came to write *Awake and Sing!* I was sore; that's why I wrote that play. I was sore at my whole life. Getting nothing done. Stuffed in a room waiting for Luther Adler to perish so I might get a chance at playing his part in *Success Story.* All my life wondering whether to act or write. But all the time acting to make a living.

When the Group came along it began to mean more, but yet it was wrong for me. What could you do with a part in another fellow's play? Could you say something was wrong with people? Not much chance.

You see, I read a lot of Emerson once. I heard a lot of Beethoven's last quartets. I looked at El Grecos. I got to have a pretty fine idea of what a man could be if he had a chance.

But I saw (and I see it every day, all over the city) girls and boys were not getting a chance. I saw—make it the present—much terror in life. I went over my boyhood and tabulated the people's lives which had touched mine. I wrote small sketches on yellow paper, and when I read back I saw a strange and wonderful sort of *Spoon River Anthology,* but deeper and more hurting to me because the memories were self-experienced.

CLIFFORD ODETS

A young man in America tries to get away from himself—tries to cancel his own experience until it resembles more the general patterns. Certainly it is true of all the workers in creative things. Some escape the general trend. I began wrong. But now—in this little room—I saw where my own experience was richest, where it hurt me most, joyed me most. So I started on *Awake and Sing!* I read lines to fellow-actors who were living in the same apartment. We were all unhappy; we listened to phonograph music. I went on writing.

Lee Strasberg moved downtown and I moved with him. The last act was finished in his kitchen, on the bread board. I didn't like to work near him where he might be wakened. When I looked it over I saw I hadn't wanted to write exactly the play that came out. But it satisfied me; I saw there was material there enough to do better next time.

The next time is over now. The new full-length one is called *Paradise Lost*. For me it spells farewell, Bronx. I'm looking at people in different places now. I've been around. Years in dramatic stock. A good play is there. Advertising offices. Another good play. Broadway—another good play. I only hope I live long enough to write out what I feel. Shortly I'm getting to the coal fields and the textile centers. Let New York see the rest of the country. Hollywood, too. Play material enough to keep six dozen writers going.[1]

Odets has answered many questions regarding his methods, his ideas on life as well as drama, and his purpose as a dramatist. Odets' statement just quoted will help us understand the characters and motifs in his plays.

"I heard a lot of Beethoven's last quartets," he writes. Perhaps that is why old Jacob Berger, the lovable grandfather in *Awake and Sing*, plays his phonograph when he is disappointed in America. That makes understandable Jacob's suicide when his ungrateful daughter breaks his records. For music is his consolation. Caruso, singing with joy in *L'Africana* as he sights land, reminds Jacob of his own joy when he beheld the shore of America, the land of his dreams and hopes. In *Till the Day I Die*, the leading character is a violinist; and mention is often made of the pleasure he took, together with other members of his family, in playing the quartets of Brahms. In *Golden Boy,* Mr. Bonaparte wants his son Joe to be a violinist, to bring joy into the hearts of all people. On his twenty-second birthday Joe was to have received a $1,200 violin as a birthday gift. What follows is perhaps the most touching scene in the play. Joe refuses to take the violin with him on his Western boxing tour and his father denies him "the good word."

Another of Odets' statements is even more pertinent, because it represents the theme of all of his plays: "I see it every day all over the city, girls and boys were not getting a chance." It is these people who never get a chance that interest the dramatist. Their frustrations—and their inferiority complexes arising from the frustrations—constitute the real subject-matter of Odets' plays. Certain critics have labeled him a propaganda playwright because of this preoccupation. How clearly the dramatist himself has answered them!

Waiting for Lefty had a functional value. This is sometimes called the propaganda angle in writing. But the important thing about *Awake and Sing* is the fact that the play stems first from real character, life and the social background of these people.

It may be said that anything which one writes on "the side" of the large majority of people is propaganda. But today the truth followed to its logical conclusion is inevitably revolutionary. No special pleading is necessary in a play which says that people should have fuller and richer lives.[2]

What greater motif can any artist have? This is not "art for art's sake." This is "art for man's sake," in the words of Dumas *fils,* and later of John Galsworthy. This explains Shaw, the early Hauptmann, Ernst Toller, Franz Werfel, Schnitzler—and where could we end? Might it not be urged that great art today must be social as distinguished from mere self-expression; that it must be aware of the submerged third and must do something about it?

The literature of the Gay Nineties, of the Yellow Book, holds no attraction for us today. Oscar Wilde and Max Beerbohm seem detached and lacking in vitality. The latter's *Happy Hypocrite* was dramatized recently and enjoyed a brief success. It was a delightful fantasy, something to escape to, but it did not stir the emotions as great drama has always done.

Millions are aware that boys and girls are "not getting a chance." But a dramatist must show the causes, the *roots;* and one who digs at the roots may by virtue of etymology be said to be a radical. The great American individualist Thoreau would have welcomed Odets for his getting at the roots of things, for did he not write in his *Walden* that a thousand were hacking at the branches of evil but only one was digging at the roots?

Realizing that Odets aims to show us the American saga of failure in contrast to the usual success stories, we are prepared to appreciate the means by which he achieves his goal. As a dramatist he must rely on character development and not on soap-box oratory to show us frustration, its causes and its tragic results.

With the exception of Chekhov, no other dramatist has brought together so many thwarted individuals in one play as there are, for example, in *Waiting for Lefty*: Dr. Benjamin (his father read Spinoza and peddled shoe laces for a living); a brilliant young chemist who refused to experiment with poison gas; Joe, who is constantly reminded by his wife Edna that "everything was gonna be so ducky . . . a cottage by the waterfall, Roses in Picardy"; Flora and Irv, who can't get married because taxi-driving doesn't pay; the young actor Philips who can't get a job because producers can't find money for new plays. Like their creator, they looked at life and saw "much terror" in it. Galsworthy saw just such terror in the inhuman prison system and wrote *Justice*. Ibsen, earlier, saw the terror in the hypocrisy of his society and wrote *Ghosts, A Doll's House, Pillars of Society, Hedda Gabler,* and *An Enemy of the People*.

Perhaps Shakespeare saw the "terror" and concentrated the misery of a large group into his individual tragic heroes, his Brutus, Hamlet, Macbeth, Lear, and Shylock. Perhaps the Greek triumvirate, Aeschylus, Sophocles, and Euripides, were actuated by the same feelings when they created their great trilogies. A survey of the history of the drama makes quite clear even to the cursory reader that its leading figures have almost invariably been moved by the miseries, the injustices, and the hypocrisies of life. It was the gift of the artists to cry out boldly, fearlessly, at the risk sometimes of life and limb, at the iniquities visited upon their contemporaries. Every generation must have its Odets to open the eyes of the dull and the sentimental.

And so, it is the theme of frustration which is the motivating force in *Golden Boy*. Poor, cross-eyed Joe Bonaparte—his very name a label that was bound to attract attention! Certainly no Alfred Adler was required to warn us that in the soul of such a man a dreadful inferiority complex was festering that must eventually lead to his tragic end. Joe tried to overcome his handicap with knowledge, by reading skeptical Mr. Karp's *Encyclopaedia Britannica;* but in a city where knowledge does not keep people off relief, where doctors drive taxis and lawyers wait on tables, the facts of Greek and Roman history and the antics of *Drosophila Melanogaster* would hardly give him peace and freedom. However, Joe found solace in music, for then he was not alone. His violin could not call him cockeyed; Beethoven and Brahms could speak to him and tell him of their own sorrows.

But Joe Bonaparte could not go through life as a cross-eyed violinist. Other human beings were cruel. The next fellow who would make fun of his eyes he would knock down. Fired with this resolve, he studied boxing. Thus began the chain of circumstances that led irresistibly to death in his Dusenberg, flattened against a tree.

Joe Bonaparte is indeed the sixth attempt by Odets to dramatize an inferiority complex; for the same type of hero is to be found in all his plays. Soft-spoken actors of the British school could not play an Odets hero, for he cannot be soft-spoken, full of charm and poise. He must yell, must be *gauche,* must scream at his tormentors, must lash out. Odets' large following would seem to be

CLIFFORD ODETS

renewed testimony to the fact that most of us are suffering under some sort of inferiority complex; we see in Joe Bonaparte, in Doctor Benjamin, in Ralph Berger of *Awake and Sing,* in Leo Gordon of *Paradise Lost,* in the young revolutionary of *Till the Day I Die,* our own hopes and illusions.

Odets has revealed not only his intentions as a dramatist, but also his methods of writing. His dramatic technique is as important as his theme. In fact, the reviewers were more impressed at first by his technique than by his subject-matter.

Odets has revealed the manner in which he developed his skill in giving life to his characters. "I went over my boyhood and tabulated the people's lives which had touched mine," he has said. "I wrote small sketches on yellow paper, and when I read back I saw a strange and wonderful sort of *Spoon River Anthology,* but deeper and more hurting to me because the memories were self-experienced." Odets' characters, therefore, are full of life, easily recognizable. Recall Grandfather Berger, with his music; Pa Berger with his memory of Teddy Roosevelt; Sam Feinshreiber, "the mouse of a man," as his wife calls him; and that grand figure Uncle Morty whom Franz Hals would have loved to paint. And in Odets' second full-length play there are Gus Michaels, the Irish janitor, and the Gordon family once wealthy but now victims of the Great Depression.

His play *Golden Boy* has the most varied collection of characters of any of his dramas. And the technique is richer. The scene is no longer confined to a single room. Odets has "been around." Eddie Fuseli, the gangster who wants "a piece" of Joe Bonaparte, is as true as Mr. Karp, the disciple of Schopenhauer. What dramatist of our day can create more vivid characters?

Art is not mere imitation of life. Cameras and dictaphones could never create living characters. Though one cannot say he has met a character just lke Eddie Fuseli or Mr. Bonaparte, yet one feels that the people on the stage are alive and that somehow we should not forget them for a long time. Odets has created altogether about forty characters, each with a distinct, vibrant personality, an unusual accomplishment for a young playwright.

In 1935 Odets said that he was leaving the Bronx. This he has done not only in a geographical but also a sociological sense. He has learned the ways of prize-fighters who are so stupid that they refuse to fight for less than $1,000 and then quarrel with their managers when $1,200 is offered; he has caught the language of the rackets; he understands the heart of an Italian fruit-peddler and there finds a love for all mankind. The character of Roxy Gottlieb is a delicious satirical creation. Siggie, the taxi-driver, who cannot buy his own cab, his wife Anna who fell in love with him when he told her a dirty story the first time he met her—these, too, are living personalities speaking a language the ordinary citizen recognizes as genuine.

Odets' language merits special attention. It is unlike that of any other dramatist in America. Stark Young states, "It seems to me the first thing about Mr. Odets' new play that we should mention is a certain quality in the dialogue. . . . The point I wanted to stress as where his theatre gift more appears is in the dialogue's avoidance of the explicit. The explicit, always to be found in poor writers trying to be serious, is the surest sign of lack of talent. To write in terms of what is not said, of combinations elusive and in detail, perhaps, insignificant, of a hidden stream of sequences, and a resulting air of spontaneity and true pleasure—that is quite another matter." [3]

Odets also informs us regarding the origin of this remarkable gift of his for creating character through dialogue. At the very beginning of his career as a dramatist he learned that, in the words of Galsworthy, "good dialogue is character, marshaled so as continually to stimulate interest or excitement." For characterization Odets has his own very definite theories:

. . . The best procedure, it seems to me, is to take your own subjective experience and self and break that up to bits. I mean to isolate a small portion of one's own personality. When I reminisce I am one character; when I greet my mother after a long absence, another, and so on.

Objectifying and amplifying these facts of one's self makes for sound and organic character. Dostoievsky is a marvellous example of this principle of creative construction. Writers should not cancel their own life experiences, but use them wherever possible.

I believe sincerely that only when this experience flows into one's work does there begin to be a fighting chance for a writer to become an artist.[4]

But the personal experiences of the playwright, rich as they have been, would not suffice were he not also a master of dramatic construction. Though the number of books on how to write plays grows steadily year after year, their authors do not seem capable themselves of writing the masterpieces which they dangle so temptingly before gullible neophytes (for the requisite tuition fee, of course). Odets, for his part, learned his dramaturgy by studying and acting in plays. For a number of years he acted in stock companies barnstorming up and down the Atlantic coast. He writes:

Although there is little time in stock to do anything else but learn lines and rehearse, it is possible to absorb a great deal of the playwright's method when it is realized that one plays thirty-two different scripts in one stock season.

The use of sound theatrical and effective technique seems frowned upon by literary people today. But if we go back to Shakespeare—and who will deny that literary glory?—we come to the greatest creator of sheer theatrical effectiveness in all its aspects. Right now (1935) I'm very busy again with an intensive study of his work and begin to realize for the first time what such greatness consists of.

In other respects, too, Shakespeare's practices are followed by Odets. Hamlet makes his own new verb when he uses the expression "to out-Herod Herod." Cleopatra says that she will "unhair" the courier who brought her news of Antony's marriage to Octavia. Odets, too, creates his own language when necessary. Tom Moody says to Lorna Moon, in *Golden Boy*, "Don't Brisbane me."

CLIFFORD ODETS

In the light of this brief description of Odets' history, technique, and philosophy of life, we can see more clearly the various stages of his development. In his phenomenal début-piece, *Waiting for Lefty*, he seemed to have done a very ordinary thing: he placed a group of men and women on the stage and gave them words. A play resulted. It was unlike any other great play the critics had ever seen. One of them called it the greatest one-act play of the century. Perhaps that sounded too much like the advertisement of a boxing-match, but the truth was that the critics were non-plussed. Here was a play that stirred one to one's very soul, yet broke all formal laws of construction. Its popularity was unprecedented. The year 1935 saw almost three hundred productions of the play in theatres ranging from South Africa to Seattle. A new talent was heralded.

Awake and Sing opened at the Belasco Theatre on February 19, 1935. It was Odets' first long play, and his sincerity, power of characterization, and "juicy language" (in the words of Percy Hammond) were quickly recognized. It was a study of an unhappy Jewish family in the Bronx. Grandfather Berger had come to America filled with noble dreams and a belief in the realization of Karl Marx's Utopia on our shores. Sadly disappointed, he was now consoled with the thought that his grandson Ralph might help build a better world. Ralph is dissatisfied because he had to work so long and so hard that he could not enjoy the things a young man was entitled to. Moreover, he is in love and wishes to marry, but his mother will not consent to the match. Hennie Berger, her daughter, is an irritable, dissatisfied person, rebelling against the lack of luxuries which she reads about and sees in the movies. Her position is further aggravated by the fact that she is pregnant as a result of an illicit relationship with the boarder.

Moe Axelrod, her lover, lost a leg in the World War. Bitter against a world which permits wars and resentful because he cannot participate in the pleasures of normal people, he has become sardonic and unscrupulous in his dealings with Hennie.

Mrs. Berger is nervous, imperious, and matriarchal in disposition. Having had the misfortune to have married a man without much backbone, she has been the guiding spirit in keeping the family together. Her husband is caught in the inexorable wheels of the depression and seems content with reminiscing of the "good old days" when Teddy Roosevelt was President.

More vigorous in character is Mrs. Berger's brother Morty, who has built up a successful clothing business. All these characters, to quote Brooks Atkinson, are "excitable, restless and at loose ends; and they are generally flying at one another's throats."

These people are sufficiently interesting to make us forget that the plot is rather thin and that very little happens. When Mrs. Berger discovers that Hennie is to become a mother, she rushes her into marriage with Sam Feinschreiber, whose character is aptly summed up in Hennie's words, "a mouse of a man." Moe Axelrod has no respect for the marriage and persuades Hennie to run off with him to Bermuda. Grandfather Berger, disappointed in his dreams, and having assured himself that his grandson would inherit the proceeds of his life insurance policy, jumps off the roof. The conclusion of the play shows Ralph rushing out from the study with a handful of books. From them he hopes to derive enough knowledge to make a more successful attempt than his grandfather to change the world.

The play was rough in style, it stood still at times, but it stirred its audience more than much better ones. It was the work of a young man writing of the frustrated young men and women all about him. Gilbert Gabriel, critic of the *New York American,* aptly summed up its theme:

> The youth of the tenements . . . that is Mr. Odets' occupation in this stirring little play. The youth which stubs its fingers on typewriter keys and packing edges all day long and which scuttles to the neighborhood vaudeville and street-corner gangdom by night.

The play was one of many folk-plays of Jewish life, but it appeared to many critics, of whom Richard Lockridge, critic of the *New York Sun,* is typical, that "of all the many pictures of this *genre,* which have been hung in the theatre's gallery of recent years, this is, in its detail, one of the most convincing and forceful."

Odets avoided the sentimentality which is found in so many folk-plays, of which the Spewacks' *Spring Song* was typical. This sentimentality is a heritage of the Golden Age of the Yiddish theatre of the Bowery days at the beginning of the century. J. I. Gordin was turning out plays with amazing rapidity. Jacob P. Adler, father of Luther and Stella, who appeared in *Awake and Sing,* was the theatrical idol of the East Side. Audiences enjoyed the stirring of their emotions, even when the melodrama fairly dripped over the stage.

Awake and Sing represented an advance over *Waiting for Lefty,* which revealed the author as a social dramatist, or as Richard Lockridge, of the *New York Sun,* expressed it, "revolutionary." The first play was written almost immediately after his observation of the unsuccessful taxi-strike in New York in the Spring of 1934. It was pro-labor or "propagandist." It seemed to be lacking in all dramatic technique. *Awake and Sing* was in the tradition of the Russian master, Chekhov. John Mason Brown, of the *New York Evening Post,* declared, "The simple fact remains that of all the American playwrights who have attempted to employ Chekhov's method, none has used it to such advantage as Mr. Odets has in *Awake and Sing.*" Unlike Chekhov's characters who take such a hopeless view of life, however, Hennie and Ralph Berger awake and struggle to find their own salvation. The play was a kind of hybrid of the spirit of Chekhov and of the American Pioneer.

In April 1935, Odets completed a play about Nazi Germany in five days and offered it on a program together with *Waiting for Lefty. Till the Day I Die* was based on a letter from a German writer which had been translated in the *New Masses.* A German communist was arrested while working in the underground movement. After weeks of torture he was released. His comrades had suffered from the treachery of stool-pigeons and were hesitant about giving him work with the movement. He was arrested a second time and tortured physically as well as by the taunts of the Nazis that his comrades had no longer any faith in him. When released a second time he unwittingly caused the arrest of all who spoke to him. Finally, he came to his brother and asked him to kill him.

Odets read the English translation and in the heat of anger wrote his seven-scene play in almost record time. Critics were somewhat disappointed because its horror was unconvincing. The author was not familiar enough with the material to give it the verisimilitude which had characterized *Awake and Sing*. For the anti-fascist audiences it had the appeal which any attack on Nazi brutality would have engendered. It did not indicate any artistic growth and indicated rather that at times Odets' emotions ran away with his artistic principles.

Till the Day I Die was nothing to be ashamed of. Its subject-matter was such as to make almost any play unbelievable. In fact, when other dramatists tried to write about Nazi Germany they were also criticized for being too melodramatic. Elmer Rice's *Judgment Day*, Leslie Reade's *The Shatter'd Lamp*, and Friedrich Wolf's *Professor Mamlock* were all criticized as unbelievable, although in each case the dramatist contended that he was merely reporting the facts. In truth, the story of Nazi Germany is so horrifying that on the stage it is unbelievable. Odets was handling material which simply refused to be molded into dramatic form.

The dramatist was obviously experimenting with dramatic types, for in April 1935, he wrote a "propaganda" monologue especially for Morris Carnovsky, who had previously created the character of Grandfather Berger. The speaker has passed up a beggar, who stares at him so pathetically that he must defend himself for not giving anything. As the confession continues, the speaker reveals his miserable existence. Like Grandfather Berger in *Awake and Sing*, he, too, had once been an idealist, but now he had become hard and calloused to all the nobler aspects of existence. He concludes with a condemnation of himself for betraying his early ideals. As an exercise in the monologue of social significance, *I Can't Sleep* was undoubtedly unique.

Paradise Lost, Odets' second full-length drama, opened on December 9, 1935. It was the fourth play of his to be presented in one year, *Awake and Sing, Till the Day I Die,* and *I Can't Sleep* being the other three. It must be admitted that the critics were disappointed. Gilbert Gabriel, whose praise for the earlier plays was unstinted, regretted that:

. . . Everything that Father Time and his mean lieutenants, the drama critics, ever feared would happen to the talents of Odets has evidently been happening now. Everything that would reduce the fiery attractiveness of an *Awake and Sing* to fog, almost to foolishness, has turned up in exaggerated quantity in *Paradise Lost* and made of it a grotesque with a dozen oratorical arms and not a leg to stand on.

Odets left no doubt as to his intentions, for he sent out an announcement prior to the performance that the hero in *Paradise Lost* was the entire American middle class of liberal tendency. The Gordon family was represented as living somewhere in the East. This time they were not definitely Jewish like the Bergers of *Awake and Sing*. Mr. Gordon had manufactured ladies' pocketbooks until the depression killed the demand for them. One of his sons is slowly dying from encephalitis; another had been a famous runner until he had developed a bad heart. The daughter is a pianist who cannot marry the man she loves because he has no job. Other characters introduced are the garrulous Gus Michaels, a family friend; Marcus Katz, the unscrupulous partner who suggests that they burn their factory and collect insurance with which to start a new business; Mr. May, a professional incendiary who has developed arson into a science; Mr. Pike, a pacifist furnace man; and various other typical members of American society.

The criticism of the play was unfavorable. Though the reviewers were willing to accept the Berger family as an authentic representation of Bronx Jewry, the Gordons were not convincing. As Robert Garland wrote, "They aren't American, they aren't middle-class, they aren't alive." Richard Lockridge, dramatic critic of the *New York Sun,* was more explicit in his disapproval.

If it were less realistically described, one might suspect the author of symbolism. As realism it is ridiculous, comic exaggeration. As a charter member of the American middle class of liberal tendency I assure Mr. Odets that it is not in the least like this; that what he has achieved is a mixture of shrill melodrama and caricature and that his religious faith in the revolution is descending like a curtain between him and the people of the real world, whom it is every dramatist's duty to observe.

Odets was not content to accept the derogatory criticisms without challenging their validity. *"Paradise Lost* is my best and most mature play," he said. "By far! And without reservation." Since most of the critics had commented on the Chekhovian echoes in the play, Odets felt it necessary to explain that "Chekhov was mentioned in that statement (released to the press before the première) as historic reference, not to point out his influence on my work—one which, incidentally, is still doubtful in my own mind. You have my word for it that I intend to read *The Cherry Orchard* tonight for the first time in my life."

Because so much skepticism has been expressed about the verisimilitude of his portrait of the American middle class, Odets attempted to defend his characterization.

Some of us are inclined to think today that we are surrounded on all sides by normal, well-juiced people (he said). We are apt to forget that day by day millions of intellectuals, professionals and white-collar workers are gently being eased out of comforts they once knew, surely being declassed and dispossessed. Perhaps many of us living in comfort, well-cushioned away from reality, know little of what is going on. Little or nothing.

Perhaps these comfortable, well-cushioned ones, able to buy drinks at Tony's or 21—surely full of sane, normal people, as John O'Hara has brilliantly shown—are not aware that twenty-eight million Americans are living on relief of various kinds. Perhaps we have not seen the delicate psychological manifestations of their degradation.

Perhaps the disappointment of the critics was due to their expectations, which only a master-dramatist could have fulfilled. It is embarrassing to be called the "white hope of the American theatre" before one's thirtieth birthday. The gifts of dramatic dialogue, vivid characterization, and theatrical sense may be granted to a young man, but the greater gift of understanding the decline of a great class comes only with age and maturity. Odets did not know enough of the American middle class whose demoralization he tried so earnestly to depict. Besides, any drama in which a "class" is a hero is bound to cause confusion. To emphasize the afflictions of his representative American family, he piled calamity upon calamity which had no connection with his economic thesis. There was no reason for introducing the slowly dying Julie, since his lingering illness might have occurred in biblical, feudal or renaissance times. Here and there, slightly overcome by the temptation to show his skill at revealing the varied elements that constitute character, Odets introduced asides and monologues which were irrelevant to his theme and plot.

The play aroused considerable discussion, which was one indication of its vitality. It was by no means a failure. Rather was it not the masterpiece his admirers were led to expect. For two years he did not produce another drama. He had received a call to Hollywood whither Franchot Tone and J. Edward Bromberg, fellow-members of the Group Theatre, had gone earlier. One of his pictures, *The General Died at Dawn,* was marked by a few speeches which revealed the social viewpoint of its author. Odets was not inactive in his playwriting. Rumors came to Broadway that he was writing a play about the prize-ring and one about business. *Golden Boy,* produced in November 1937, is the first; *Rocket to the Moon,* produced in the Fall of 1938, is the second. It is generally assumed that *Golden Boy* is his most important

CLIFFORD ODETS

play to date and that Hollywood did not have the deteriorating effect which it usually has upon the gifted young dramatists lured there by high salaries. If anything, Odets has become keener in his perception of men and women, more precise in his dramatic idiom, and more aware of the intricacies of human nature.

Golden Boy is the story of the rise and fall of a cross-eyed, sensitive Italian boy who becomes a famous pugilist and finally dies in an automobile crash after his most successful fight. In telling this story Odets introduces the machinery of fight promotion, racketeering in the boxing-game, and the family life of the Bonapartes, hard-working, simple, kindly Italians. The "collapse of the American middle-class" which was pictured in *Paradise Lost* has given way to the study of the making of an individual, in the manner of Shakespeare, rather than Chekhov. Not that Odets has lost his awareness of the class struggle. Joe Bonaparte's brother is a C. I. O. organizer, who is working among the Southern textile laborers. Mr. Karp is a favorite character with Odets—the commentator on the sadness of the *status quo*. In *Awake and Sing* it was Grandfather Berger; in *Paradise Lost* it was Gus Michaels. Siggie's inability to buy a taxi so that he can be independent of the "bosses" is another indication of Odets' interest in the difficulties of the working class.

The superiority of *Golden Boy* to the other dramas is apparent in the diversity of characters, in the coherence of his plot, and in the omission of the non-essential elements which cluttered up the earlier dramas. In his experimental stage, in the heat of his emotions, Odets was inclined to permit speeches which were good in economic theory but bad as dramatic dialogue. In *Golden Boy* the dialogue proceeds inevitably from the characters and the plot proceeds from the dialogue in a manner that would have warmed the heart of John Galsworthy.

Clifford Odets in his *Rocket to the Moon* does not directly discuss fascism, but, as in all his plays, uses the current spiritual unrest as a background for his story of marital unhappiness and thwarted ambitions. In the words of the disappointed Mr. Prince,

CLIFFORD ODETS

Odets puts his philosophy and disenchantment, which in *Golden Boy* came from Mr. Karp, and has appeared in earlier dramas. The economic ills afflicting our society account for the character of Cleo Singer, the love-starved, art-starved little assistant who takes Dr. Stark away from his wife, only to abandon him later in her quest for true love. Odets reveals once again his mastery of dialogue and characterization. Each of his characters lives before us to be added to the other creations of his fertile genius.

In summing up Odets' qualities as a writer of drama one can distinguish several outstanding virtues. First, he is concrete, dramatizing in vivid terms the ideas and acts of his characters. Secondly, he has used his knowledge and love for music to give his dramas a symphonic quality which naturally enriches them. Life is not a matter of a simple melody, and in telling of the rise and fall of one person, one would be untrue to life to omit the strands of minor plots of other persons in the play. Odets has always woven several life-stories into his dramas. In *Waiting for Lefty* about a dozen victims of the depression were analyzed. In his larger dramas he has always tried by skillful exposition to present the past of each character, sometimes too generously. In *Golden Boy* all these themes are combined into a dramatic symphony, with a skill found in few dramatists writing today.

Thirdly, his dialogue is pungent, revelatory of character, memorable for its quotability, devoid of any unnecessary elements, and charged with dramatic intensity. Even when the critics were disappointed with the confused thinking of *Paradise Lost,* they still admired the brilliant dialogue. It may lack the poetry of which Maxwell Anderson is the master; it has not the recognizability of Elmer Rice's language in *Street Scene;* nor has it George S. Kaufman's gag-like smartness. It has, however, force and inevitability.

Finally, Odets aims to write plays of social significance and interpretation. He is following in the footsteps of Ibsen, of the early Hauptmann, of Shaw, and of their numerous imitators. Perhaps he expresses best his philosophy of playwriting in his own words, written after the première of *Golden Boy*:

It is about time that the talented American playwright began to take the gallery of American types, the assortment of fine vital themes away from the movies. This was attempted in *Golden Boy*. Some critics were surprised at the choice of theme. Where is there a more interesting theme in this country than a little Italian boy who wants to be rich? Provided, of course, you place him in his true social background and show his fellow-conspirators in their true light, bring out the essential loneliness and bewilderment of the average citizen, do not blow trumpets for all that is corrupt and wicked around the little Italian boy, do not substitute a string of gags for reality of experence, present the genuine pain, meaning and dignity of life within your characters.

As spokesman for the Americans who are not found in the 4% tail which wags the 96% dog, for the Americans who are not mentioned in Lundberg's *Sixty Families*, but of the Americans who sought in our cities and on our plains a land where human liberty would be a reality, where human labor would earn its just reward, and where human dignity would be cherished, regardless of creed or race, Clifford Odets deserves the laureateship.

5. S. N. BEHRMAN AND THE

AMERICAN COMEDY OF MANNERS

In 1938 a group of five American playwrights decided to do away with producers, agents, and entrepreneurs of all kinds and to produce their own plays. This quintet included Maxwell Anderson, Robert E. Sherwood, Sidney Howard, Elmer Rice, and S. N. Behrman. With Sherwood's *Abe Lincoln in Illinois* and Anderson's *Knickerbocker Holiday* opening in October, the Playwrights Company rapidly became the most important new organization in the American theatre. The variety of talent possessed by the individual members undoubtedly played some part in bringing them together. Thus Maxwell Anderson could contribute his gift for poetic speech and re-creation of historical characters, already revealed in *Elizabeth the Queen, Mary of Scotland, Valley Forge,* and *The Masque of Kings.* Robert E. Sherwood, with varied success in the comic, pseudo-historical play as in *The Road to Rome* and *Reunion in Vienna,* the anti-war *Idiot's Delight* and the socially significant *Petrified Forest,* turned to a biographical portrait of Abraham Lincoln, which became overnight the hit of New York.

The individual achievements of S. N. Behrman are not approached by his four associates for in the department of the American comedy of manners, in the grand tradition of Sheridan and Wilde, he is the master in our drama. Critics have learned to expect from his works perfection in form, language, and plot, so that they come to a Behrman play ready to acclaim. George Jean Nathan in *Testament of a Critic* (1931) mentions his own weakness of a prejudiced attitude when witnessing the new work of inferior dramatists. Almost all the members of the critical fraternity will admit that their expectations on the first night of a Behrman play run high and that they have seldom been disappointed.

The explanation of Behrman's remarkable gifts as revealed in his first full-length play, *The Second Man*, in 1926, was difficult to find. A few facts of his life were ascertained but they were hardly illuminating. It was learned that he was born in Worcester, Massachusetts in 1893; that he had studied at Clark University; and that he had attended Professor George P. Baker's course in playwriting at Harvard.

While still in college, Behrman wrote a vaudeville sketch, *Only a Part*, which was produced in Worcester. A vaudeville booking agent saw it and brought it to one of the theatres in Fourteenth Street in New York. Behrman followed his play as an actor. He might have become a second Noel Coward, for he enjoyed acting but his parents prevailed upon him to return to college and obtain his degree. The course with Professor Baker decided his career. The dramaturgic tendency conquered the histrionic, and Behrman, like so many hopeful young dramatists, came to the metropolis to offer his wares.

As one might have expected, New York, which is represented in the cinema as being so generous to bright young artists who have pawned their last shirt to come to the Big City, did not give Behrman the golden key to the city or even the smaller key to Broadway.

Behrman tried his hand at various kinds of writing. He wrote magazine articles, such as the one on "Movie Morals" for the *New Republic* in 1917. Eventually he became the assistant editor of the *Times Book Review*. The *New York Times* seems to have been the early training ground of another great dramatist, George

S. Kaufman, who was its dramatic editor before he wrote any plays. Although Behrman's field was in the written word, he did not forget the spoken drama. In 1924, there was performed in Peekskill, New York, a one-acter, written in collaboration with Kenyon Nicholson, whose comedy *Sailor, Beware!* later proved so successful. This one-act play, *A Night's Work,* lacks any clue to the future excellence of the collaborators. In this respect it contrasts vividly with the one-act plays of Eugene O'Neill, which after repeated performances for twenty years, are still capable of being revived with success.

A certain distinction was given this early effort by the presence of Beryl Mercer, who played one of those scrubwomen roles which have endeared her to her admirers. A brief summary of the plot will reveal the step which Behrman took between 1924 and 1926, when *The Second Man* startled Broadway by its sheer brilliance.

The scrubwoman is cleaning her employer's office at two in the morning. A young man enters, opens the safe, and steals ten thousand dollars. Mrs. O'Reilly stops him, learns that he is stealing it for a Miss Navarre, with whom he is hopelessly infatuated. Lying ingenuously, Mrs. O'Reilly informs the thief that she is Miss Navarre's mother and that her daughter is accepting his employer's attentions also. This is enough to make him give her up completely. Just then the employer enters, discovers the theft, and is ready to send for the police. Mrs. O'Reilly saves the day by saying that she stole the money, and that she is the mother of the young man. Both men renounce Miss Navarre; employer and employee forget the earlier recriminations.

Nothing could have been more in the tradition of sweet sentimental vaudeville drama, and nothing more uncharacteristic of Behrman's later work. It is like trying to find the Bernard Shaw of *The Apple Cart* in *Candida* or finding the Ibsen of *An Enemy of the People* in *Love's Comedy.*

Behrman continued working in the practical field of the theatre. He became a play-reader for Crosby Gaige, and future candidates for Ph.D.'s on *The Dramatic Development of S. N. Behrman* would find some illuminating criticism in Behrman's marginalia on the scripts submitted. In 1926 Behrman was the press agent for Jed Harris' success, *Broadway*.

Another collaboration, *The Man Who Forgot*, was produced out of town, but never reached New York. To complete his success story, it must be revealed that just as he was becoming discouraged with his talent in drama, two of his plays were accepted by producers simultaneously. The Theatre Guild produced *The Second Man* (1926) and Jones and Green presented *Love Is Like That,* written with Kenyon Nicholson. Behrman had found himself. Pure comedy was his forte, and in seven original plays he has not compromised with the tastes of his audiences or the gentle admonitions of his well-wishing critics, who felt that his art would not appeal to the masses, but would always be intellectual caviar for the élite.

As T. H. Huxley said, one must begin a discussion by definitions. The term "comedy" has been misused and abused so long that in these days of societies formed to uphold this and defend that, one would not be surprised if a "Society to Uphold the Meaning of Comedy" were organized. The average person thinks Joe Penner, Popeye, Bert Lahr, the weather, the baby's face all comic, while the dictionary writer squirms with uneasiness at the perversion of a grand old term in drama.

Joseph Wood Krutch, critic of the *Nation,* in discussing a Behrman play makes it his point again and again to define comedy, the comic spirit, and the purpose of comedy. Of all the writers on this subject, including Henri Bergson (*Essay on Comedy*), Sigmund Freud (*Wit and the Unconscious*), and John Palmer (*Comedy*), he seems one of the most lucid. Concerning the final business of comedy, he writes:

> It first deflates man's aspirations and pretensions, accepting the inevitable failure of his attempt to live by his passions or up to his enthusiasm. But when it has done this, it demonstrates what is still left to him—his intelligence, his wit, his tolerance, and his grace —and then, finally, it imagines with what charm he could live if he

were freed, not merely from the stern necessities of the struggle for physical existence, but also from the perverse and unexpected quixoticisms of the heart.

Behrman's seven plays are remarkable examples of the type of drama indicated in Krutch's definition. Their distinction is all the more unusual, insomuch that they represent only a recent addition to American drama. For it can be truly said that genuinely great American drama is only about twenty years old. When did an American play win success in London or Paris before the war? Was not American drama almost exclusively importations or imitations of successful European products?

Today American drama is the most significant in the world. This opinion has been expressed by Max Reinhardt, greatest of all producers, Ernst Toller, famous German dramatist, and any number of critics who have had the opportunity to compare plays in different countries. Behrman plays a definite role in the supreme position of American drama. Only two or three living writers of English can write dialogue with such charm, wit, polish, and brilliance. Noel Coward's dialogue may seem brilliant when interpreted by himself and Gertrude Lawrence, but in the reading of it one is impressed by its emptiness. Behrman's plays are a delight to read. The reader feels clear-headed, stimulated, and amused, as those in the inner circle of true devotees of art can be amused.

A survey of the subjects which interested the playwright ought to help to an understanding of the greatness of the man. For no writer who is mean in soul and spirit has ever created works which were noble. In *The Second Man* (1926) Behrman probed the personality of a second-rate writer confronted with the decision of maintaining his relationship with a wealthy woman who supports him, or of marrying a beautiful young girl of twenty who idolizes him. In the end he lets his mind defeat his heart and he continues his parasitic existence at the expense of his wealthy admirer. The solution is that of the comic dramatist, who likes to present an interesting human situation, to discuss it intelligently and brilliantly from all angles, and finally to settle the problem calmly and urbanely.

Certain playgoers will resent such a play, and such an attitude on the part of the playwright—the discussion of petty personal problems in the midst of a world always on the verge of political and social explosions. That it is characteristic of the comic spirit to concern itself with a subject which most people would consider trivial, is exemplified in Oscar Wilde's *The Importance of Being Earnest*. Algernon and Jack are discussing most earnestly:

JACK: How you can sit there calmly eating muffins, when we are in this horrible trouble, I can't make out. You seem to me to be perfectly heartless.

ALGERNON: Well, I can't eat muffins in an agitated manner. The butter would probably get on my cuffs. One should always eat muffins quite calmly. It is the only way to eat them.

JACK: I say, it's perfectly heartless your eating muffins at all, under the circumstances . . .

ALGERNON: I am eating muffins because I am unhappy. Besides, I am particularly fond of muffins.

Behrman's characters, it must be admitted, are far more socially conscious than Algernon, but they are just as loath to be disturbed. In *Rain from Heaven* Lady Violet Wyngate refuses to believe that a world responsible for the Russian Revolution and the Nazi tyranny is really such a terrible world. She tries to persuade the German exile, Hugo Willens, to remain in England and be her guest in much the same manner as Mrs. Kendall Frayne invites Clark Storey to partake of her bed and board in *The Second Man*. In the former play, again, a decision of the mind conquers the dictates of the heart. Hugo Willens and Lady Wyngate are attracted to each other, and were Willens a hero of the movies, he would undoubtedly have remained in England in comfort and peace. But his mind impels him on to fight against tyranny and barbarism which drove him out of his native land. Willens returns to his fellow exiles on Germany's borders, who are secretly waiting for their day of reckoning.

S. N. BEHRMAN

In *End of Summer,* Behrman turned the searchlight of his intelligence and wit upon the problems in America. In the home of the wealthy Leonie Frothingham, a group of victims of America's depression are gathered. Two young college graduates have embraced Communism for lack of any better philosophy. A psychologist tries to woo both the mother and daughter and in the end is refused by both. The alternatives to the present muddle in America are discussed and at the end of the play the audience is left uninformed of any way out. For it is not the function of the comic dramatist to solve his problems with any degree of finality. His purpose is to examine problems, to chip away the excrescences, the prejudices, the irrelevancies, and then with charm and brilliance to create characters who can discuss these problems as civilized human beings.

Wine of Choice (1938) is in many respects his most characteristic play and yet his weakest. The "formula" is most obvious and hence tends to make the work more of an intellectual exercise than a representation of living characters in the process of social and individual development. Ever since *Rain from Heaven* the plays of Behrman have become centers of brilliant discussion rather than scenes of emotional and intellectual crises. When the conversation was clever and the characters interesting, the play provided a rare entertainment, rather cerebral, but delectable.

As in *Rain from Heaven* and *End of Summer,* we have a host who manages to preserve equanimity while others around him are "losing their heads and blaming it on you." In the former the central character was a titled Englishwoman; in the latter a leader of the Newport set. In *Wine of Choice* the representative of equanimity is a man, and his satellites belong to the "horsey set" of Long Island. Binkie Niebuhr is trying in his own way to bring happiness to his friends as Lady Violet Wyngate and Mrs. Leonie Frothingham tried in theirs. Again we have a radical similar to the one in *End of Summer.* The discussion is only slightly different from that in the last two works. The references are to more recent events, but by no means more significant. Thus the radical Dow Christophsen writes of a strike of Southern sharecroppers, since in the three years since 1936 they have been receiving more attention than formerly. Ryder Gerrard is a good stage representation of the late Senator Bronson Cutting. Larry Sears obviously is an imitation of millionaire dabblers in the theatre.

All of this would not be objectionable if it were concerned with some significant plot or theme, but in these respects Behrman reveals his greatest weaknesses. In *Rain from Heaven* he discussed the subject of intolerance, using as his central character a German-Jewish intellectual who was interesting as an individual and as a representative of his persecuted fellow-non-conformists. The audience was carried away by the theme and the personality of Hugo Willens.

In *End of Summer* Behrman returned once again to his favorite practice of analyzing indecision. In his first play, *The Second Man,* the man of indecision was a novelist who could not make up his mind between falling in love with youthful and beautiful Monica Grey or living off the largesse of middle-aged but indulgent Mrs. Kendall Frayne. In *Brief Moment,* the indicision was represented in Roderick Dean, scion of a wealthy family who could not tie himself down to any worth-while occupation or purpose in life. In *End of Summer* it was the ever-youthful Mrs. Leonie Frothingham who seemed to go from one lover's bed into another. In *Wine of Choice* the indecisive character is Wilma Doran. She had been married to an artist, but she had left him. Then she had fallen in love with a millionaire publisher, who was ready to marry her whenever she was willing. In the "horsey set" of Long Island she had come in contact with Larry Sears, who made up in charm for his lack of brains. Having tried explorations into unknown regions as means of escape from life's boredom and having found them dull, he had discovered a new interest in motion pictures. Of course, his love for Wilma helped somewhat, since she was to be his star. Not content with having two wealthy and chivalrous men in love with her, Wilma falls in love with young

Dow Christophsen, proletarian novelist, obviously a caricature of his class.

Wilma flounders around in a morass of love in much the same way as does Mrs. Frothingham. The sad thing about it is that the audience is made to suffer her confusion. It is difficult, if not impossible, to become emotionally stirred by the problem of this alluring woman upon whom love is heaped lavishly, but who cannot make up her mind. The tragedy of love is important and can be made intensely moving as Thomas Hardy makes it in *The Return of the Native* and in *Jude the Obscure*. Here, however, we are prevented from feeling any sympathy for the character. It is like feeling sympathy for Alexander the Great when he sighed because there were no more worlds left to conquer. When an audience cannot sympathize with the heroine, the play is doomed as an emotional experience.

Like all Behrman's plays, *Wine of Choice* is a high comedy, a presentation of the human mind exercising itself upon the problems of life. Many of our contemporary problems are mentioned, but the intellectual exercises are puerile. Binkie Niebuhr refuses to concern himself with anything more social than his food and his friends' love affairs. He is completely insulated against the realities of the world. He has no respect for the masses, proletarian novelists, democracy, or the movies. He is a parasite and to his friends, a lovable one. To the ordinary theatre-goer, fresh from the robust gayety of *A Shoemaker's Holiday* or the provocative insouciance of *Pins and Needles,* Binkie is a trifle unreal and, sad to say, a trifle boring.

Not that he does not mean well. In his little black book he lists all his deeds of mercy. Now he is arranging a luncheon at the Colony between Siebert the publisher and Dow Christophsen. Now he is assisting in the divorce of one of his friends and manages to throw in an interior-decorating commission at the same time. In the course of the play his greatest concern is in marrying Wilma and Larry Sears. As Leo Traub, the brilliant movie director, expressed it, Binkie is the best "shotgun" or-marriage-broker on the Island.

We might have been interested in this Angel of Mercy, and for a time we are. The Little Black Book gets a few laughs, but no book can remain dramatically moving for long. Occasionally Behrman gives Binkie amusing lines but they are not memorable and many are not even amusing. He speaks of some one as the "Napoleon of indecision"; he defines democracy as the "substitution of one feudal system for another." He says that the only person who serves good food in Russia is Litvinoff. He condemns the senatorial ambitions of chivalrous Ryder Gerrard as "pouring chili on ignorant Spaniards." Proletarian fiction is to him all "genital and intestinal." All these remarks occasionally cause a ripple of laughter, but they are soon forgotten. Binkie is a creature of the dramatist's imagination, but unlike his other creatures, uninteresting. Woollcott was far more delightful in *Brief Moment* in 1932. As Binkie he is merely reiterative.

Ryder Gerrard stirs us emotionally at times because he seems to possess worthy motives. He wants to divorce "conservatism from reaction," because the British conservatives are more socially minded than the most radical of the New Dealers. He wants to distribute the blessings of democracy from above, he wants to preserve democracy even at the cost of his life. As the representative of a point of view he is interesting. To believe in him is difficult when one knows the true nature of so many of these guardians of democracy who wish to shower its blessings on the unfortunate poor. At times one is almost won over to Gerrard and his kind. He relates a touching story of visiting a squatters' colony with some wealthy slummers. One woman exclaimed that a half-starved dog was being badly treated, entirely oblivious of the thousands of human beings who were living in sub-human conditions. Yet these protestations of sympathy with the submerged one-third ring false. Gerrard becomes intolerant in the third act in the face of Christophsen's determination to keep to his chosen path. Gerrard is only the benevolent despot, more despotic than benevolent.

Nevertheless, as a representative of a class whose "grandfathers bribed aldermen for franchises" and whose members now bribe senators to pass favorable legislation, he is more to be admired than Larry Sears. Larry is simply over-flowing in wealth and charm. If his girl friends could all get together and vote for him, he might also be elected Senator, but, as he says, "The girls I know don't vote." After trying unsuccessfully many distractions, much in the same way as Roderick Dean in *Brief Moment* tries leading a dance orchestra, he has become interested in Wilma Doran. At the beginning of the play he has just taken a screen test of Wilma. He cannot make up his mind to go ahead with the venture, but Binkie eggs him on with the warning that unless he makes the picture, Wilma will marry Ryder Gerrard and go to New Mexico to take up the duties of political hostess. Having as his only other choice the financing of an expedition to locate the sources of the Orinoco River, he decides in favor of Wilma and *The Princess of Java*, an inferior little vehicle whose germinal idea is supplied by Binkie, but whose development is in the capable hands of Leo Traub, master purveyor of movie-pap to millions.

Behrman's remarks about the moving pictures are among the most brilliant in the play. To Dow Christophsen, they are escapes and as such need no discussion. Binkie's description of the reaction of the "horsey set" to a movie is quite amusing. They enter a movie house, he says, wearing spurs and sit through the picture without a sound except now and then an approving neigh. To Ryder the movies are more dangerous. They are not escapes. They are to many people the realities of life. Every girl may become the Princess of Java, just as every boy thinks he may love the Princess of Java. Ryder despises the movies because it prevents the millions of movie-goers from seeing the realities of life.

Binkie is as contemptuous of the intelligence of the masses in their reaction to the cinema as he is of all their behavior. Leo Traub is more cynical about the audiences who jam our entertainment palaces. Incidentally, Traub is one of the few believable characters in the play. He is quite aware of his powers, knows what his audiences want, and gives it to them every time. Satirical in his daily life, he cannot permit a trace of satire in his films, not even a trace of an idea. His point of view is frank and clear in an environment where a clever circumlocution is considered a solution to a vital problem.

Dow Christophsen is the bull who broke into this Long Island china shop. Perhaps his whole philosophy of life is summed up in his remark to Wilma, "Because we slept together once, you think we're soulmates." Surely Behrman did not intend him to be a representative of the class of revolutionary proletarian novelists. It is obvious that none of the characters of the play and surely S. N. Behrman have any respect for the type of fiction written by them. They admit its hold on people, however. As Wilma expresses it, "Your pages are not brilliant, but somehow you give people the idea that you have talent."

Dow is an outsider, not only to this set, but to any set. He comes to Binkie's cottage only because his uncle, Charles Don Hanlon, is also living on the estate of Kingdom Sears. He is the son of a canner and his early recollections are not the kind to inspire patriotism. An emotional dialogue between Ryder and Dow in the last act has elements of good drama in it and reveals the reasons for Dow's unshakeable faith in the inevitability of the success of his cause. Dow is planning to leave America and has no intentions of returning. Ryder sneeringly asks if he is going to Russia to be liquidated. Dow does not know where he is going, and as far as his writing is concerned, he does not care because he can write anywhere. In fact, "He can't help writing anywhere."

Ryder asks if Dow hasn't any recollection of any happy boyhood scene to which he might be drawn. Dow relates the environment of his boyhood and concludes that it was not the kind to inspire nostalgia. It was another example of Behrman's gift for crystallizing a lifetime of experience into a few moments of emotionally charged dialogue. Dow's inhuman pre-occupation with his writing is unpleasant to his associates, to the audience, and is difficult to believe. Perhaps such unshakeable confidence in one's ability is to be found among proletarian novelists, but Behrman has not made it convincing on the stage. When Wilma asks him why he does not wait for the critics' opinion of his first novel before he begins the second, he replies, "When it got by me, I was no longer interested in the critics." If Behrman wanted to incarnate in Dow the characteristics of revolutionary novelists, he has succeeded but he has failed to make him believable. We are totally unprepared for his little afternoon tête-à-tête with Wilma in his bedroom, or for his passionate kiss preceding their trip upstairs, unless as the outcome of his technique of making love, which consisted of two insults in answer to one of her compliments.

One cannot escape the feeling that Behrman transported this couple upstairs in order to lead up to his second-act curtain and not from the inner necessity of the situation or of the development of character. That Wilma would fall in love with Dow, we might possibly expect, because she is reminded of her first husband, Crain, almost the moment he enters Binkie's cottage. That Dow should stoop (in his opinion) to the all-too-human weakness of loving the delights of the flesh in mid-afternoon like any Casanova, is beyond credibility. The dramatist has not prepared us for this sudden emergence of sex.

Perhaps Behrman, like Sinclair Lewis in his novel, *The Prodigal Parents,* was not interested in presenting a believable character, but a composite of all the traits of revolutionary writers which may have offended him. Like so many other things, it all depends on the point of view one takes. When a research scientist refuses to let love interfere with his research, we are asked to admire his devotion to science and to the human race, which is ultimately to benefit from his sacrifices. When a proletarian novelist refuses to permit an emotionally unstable woman to interfere with his plans for benefiting the human race (albeit his means are revolutionary) he is condemned by other characters in the play and obviously by the author.

From the point of view of humaneness, Dow is a monster. He

has caused Wilma to fall in love with him, although he seems to have given her no visible encouragement. Ryder, following in the tradition of chivalry, would have him marry her and settle down. His uncle, the retired novelist, who was "immortal" at forty, was willing to leave his fortune to him, although he had already made up his mind to leave it to a home for indigent cats. When Dow tries to defend himself for leaving the house alone, Ryder simply explodes into vituperation. Yet Dow wanted nothing from people. It was Wilma who wanted Dow. We are made to feel that he is contemptible when after all he was only being true to himself.

This truth to one's self is at the core of all Behrman's characters, in this play and in his other comedies. In high comedy each character must be right. In his own way Binkie was to be admired. It is true that he borrowed money from his friends to play the market on tips from these very same friends. Yet he was harmless. Certainly the world was never injured by its Binkies. Ryder, too, wins our sympathy. To free one's self from the shackles of wealth and upper-class society and to try to bring more of the good things in life to the masses, is true nobility, is truly an indication of *noblesse oblige*. Yet he could be intolerant of the means and personalities of other reformers and would be willing to kill them to defend his own class. To Dow, such renegades from the wealthy class were more dangerous than the most detestable plutocrat. They claimed to be waging a war for democracy when they actually were trying to prevent the hungry masses from dispossessing them of their wealth founded with "franchises obtained by bribing aldermen." Dow saw through Ryder's humanitarian pretensions and disapproved of them. When Ryder, after all sorts of cajolery, failed to make a disciple of Dow, the older man felt that the younger was unjust. Perhaps the millionaire editor and politician did not see the beam in his own eye, while he magnified the mote in Dow's.

Larry Sears is, as the late James M. Barrie liked to say of his own characters, "inoffensive." The final product of all that wealth could do, he reminds one so strongly of the scions of ancient Teutonic families in the novels of Jakob Wassermann and Arthur

Schnitzler. If the evils of the present day were not somehow connected with these end-products of a predatory civilization in which a few cunning or capable individuals in each country managed to amass most of the wealth of their respective countries, they could be ignored. They seldom did people harm. They bore no prejudice toward different creeds; both Binkie and Leo Traub were of Jewish origin. Larry Sears was considerate because he could afford to be. True, he spent a quarter of a million dollars for *The Princess of Java,* but he had been assured that he would profit from his investment. When his honorable intentions toward Wilma are thrown to the dust by her attraction to Dow, he gallantly accepts the inevitable and wishes her happiness. We can find little fault with Larry and we are inclined to be sorry for him in the end.

It is in Wilma that Behrman concentrates his forces. He tries very hard to make her a human being, but in the end he endows her with so many traits that she is unconvincing. We discover at the very end of the play that she had been born to poverty; that she had been compelled to entertain in night clubs; and that she had been the model of the artist whom she married. One hears echoes of *Brief Moment,* in which a night-club singer marries into the wealthy set, only to disappoint her husband. Wilma also reveals herself as an impetuous, impulsive creature. It was only in Ryder's and in Larry's eyes that she appeared as the goddess. In the presence of Dow she could throw off her pretenses. After all, he said, why pretend, when it is so obvious? Though two wealthy men could not persuade her to marry them, she walked into the bedroom of an egocentric novelist who seems to have won his way to her heart by ignoring her.

Wilma is incapable of keeping her resolutions. At the very beginning of the play she resolves to be "hard and casual"; a moment later Dow walks in and one almost can hear her heart pumping wildly. Now she wants to be herself and become a star in pictures, and in the third act she wants to give up everything and go with Dow to starve in a garret. No wonder he said that she would change her mind in six months. From what she does in the play, we are inclined to think that she would change her mind in six hours. In the third act, for example, Dow and Wilma come back from the private showing of *The Princess of Java*. She expresses her love for him with feeling so powerful as almost to appear indelicate. Five months later, when he has steadfastly refused to be weakened by her pleas, she exclaims "I hate you. If I only knew how I could hurt you." Her words sound too much like the *clichés* in the pulp magazines to be worthy of Behrman.

One cannot expect an audience to be sympathetic to a woman who has just refused honorable offers of marriage and falls madly in love with a revolutionary novelist. Women have the privilege of falling in love with whomever they wish, but on the stage such antics as are exhibited by Wilma seem more like an exhibition of distraught nerves than true emotion. In the very last line she repeats her words of the first few minutes of the play, "From now on I'm going to be hard and casual. Oh, but I've said that." The curtain descends on an unsolved problem.

Of course, the comic dramatist is not a reformer or social-planner and it is not his function to set the world aright. It is sufficient that he writes cleverly and, sometimes, wisely, of some human problem. Behrman has been quite successful, with the exception of *Wine of Choice,* in presenting interesting problems and discussing them with charm, *savoir-faire,* and a modicum of wisdom. It was an exhilarating experience to hear his discussion of religious and intellectual persecution in Germany. *Rain from Heaven* was mature entertainment. One felt that a razor-keen intelligence was behind it all. The discussion was civilized, cultured, witty, and quotable. Compared with *Wine of Choice, Rain from Heaven* was a masterpiece.

What is Behrman trying to discuss in his latest play? Is it a satire on proletarian novelists? Is it an amusing exposé of the "horsey set"? Or is it a case-history in feminine instability? Sometimes, as in *End of Summer,* Behrman could combine all these elements and produce an enjoyable concoction. This time he has not succeeded. It is not to be implied that his powers are diminishing. In his own special field of high comedy he is still the master. Perhaps the change has come about in the audience. In a theatrical season (1937) which brought such serious productions as those of the Mercury Theatre, Thornton Wilder's *Our Town,* Paul Vincent Carroll's *Shadow and Substance,* and *On Borrowed Time,* the love problems of a beautiful woman seem inconsequential. To Behrman, noble living, good food, clever discourse, and intellectualism are still of paramount significance; but to the world at large, outside of the "horsey set," other realities rear their ugly heads: war, dictatorship, unemployment, the reversion to barbarism. Is Behrman still living in the world of 1926 when his *Second Man* was presented? At that time Freudianism, introspection, lost-generationism were the topics of the day. In a world where hundreds of millions are forbidden the privilege of thinking, Behrman's preoccupation with the emotional instabilities of a few selected individuals seems ivory-towerish. Of course, we can all have our wine of choice, and Behrman has partaken so long from his particular vintage, that he finds it difficult to change. Perhaps the Coca-Cola drinkers who fill the Labor Stage Theatre and the beer-drinkers who laugh so heartily at *A Shoemaker's Holiday* have no taste for any kind of wine, dramatic or liquid.

6. IRWIN SHAW

New York playgoers who can recognize a potential Pulitzer Prizewinner when they see one are making all kinds of complimentary predictions about Irwin Shaw, whose *The Gentle People* was the 1939 success of the Group Theatre. It served also as the vehicle for Franchot Tone's long-awaited return to the legitimate stage. In his second full-length play, Shaw leaves no doubt as to his amazing skill in the creation of recognizable and long-remembered characters, the most important acquisition of any young dramatist.

In 1934 Clifford Odets' *Waiting for Lefty* startled a dull and uninspired theatrical season, and all the critics tumbled over each other, throwing compliments to the young and perhaps surprised author. Since that time Odets has definitely made his mark on the American stage and in 1939 he enjoyed the enviable distinction of seeing his *Awake and Sing* performed simultaneously in English and Yiddish while *Rocket to the Moon* alternated with his first play.

Now the critics like to make prophecies for Irwin Shaw. The encomia liberally showered upon the two young dramatists read very much alike. If Shaw improves in the next play to the extent that *The Gentle People* is an improvement over *Bury the Dead,* the Pulitzer Prize should be his very soon.

IRWIN SHAW

Everybody who knows the American social theatre of recent years has heard of or seen *Bury the Dead*. It seemed too ghastly a subject—this portrayal of six dead soldiers "of the next war" who refuse to lie down and be buried, but this is what Robert Garland, drama critic of the *New York World-Telegram* wrote:

Nobody has seen fit to deny that Mr. Shaw's is one of the most stirring plays ever fashioned by an American, even as at the same time it is one of the most dramatically denunciatory of the anti-war, anti-munition-makers, anti-jingo dramas.

Richard Lockridge, drama critic of the *New York Sun,* who rarely uses superlatives in his critical vocabulary, wrote:

Angrily satirical at its best and giving evidence at all times of the arrival of a new and vigorous talent in the theatre. At the opening it received applause which has not, either in volume or enthusiasm, been surpassed this year.

Bury the Dead was originally submitted for a one-act play contest conducted by the New Theatre League, which has the distinction of producing for the first time Clifford Odets' *Waiting for Lefty*. Although the play arrived two weeks after the closing date of the contest, it was accepted and printed in *New Theatre Magazine* and later by Random House. Almost nothing was known about the author at the time, except that he had attended Brooklyn College, had played on its football team, and had been writing radio scripts.

More is known now (1939) of his early life (there are only twenty-four years of it altogether). He was born in Brooklyn, New York, went to one of the local high schools and began his literary career writing for the school paper. In Brooklyn College he conducted an essay column on the newspaper. For four years he played quarterback on the varsity team, a fact which explains certain lines in his newest play. Semi-professional football followed.

His first experiences with playwrighting were with his college dramatic society for which he dashed off half-a-dozen one-acters.

IRWIN SHAW

After graduation, he wrote radio scripts in the form of serial dramatizations of famous comic strips. Two of them, The Gumps and Dick Tracy, were very successful.

The success of *Bury the Dead* led to a Hollywood contract, the most conspicuous result of which, as far as the public was concerned, being the script of *The Big Game*. He returned to New York after a brief stay and wrote two plays, *Salute,* a satire on false patriotism, and *Siege,* a drama about the Spanish War.

Siege was produced on December 8, 1937, and ran only six nights. The critics noted a definite artistic growth and knew that with the discovery of a theme worthy of his talents, Shaw would produce a full-length drama as successful as his initial one-act play.

Shaw's idealism and hatred for war are exemplified in *Siege*. The scene is the garrison of a Loyalist Spanish citadel in the path of the advancing rebels, waiting for the relief column that never comes. Shaw's characters were vividly portrayed, a trait noted in his first drama. It was the first play of the Spanish Civil War to be produced on Broadway.

In *The Gentle People,* Shaw is describing the human beings he has lived with and knows, with the result that one leaves the theatre remembering half a dozen people who refuse to leave your mind. Included in this band is the Goodman family, Jonah, Florence and Stella, a Jewish family which takes its place among the memorable portraits of Jews in the contemporary theatre. Other Jewish characters are Eli Lieber, the barker, and Lammanowitz, the bankrupt retail merchant, whose portrait is the work of a first-rate artist.

Thus Irwin Shaw joins the ranks of the Jewish writers in America, in his portrayal and interpretation of this Jewish family, alike in many respects to other Jewish families on the stage yet original in many ways. Shaw has not imitated what Montague Glass, Anne Nichols, Bella and Samuel Spewack, Clifford Odets and Augustus Thomas have done. Each of these dramatists has described Jewish life in the American scene. Shaw's picture—a true *genre* portrait of the theatre—is an original creation. One scene, that in the sweat-bath, is probably the first such scene in the history of the American, and possibly, world drama.

Jonah Goodman is a W.P.A. worker, who admits his failure in life, yet is definitely one of God's gentle creatures. His life revolves around the happiness of his daughter Stella and his fishing, which he shares with his old friend, Philip Anagnos. As the play opens, they are discussing the purchase of a little motor-boat which will take them to Southern waters, where fishing is all one could wish for.

Mrs. Goodman is a complaining shrew, who is definitely maladjusted and dissatisfied with Jonah's failure, but her nagging cannot take away his simple faith in the goodness of human nature and in the pleasures of life. Stella Goodman is a typical product of a poor environment, plus illusions fed by glamorous movies and the cheap magazines.

Into this quiet household there enters the sinister figure of Harold Goff, petty racketeer, whose vicious character seems like a scourge from heaven. To all his demands, Jonah and Philip finally give in. They must pay "protection" so that their little boat will not be cut adrift. Goff insists upon taking Stella away from her faithful boy-friend, and treats her as his mistress. The climax of Jonah's sufferings is reached when Goff demands the money saved up by the two fishermen so that he may take Stella on a Southern cruise.

Jonah tries to rebel and goes so far as to bring Goff to the magistrate on charges of forced "protection." The latter is a friend of Goff and chastises the two fishermen for wasting his time. In the cruelest scene of the play, Goff beats Jonah with a rubber hose, as a lesson in manners. This is too much. Jonah and Philip resolve to kill Goff and follow through. They recover their money, Stella goes back to Eli, and the gentle people continue their plans for their Southern trip.

The plot has the simplicity of life, yet with the dash of sensationalism given by an account of a racketeer's death as printed in the daily newspaper.

Shaw has created characters who live for us and thus has made a definite advance up the ladder of his dramatic success. Jonah Goodman is one of the most likable Jewish creations in the contemporary drama. He invites comparison with Esdras in Maxwell Anderson's *Winterset* as a man of ideals and innate goodness. His courage in the face of seemingly hopeless odds, his uncomplaining acceptance of the inhuman rubber-hose beating at the hands of the bullying Goff, give him an almost Job-like patience and capacity for suffering. Murder cannot be made attractive on the stage, but if ever a murder was deserved and sincerely applauded by the sympathetic audience it was the murder of Goff by these two gentle people.

What dramatic path will Shaw now follow? His interest in the drama of social protest seems to have waned temporarily in favor of an interest in human beings who can be made to live. Whereas one left *Bury the Dead* with only vague memories of the individual participants, one cannot forget the half dozen unusual personalities of *The Gentle People* who in the brief two hours granted by the exigencies of the theatre have somehow managed to become part of you.

If Shaw retains his mastery of the creation of character and employs a significant theme in his next play, he cannot fail to make a truly important contribution to American drama.

7. BELLA AND SAMUEL SPEWACK

The American theatre has several distinguished family collaborators like the Lunts, the McClintics, the Heywards, the Langners, the Emersons and the Spewacks.

New York is so accustomed to one success after another at the hands of this capable dramatic team, that the failure of their play, *Miss Swan Expects* (1939), amazed their many admirers as much as success would have done earlier in their career. Their great hit to date has been *Boy Meets Girl* (1935), one of the greatest satires on Hollywood, which closed after 669 performances.

Bella Cohen was born in Hungary and Samuel Spewack in Russia in the same year, 1900. She attended Washington Irving High School in Manhattan and is still remembered as a precocious young girl who has more than fulfilled her early promise. She edited her high school magazine and later worked on the *New York Call,* with many other now celebrated Jewish authors, including Edwin Justus Mayer, Louis Weitzenkorn, Anita Block, and David Karsner. She made her entry into theatrical writing via press-agenting for various art groups.

She was gifted as an actress, having sung in the Victoria Music Hall at the age of four. In high school she participated in and directed plays. She was press-agent for Max Reinhardt's *Miracle* and Balieff's *Chauve Souris.*

BELLA AND SAMUEL SPEWACK

Samuel Spewack was a reporter and later a foreign correspondent in Moscow and Berlin. His experiences in Russia may have led to his writing *Clear All Wires* (1932), which he later turned into the musical *Leave It to Me*. It is significant that in 1929 Samuel Spewack wrote a series of articles on the sad state of the American theatre, to whose gay resurrection he has contributed so much.

In 1926 their first collaboration appeared, *The Solitaire Man*. In 1928 two plays, both of Jewish interest, were produced. Neither *Poppa* nor *The War Song*, which served as a starring vehicle for George Jessel, revealed phenomenal talents. Broadway was aware that a new comedy-writing team was performing but it was not terribly excited.

In 1932 *Clear All Wires* gave every indication of a long and successful run, as it satirized Russian life and gave New Yorkers an idea of the daily experiences of a foreign correspondent in the days before United States recognition. The movie made subsequently was more successful than the play.

The greatest interest the Spewacks have for the students of the portrayal of Jewish life in American drama, lies in their collaboration, *Spring Song* (1934). It remains to date (1939) the last of the English dramas of New York's East Side Jewish life. A number of plays depicting Jewish households have appeared since *Spring Song*, but they are definitely away from the New York East Side. Clifford Odets' *Awake and Sing* (1935) takes place in the Bronx. Maxwell Anderson's *Winterset* occurs somewhere near the Brooklyn Bridge; Irwin Shaw's *The Gentle People* is in the Sheepshead Bay section of Brooklyn.

Spring Song portrayed a typical Jewish mother whose only reason for slaving away in her little confectionery shop was the happiness of her two daughters. One of them, Florrie, has her head filled with all sorts of notions derived mostly from the movies and the magazines. At times Florrie of *Spring Song* and Stella Goodman of *The Gentle People* seem to be using the same words, as do Hennie Berger of *Awake and Sing,* and Florrie in *Waiting for Lefty*. They are all emotionally and artistically starved. They dream like their millions of American sisters, of ermines and duplex apartments, yachts and cruises. Pathetic in their credulity, they almost always are bound to be disillusioned or to make an ignoble compromise.

Florrie carries on an affair with the sweetheart of her older sister. She becomes pregnant and dies in childbirth after marrying the man who seduced her, but whom she does not love. In the long-established tradition of the Yiddish theatre, Florrie dies on the stage, a victim of her uncontrolled restless strivings to escape from her sordid environment.

Although the critics and the audiences indicated only lukewarm interest in the Spewacks' attempt at tragedy, they admitted that the characters of Mrs. Solomon and her friend the butcher were living creations and more memorable than even the starring role. The Spewacks had not yet found their *métier*. It needed a protracted sojourn in Hollywood, writing scenarios, to give them the material and the skill to concoct *Boy Meets Girl*. Like George S. Kaufman's *Once in a Lifetime* it satirizes the inanities of the movie world and the authors emerged as a comedy-writing team of the first magnitude.

The authors began with the idea of satirizing the Boy-Meets-Girl formula of every movie scenario and ended after three hilarious acts of strange movie interludes with the old formula coming out on top once again; the waitress marrying a real Lord.

The Spewacks found room for some brilliant satire on the musical ignorance of production heads, the artistic integrity of scenario-slaves, authors with desires to "escape from it all and go off to Maine and write real literature." Hollywood did not object to its lambasting, for a moving-picture version was soon made.

Their latest effort is a revamping of *Clear All Wires*, their venture into the biography of a foreign correspondent. With Cole Porter's music and lyrics and William Gaxton and Victor Moore, *Leave It to Me* was definitely one of the bright spots of the 1938 dramatic season. Devotees of the theatre know the much discussed scene in which Victor Moore as American Ambassador to the U. S. S. R. kicks the nazi envoy. For a time the press agents welcomed the news that Prince Obolensky, who had a part as a member of the U. S. S. R. officialdom, was expelled from the society of Russian nobles in America for playing such a role.

Their latest collaboration, *Miss Swan Expects,* a farce about book-publishing, opened in New York on February 21, 1939. Their portraits of literati were the funniest of their kind in many years. Not since Ben Hecht's movie, *The Scoundrel,* was there such a collection of auctorial idiosyncrasies. Josie Swan is an editor married to a ghost-writer. There is a crack-brained sandwich man who is trying to sell his life-story. A taxi driver quietly steals the erotic books belonging to the firm. Throughout all the commotion Miss Swan is expecting to be initiated into the mysteries of motherhood. Her husband is arrested for selling erotic literature; the firm almost collapses, and is saved by the wealth of the millionaire whose book the husband is ghost-writing.

The Spewacks, having apparently exhausted the fun-provoking possibilities of Hollywood and newspaper life, tried their hand at another phase of American life which they knew and in which they saw comic possibilities. That the play failed to live up to the high expectations set by their success earlier is no fault but their own. Yet farce, once successful, is very difficult to repeat. If the same funny situations are repeated, there is always the tenacious memory of the dramatic critic to remind the authors of the repetition of tried formulas. If a new situation is attempted the recollection of earlier success is often brought up to make an odious comparison.

To date the Spewacks can boast of two unquestioned successes in *Boy Meets Girl* and *Leave It to Me,* and several hopeful attempts. Both still under forty, they will undoubtedly add much to the gayety of Broadway's jaded appetite. Their versatility and sheer *joie de vivre* are amazing. They have attempted to interpret the life they know best, even though their presentations of

Jewish life were not so successful as their satires of Hollywood and newspaper life.

Ten years after Samuel Spewack interviewed leading personalities of the American theatre on the imminent demise of the Fabulous Invalid, the American drama, he has contributed to a drama which is now the leader in the world. With his wife he has given us the comic aspects of certain intensely American phenomena and has made us see them as perhaps we never saw them before. They may not have the stature of S. N. Behrman or George S. Kaufman with their mastery of the comic gift, but they are definitely determined to try to improve their technique and broaden the scope of their activities.

8. JEWISH NOVELISTS AND

THE CONTEMPORARY AMERICAN NOVEL

The novel as a literary medium for American Jews is almost exclusively a product of the twentieth century. When it was first employed it was most often used as documentary studies of Jewish life and hence lost its interest and value when the transitory conditions depicted no longer existed. Thus the entire output of Ghetto fiction in America is gradually assuming difficulties for the reader of the 1930's and will become more and more strange as the Ghetto slums and streets and pushcarts disappear and a new East Side (in New York, Chicago, or elsewhere) is born. In the final judgment upon the literary significance of the contributions of Jewish novelists in America, those who confined themselves too closely to case histories of the immigrant will inevitably assume less importance. Those novelists who have universal appeal, who dealt with eternal problems rather than with local difficulties, deserve greater credit for their work.

The list of Jewish novelists writing at the end of the 1930's is impressive and makes extremely difficult the task of organizing and evaluating their literary output. The most prominent are: Benjamin Appel; Nathan Asch; Konrad Bercovici; Rion Bercovici; Maxwell Bodenheim; Lowell Brentano; Myron Brinig; Catherine Brody; Ezra S. Brudno; Abraham Cahan; Lester Cohen; O. R. Cohen; John Cournos; Alvah Bessie; Beatrice Bisno; Her-

JEWISH NOVELISTS

man Bloom; Edward Dahlberg; Hermann Deutsch; Lawrence Drake; Leonard Ehrlich; Edna Ferber; Nat J. Ferber; Irving Fineman; David Freedman; Daniel Fuchs; Gilbert Gabriel; Milton Goldsmith; Joseph Gollomb; Albert Halper; Ben Hecht; Sam Hellman; James Henle; V. D. Hersch; Fannie Hurst; Joseph Israels; Aben Kandel; McKinlay Kantor; Lincoln Kirstein; Manuel Komroff; Bruno Lessing; Meyer Levin; Melvin P. Levy; Ludwig Lewisohn; Harold Loeb; Miriam Michelson; Robert Nathan; Sidney Nyburg; Samuel Ornitz; Charles Recht; Charles Reznikoff; William B. Richter; Henry Roth; Emanie Sachs; Edwin Seaver; Edgar Selwyn; Tess Slesinger; Marion Spitzer; Irving Stone; L. C. Stone; Jerome Weidman; Thyra S. Winslow; Anzia Yezierska; Leane Zugsmith.

A few well-defined groupings can be made. Thus Michael Gold, Albert Halper, Nathan Asch, Edwin Seaver and Leane Zugsmith might be classified as "proletarian novelists," a term applied in the depression period (1929-   ) to writers depicting the poverty and misery as a result of the breakdown of the economic order.

America's colorful past has occupied Edna Ferber, Gilbert Gabriel, McKinlay Kantor, and Leonard Ehrlich. Octavus Roy Cohen has specialized in negro life. Samuel Ornitz has laid bare the corruption in municipal politics, Konrad Bercovici has written of gypsy life and of the East Side of New York. Ludwig Lewisohn, Marion Spitzer and Emanie Sachs have discussed marital problems. Robert Nathan is perhaps the finest stylist among the American Jewish novelists and is a favorite with the critics.

To be specific, among the proletarians one notes Michael Gold. He was editor of the *Liberator* from 1919 to 1921; and then edited the *New Masses* from 1924 to 1927. *Jews without Money* (1930) is one of the most vivid studies of the New York East Side. He wrote one play about Mexico, *Fiesta,* a one-act play *Money* (1930), 120 *Million* (1929), sketches of the American worker and *Charlie Chaplin's Parade* (1930), a book for children. Gold is primarily interested in social protest and was among the first to write courageously of the sufferings of the American working class.

Albert Halper has followed the American worker in New York (*Union Square,* 1933), in a steel mill (*The Foundry,* 1935), and in a mail-order establishment (*The Chute,* 1937). In *The Company* (1930) Seaver writes this "collective" novel in a skeletonized prose style which conveys the barrenness of lives in dull subservience to a well-run machine, The Company. No character in the book is truly flesh and blood; they have become automatons and lost their human values under the hand of an industrial despotism. The only person who views his enslavement to The Company with a cynical and understanding eye that ultimately leads to a self-given freedom is a Jew, Aarons. Written about a similar theme and in a similar pattern is Nathan Asch's *The Office* (1925). Although a youthful work which is not enhanced by an unintegrated experimentalism, it yet displays the beginnings of a vigorous pen.

American history has supplied the subject-matter for many of the novels of Edna Ferber. Only one novel, *Fanny Herself* (1917), deals with a Jewish subject. In the latter the difficulties of a Jewess in a mid-Western town who has not been considered Jewish are given sympathetic treatment. More characteristic of the novelist, however, are *Show Boat* (1926), *Cimmaron* (1929), and *American Beauty* (1931). She has acquired a reputation for her sympathetic treatment of women in industry and business in such books as *Emma McChesney & Co.* (1925), *The Girls* (1921), and in her play *Stage Door* (1936).

McKinlay Kantor has written *Long Remember* (1934), a study of the Civil War, which was well received by the critics, *The Voice of Bugle Ann* (1935), *Turkey in the Straw* (1935), and *Arouse and Beware* (1937). He is especially gifted in the powers of description, employing a style marked by simplicity and picturesqueness.

Leonard Ehrlich in *God's Angry Man* (1931) novelized the life of John Brown and produced one of the best first novels of the early 1930's.

Since Robert Nathan is discussed in another chapter, only his characteristics as a stylist and ironist will be mentioned. His dozen novels since his first in 1919 are all marked by a fine sense for the language, a love of nature, a nobility of character which is exemplified in his heroes.

The problem of living in the complex civilization of America during the prosperity of the Calvin Coolidge period and the subsequent depression were not always economic. The social and particularly Jewish difficulties are discussed in the section on Jewish Writers on Jewish Life. Occasionally Jewish novelists described their non-Jewish environment. Ludwig Lewisohn in *Stephen Escott* (1930), *The Case of Mr. Crump* (1927), *Don Juan* (1923), and *Forever Wilt Thou Love* (1939), attempted to deal with marital incompatibility. Tess Slesinger in *The Unpossessed* (1933) delineated a social set whose principal activities seemed confined to the arts of drinking and gallantry.

Perhaps the most commercially successful of the Jewish writers in America is Fannie Hurst. She was born in Hamilton, Ohio. In 1914 she made her literary début with *Just Around the Corner*. The career of Fannie Hurst is especially instructive, in view of its uneven line. One moment she is signing a book that makes one blush for her; the next, she produces a work that raises her to the heights of American authorship. She is a best-seller that has attracted at once the multitudes and the critical few. Something in her keeps alternating between East of Suez and the West. Outwardly, such a novel as *Apassionata* (1925) may be Catholic in environment; inwardly, one may discover the soul-searching of a Jew. Outwardly, her story *Five and Ten* (1929) may deal with a department store millionaire as far removed from a Jewish atmosphere as Alaska from Arabia, yet inwardly there is a sternness of mood and dedication to the spirit that comes right out of the Psalms.

Ben Hecht has displayed remarkable versatility in the dramas *The Front Page* (1928) and *To Quito and Back* (1937), as well as in the novel. *Erik Dorn* (1921) is a novel characteristic of his style and method. He has an amazingly rich vocabulary which he employs with great power. His plots are not memorable, and his themes difficult to comprehend. His short stories of Chicago are among his best work.

Waldo Frank is another novelist of distinction; in *Rahab* (1922) and *City Block* (1922) he made some important contributions to the structure of the novel. Some of Frank's work abounds with a mysticism which is sustained to the enhancement of the work. *The Death and Birth of David Markand* (1934) is profoundly philosophical in regard to the place of a man in a modern complex society, and it has placed him among the ranking American novelists of the day.

9. JEWISH NOVELISTS

PORTRAY THE JEW, 1867-1939

The history of Jewish life in America from the Civil War to the present is written in the fiction by American Jewish novelists. The recent literature is in vivid contrast to that of the American Jewish writers of the early nineteenth century, who seldom introduced a Jewish character or a Jewish problem in their works. In 1818 the Jewish population in America was estimated at 3,000; in 1824, at 6,000; in 1848 at 50,000. By 1880 it had risen to 230,000, and material for the novelist was at hand.

In 1867 Nathan Mayer wrote a novel of the Civil War, *Differences,* in which the participation by Jews on the side of the Confederacy is presented. Twenty years later Henry Harland, who was not a Jew, but who wrote under the pseudonym of Sidney Luska, in an obvious attempt to suggest Jewish origin, described several interesting Jewish personalities in his novels. *As It Was Written* (1885) concerned a Jewish musician in America. *Mrs. Peixada* (1886) delineated contemporary German-Jewish life in New York City. *My Uncle Florimond* (1888) illustrated the philanthropic character of a group of New York Jews who befriended and protected an orphan. Perhaps his most significant study of Jewish life was *The Yoke of the Torah* (1887). The hero, a German Jew, is in love with a Christian. Upon the strong insistence of his uncle, a rabbi, he breaks the relationship, marries a commonplace Jewess and dies soon after. Harland's work was among the best which dealt with the life of the German-American Jews. The influx of the Russian Jews changed the subject-matter and introduced new problems. New novelists arose to utilize it.

The forces that operated in the development of their material in America have been swift, dramatic and abundant. The collapse of the traditional culture and religion of the immigrant Jew in the New York Ghetto, the manner in which he was exploited in the sweatshop, his conflict with a rising generation of American-born sons and daughters, tempted a literary treatment that sought for effects in pathos, rhetoric and picturesqueness.

As a result, there was a flood of novels on immigrants and peddlers, bearded fathers and bewigged mothers, set against the East Side's teeming background, whose prototypes and flat outlines became increasingly familiar. Bruno Lessing, Elias Tobenkin, Anzia Yezierska, Fannie Hurst, Abraham Cahan, Herman Bernstein, and a host of innumerable other American Jewish writers turned out novels and short stories that followed the curve of this pattern with more or less moderation. Their works became typed.

As far back as 1896 Abraham Cahan began to write of the newly-arrived Russian-Jewish immigrants in such stories as *Yekl* and *The Imported Bridegroom* (1898). Herman Bernstein was writing similar stories, which he collected in 1902, in *In the Gates of Israel*. American readers, through the fiction in magazines and later in collected volumes and in novels, were learning about the East-European Jews. Occasionally one of them would write an autobiography which would help to explain the plight of the new immigrants. Such a writer was Mary Antin, author of *From Polotsk to Boston* (1899), *The Promised Land* (1912), and *They Who Knock at Our Gates* (1914).

In 1917 Abraham Cahan published *The Rise of David Levinsky* and M. E. Ravage, *An American in the Making*. The first has become a classic of its kind. The characters, sharply outlined, present a rich welter of the many-sided life of Jews, which comes to the surface in pages written with force and restraint, and is crowded with business rivalries between German and Russian Jews goaded by ambition and desires. The author skilfully weaves his theme around the main character of the book, David Levinsky, a student of the Talmud without any love for Jewish ideals and learning. He emigrates to America where, after years of toil in sweatshops, he enters business and ultimately the "higher life," as opposed to his own of gaudy splendor. He offers his hand in marriage and when refused he considers his success a hollow mockery and his life, he feels, lacks an inner solidity.

The struggles of the Russian-Jewish immigrants in other American cities were also portrayed. Isaac Kahn Friedman in *The Lucky Number* (1896) described the Chicago Ghetto, establishing a tradition that was followed by Meyer Levin's *The Old Bunch* (1937), in which the activities of the American descendants of the Russian immigrants are chronicled.

Several women have found rich material for their stories in New York's East Side. Of these, Anzia Yezierska and Fannie Hurst have been most successful. The former was born in Russia in 1885 and came to America in 1901. She went through many of the economic and spiritual difficulties which beset her characters until she finally learned enough about the English language to put her bitter experiences into words. In 1918 she began to write short stories of the life she knew. In 1919 Edward J. O'Brien designated her story *The Fat of the Land* the best of the year. She has written two novels, *Salome of the Tenements* (1922) and *Bread Givers* (1925), and numerous short stories. Throughout her work she emphasizes her solution of the immigrant problem, that of providing the means by which the newcomers can realize their dreams.

Anzia Yezierska invites comparison with Fannie Hurst. The latter, however, is a native American, having been born in Hamilton, Ohio, in 1889. In 1911 she began to publish her short stories. Having come to New York, she quickly realized the wealth of fictional material which the Ghetto offered. *Humoresque* (1918), *Lummox* (1923), and *Apassionata* (1925) deal with Jewish characters, particularly in their strivings toward self-fulfillment. She is also the author of the scenario of *Symphony of Six Million,* a very sympathetic treatment of a Jewish-American family and of the rise of a brilliant surgeon, one of its members.

In 1917 Edna Ferber, who although of Jewish parentage, has been more interested in the aspirations of American Westerners than of Jewish immigrants, published *Fanny Herself.* It is a penetrating study of a Jewish business woman, Fanny Brandeis, who is accepted in a Western Gentile community as one of their own folk. The novel offers some interesting discussions on the business and general characteristics of Jews, of which one of the most penetrating is:

I tell you, Fanny, we Jews have got a money-grubbing, loud-talking, diamond-studded, get-there-at-any-price reputation and perhaps we deserve it. But every now and then, out of the mass of us, one lifts his head and stands erect, and the great white light is in his face. And that person has suffered, for suffering breeds genius.

Again, when Fanny speaks of her race as a handicap, her friend, the Irish priest, says:

That's not a handicap, Fanny. It's an asset. Outwardly you're like any other girl of your age. Inwardly, you've been molded by occupation, training, religion, history, temperament, race into something . . . You've suffered, you Jews, for centuries and centuries until you're all in it, emotional, over-sensitive, cringing, or swaggering, highstrung, demonstrative, affectionate, generous.

The early years of the twentieth century saw new collections of stories or new novels of the new Jewish immigrants. Many of the old problems of Israel in Exile occur in fiction time and time again. The relation of Jew and Gentile was the subject of Ezra Selig Brudno's *The Fugitive* (1904). Brudno wrote copiously on this subject, including the novels *One of Us* (1908), which was concerned with the supersensitiveness of a Jewish artist and musician, burdened with a physical deformity; and *The Tether* (1908), which was one of the earliest studies in American fiction of the Jewish writer. Brudno knew the Russian immigrant at first hand and his *Little Conscript* (1905) is a sympathetic study of the sufferings of the Jewish soldier in the Russian army.

The element of humor in this type of fiction is at first a rarity, but with the stories of Montague Glass the saga of the Jew in America is no longer one of tears and struggles. For twenty years his "Abe" and "Mawruss" were popular as representatives of the immigrant Jew who had gained financial success. Beginning in 1910 with *Potash and Perlmutter* and in the succeeding volumes *Abe and Mawruss* (1911), *Object Matrimony* (1912), *Elkan Lubliner, American* (1912), *The Competitive Nephew* (1915), *Worrying Won't Win* (1918), *Potash and Perlmutter Settle Things* (1919), *Y' Understand* (1925), *You Can't Learn 'em Nothin'* (1930), Glass created characters which became almost as well known as Finley Peter Dunne's Mr. Dooley. The fact that he could provide material about them for twenty years, running through the pre-war prosperity, the World War, the Peace Conference, and the post-war prosperity indicates an inventiveness which critics readily granted to the author. These books were well received by the public and critics and represent a distinct contribution to the literature of the immigrant American Jew in business.

Many of the Russian-Jewish immigrants had been associated with social-reform movements in their native land and before long there arose in New York various literary, debating, and fraternal organizations devoted to fostering social improvement. American fiction by Jews soon responded. Henry Berman's *Worshippers* (1906) delineates the Bohemian existence of the intellectual Russian Jews in New York. *Comrade Yetta* (1913) by Arthur Bullard presents sympathetically the evolution of a Jewess from worker in a sweatshop to leadership in trade unions and to literary prominence in the workers' cause.

Other types of idealistic Jews were subjects of fictional treatments. James Oppenheim's *Doctor Rast* (1909) was a forerunner of Sinclair Lewis' *Arrowsmith* (1926) and Sidney Kingsley's *Men in White* (1933) in the presentation of the Jewish scientist who thinks more of his science than of his material advancement. Dr. Rast definitely rejects a prosperous practice to minister to the spiritual and physical disabilities of his own people on New York's East Side.

When the immigrant Jew did not remain in New York but travelled further into the interior or to the far West, novelists quickly chronicled his trials and tribulations. Elias Tobenkin concerned himself particularly with these Jewish pioneers of the twentieth century. *Witte Arrives* (1916), *House of Conrad* (1918), and *God of Might* (1925) are studies in the winning of the West by the new immigrant. The problem of intermarriage is also discussed.

With the elevation of the Jews economically and socially, the cultured, artistic, and intellectual Jew appeared in American fiction. The Jewish thinker of the 1930's did not speak with any accent, nor was he confined to the New York East Side. As early as 1911 in Augustus Thomas' *As a Man Thinks* the cultured American Jew had been portrayed in drama. One of the most discussed of these novels was Nyburg's *The Chosen People* (1917), which treated critically, though fairly, of the efforts of Jewish groups attempting to climb the social scale. A chronology of the outstanding novels of Jewish life in America between 1920 and 1939 will reveal at a glance the main problems which concerned their writers:

1920 Anzia Yezierska's *Hungry Hearts*.
1921 John Cournos' *The Wall*.
1921 Ben Hecht's *Erik Dorn*.
1922 John Cournos' *Babel*.
1922 Anzia Yezierska's *Salome of the Tenements*.
1923 Anzia Yezierska's *Children of Loneliness*.
1923 Fannie Hurst's *Lummox*.
1924 Marion Spitzer's *Who Would Be Free*.
1924 James Henle's *Sound and Fury*.

1924 Samuel Ornitz's *Haunch, Paunch and Jowl.*
1924 Charles Recht's *Rue with a Difference.*
1925 Anzia Yezierska's *Bread Givers.*
1925 Montague Glass's *Y' Understand.*
1925 Elias Tobenkin's *God of Might.*
1925 Irwin Edman's *Richard Kane Looks at Life.*
1927 Elias Tobenkin's *Lucky Numbers.*
1927 Nat J. Ferber's *The Sidewalks of New York.*
1928 Ludwig Lewisohn's *The Island Within.*
1928 Paul Rosenfeld's *The Boy in the Sun.*
1929 Paul Reznikoff's *By the Waters of Manhattan.*
1929 Myron Brinig's *Singerman.*
1929 Lawrence Drake's *Don't Call Me Clever.*
1930 Glass's *You Can't Learn 'em Nothin'.*
1930 Michael Gold's *Jews Without Money.*
1930 Lester Cohen's *Aaron Traum.*
1931 Ben Hecht's *A Jew in Love.*
1933 Virginia Hersch's *Storm Beach.*
1933 Irving Fineman's *Hear, Ye Sons.*
1933 Albert Halper's *Union Square.*
1934 Henry Roth's *Call It Sleep.*
1934 Melvin P. Levey's *The Last Pioneers.*
1934 Nat J. Ferber's *One Happy Jew.*
1934 Maurice Samuel's *Beyond Woman.*
1934 Waldo Frank's *The Life and Death of David Markand.*
1934 Ludwig Lewisohn's *An Altar in the Fields.*
1935 Isidor Schneider's *From the Kingdom of Necessity.*
1935 Daniel Fuch's *Summer in Williamsburg.*
1936 Daniel Fuch's *Homage to Blenholt.*
1937 Myron Brinig's *The Sisters.*
1937 Jerome Weidman's *I Can Get It for You Wholesale.*
1937 Meyer Levin's *The Old Bunch.*
1937 Daniel Fuch's *Low Company.*
1938 Beatrice Bisno's *Tomorrow's Bread.*
1938 Aline Bernstein's *The Journey Down.*
1938 Jerome Weidman's *What's in It for Me.*
1939 Irving Fineman's *Dr. Addams.*

The new notes in fiction were Marion Spitzer's study in the

futility of a Jewess's attempt to break away from her own people with the consequent disillusionments; Samuel Ornitz's bitter study of an East Side judge who attained a high position on the judiciary by methods not always acceptable; and Ludwig Lewisohn's and Paul Rosenfeld's studies of the new Jewish intellectual.

These two novelists are among the first American Jewish authors who have not hesitated to describe their own set, with its special problems. No longer is the struggle one of bare existence as it was portrayed in the fiction in the early years of the century. These heroes have wealth and leisure, but they now suffer mental and spiritual crises which are just as acute as those of the earlier protagonists.

Ludwig Lewisohn is a pioneer in the special field of relating the American Jew to his entire racial tradition. His *Island Within* (1928) introduced the American Jewish man of intellect, whose attempts to achieve an inner poise amidst material comfort became the subject matter of many other fictional studies. As a contribution to the study of intermarriage in America, it is one of the most penetrating treatments, which include such excellent plays as Rita Wellman's *The Gentile Wife* (1919), Elmer Rice's *Counsellor-at-Law* (1931), and the novels of Elias Tobenkin.

Paul Rosenfeld's *The Boy in the Sun* is a story of a sensitive and brilliant son of German-Jewish parents who is harassed by the subtle restrictions of Jewishness. It employs the stream-of-consciousness method. Another excellent case-history of the effects of American experiences upon traditional Jewish customs and behavior patterns is Thyra Samter Winslow's short story *A Cycle of Manhattan*. The author shows a keen insight into the evolution of an immigrant family into almost complete Americanization. The "conflict of the generations" is found frequently in American-Jewish fiction. *The Island Within* presents it vividly; so, too, does Irving Fineman in *Hear, Ye Sons* (1933).

The Jewish immigrant as business man has received adequate treatment in Abraham Cahan's *The Rise of David Levinsky* (1917). After two decades he emerged again completely Americanized in Jerome Weidman's *I Can Get It for You Wholesale* (1937). In most cases the tales are sordid and unpleasant, as are the corresponding sagas of American business men in Frank Norris' *The Octopus* and *The Pit* or any number of presentations of the tycoons of the American business world. These analyses of Jewish characters are also valuable as historical records of a period in financial life that seems to have passed.

The differences between German Jews and Russian Jews has been the subject of considerable American literature. As recently as 1931 in Lawson's play *Success Story,* Mr. Sonnenberg, a German-Jewish banker, warned his Gentile friend that the young Russian Jew, Ginsberg, like others of his class was unbeatable, and was to be watched closely. As described in the early American fiction on this topic, the attitude of the German Jews was originally one of sympathy for the victims of the Russian pogroms of the 1880's. When competition arose and economics entered into the field, then the attitude changed. *The Rise of David Levinsky* discusses this antagonism with frankness and understanding. Emanie Sachs in *Red Damask* (1926) offers the prosperous German-American business man, envied by the new Russian arrivals because of his social position.

An interesting variation of the fiction of the American Jew is to be found in the novels of Daniel Fuchs: *Summer in Williamsburg* (1935), *Homage to Blenholt* (1936), and *Low Company* (1937). Fuchs has been aptly termed the "Charlie Chaplin" of the newer novelists. His book, *Homage to Blenholt,* possesses a wistful serio-comic charm that makes us forgive the impractical dreaming and blundering of its hero, Max Balkan, who eventually discovers that a hard world demands a realistic outlook. Fuchs has written something of social import, for if we readily forgive Max Balkan, we find it hard to forgive the world that has produced him. The other characters in the book are drawn with sharp lines, but sometimes Fuchs lacks the warm deep understanding that makes for a really great novel.

Three novels of Jewish interest of 1934 to win distinction are

THE JEW PORTRAYED

Waldo Frank's *The Death and Birth of David Markand,* Maurice Samuel's *Beyond Woman,* and Ludwig Lewisohn's *An Altar in the Fields.* Curiously, all three of these penmen are consumed with pet theories for the reform of society and the solution of the Jewish problem.

With the shutting of the gates to new immigrants during the 1930's, writers on Jewish life in America found their subject-matter in cities other than New York. Myron Brinig in *Singerman* (1929), *Sons of Singerman* (1934), and *The First Book of Michael Singerman* (1935) paints the life of a Jewish family in a town of Montana, while Lawrence Drake in *Don't Call Me Clever* (1929) describes a family in Milwaukee.

Troubles in Europe, which caused the emigration of many cultured Jews, led to considerable fiction in which a new type of Jew was the hero—the professionally prominent exile attempting to find a new home in America and opportunities for his special gifts. Irving Fineman's *Dr. Addams* (1939) is characteristic of this new type.

Fiction of the Jew in America is ever changing with the status of the Jews who are present in America. When they are completely assimilated and indistinguishable from other Americans, the Jews will probably no longer be subjects for special fictional treatment. As long as Jewish problems exist, these problems will occupy the talents of Jewish novelists.

10. **ROBERT NATHAN:**

MASTER OF STYLE AND MOOD

Robert Nathan's contributions to American literature have consisted of thirteen novels, three volumes of poetry, and one play. His reputation among critics is secure and his discriminating audience increases with each new work. Typical of the respect in which he is held is Burton Rascoe's tribute:

> A new novel by Robert Nathan is one of the happier expectations some of us have left in a disappointing world.[1]

Throughout the literary period extending from the end of the World War, Nathan has produced his carefully-wrought studies of phases of contemporary life, never abandoning his artistic principles, his faith in the dignity of his profession, his love for mankind, his pride in his racial and religious heritage. Robert Nathan is a Jewish novelist, not only by reason of birth, but by his attitude to the problems afflicting Jewry of today and of all time. As he has grown more mature, his interest in Jewish problems has progressed from the preoccupation with a single Jew as in *Jonah*, a study of the Prophet, to his treatment of so vast a subject as the expulsion of all the Jews from all lands and their long trek to a new homeland in the Gobi desert, in *Road of Ages*.

Robert Nathan interests the critical reader as novelist, as poet, as Jew, and as commentator. Each of these four larger interests might easily be subdivided. For example, much discussion might follow Nathan's treatment of the subject of Jewish participation in Christian philanthropy (Mr. Cohen in *The Bishop's Wife*); his treatment of the Jewish convert to Christianity (*There Is Another Heaven*); his attitude toward biblical personalities *(Jonah);* his characterization of the Jewish musical genius (Morris Rosenberg in *One More Spring*); and his ironic portrayal of Jewish types in *Road of Ages.*

Robert Nathan illustrates so well the method of a novelist's artistic development that one is irresistibly tempted to write of him chronologically. For he, too, like the long-deceased literary figure under the eye of the analytic critic, has had his literary periods.

Nathan's writing career began while he was a student at Harvard University. In the winter of 1913-1914 he joined four other now famous Harvard *literati* in frequently contributing to the *Harvard Monthly.* These writers were Gilbert Seldes, Robert Hillyer, E. E. Cummings, and John Dos Passos. Their literary directions in the twenty-five years that have elapsed have diverged widely, and a more diversified group of contemporary writers could hardly be found. Yet the fact remains that Nathan was in close contact with these writers, with whom he undoubtedly had many literary discussions, and by whom he was influenced. Though Dos Passos, Hillyer, and Cummings would not be particularly proud of their contributions of that year, Robert Nathan already was demonstrating signs of his talent which developed later.

Two one-act plays and several poems were submitted by him. Nathan has never given up his poetry, which will be found quite frequently in the *Atlantic, Harpers,* and other "quality" magazines. In 1935 he wrote another play, *Music at Evening.* In his early poems (he was only nineteen years old), he exhibited that clarity of image, that sharpness of vision, and that sense of wonder, which distinguish his more mature works. Writing of a freight train passing at night, he said:

A red glow hissing in the night,
Then a long, long rush of darkness into the wind,
Clanking and grinding and bumping in slow rythm,
A brutal, lonely power—or a dream
From nowhere to nowhere.[2]

One recalls Rudyard Kipling's opening sentence in his story ".007":

A Locomotive is, next to a marine engine, the most sensitive thing man ever made.

Nathan has been associated with the humorous touch, of which the following is an early example:

Off on the road with hearts asong
And a little brown dog to patter along
In a fat little way.[3]

Nathan's juvenilia, indicative as they are of the future poet, gave no indication of his future mastery of the novel form. There can be no doubt that he destroyed much of what he wrote before he submitted his first novel to the publishers, for as a first novel it was surprisingly mature. *Peter Kindred,* published in 1919, was the work of a man of twenty-five. True to the literary principles of Arnold Bennett and H. G. Wells, whose novels he read enthusiastically, he wrote as a realist. It is a critical platitude that one's first novel is usually autobiographical. Nathan's was no exception. His hero Peter studies at Exeter Academy and at Harvard. The heroine is named Joan, perhaps as a tribute to the *Joan and Peter,* which appeared in 1918. In this first novel Nathan exhibits a literary tendency which he has incorporated into almost all the others. He likes to represent an experienced older person offering his wisdom and experience to a younger couple. In *Peter Kindred,* Professor Carver of Radcliffe is the apex of this triangular arrangement. In *Autumn* it is Jeminry the schoolmaster; in *The Puppet Master* it is Papa Jonas; in

Jonah it is Nassan; Otkar in *One More Spring;* Professor Wutheridge in *The Bishop's Wife;* Dr. Pembauer in *The Orchid*. This constellation of characters is welcomed in each successive novel since the author shows such admirable ingenuity in avoiding mere repetition of plot.

Joan and Peter take Professor Carver's social philosophy seriously. They marry and establish themselves in New York, Peter's birthplace. Nathan loves the open country, as his later novels, *Autumn, The Fiddler in Barly,* and *The Woodcutter's House* demonstrate. It is not surprising that his hero Peter describes the city thus:

> The air was hot and lifeless in the subway; there was a stale smell of cigarettes and papers and dust.[4]

There follows for Joan and Peter the usual experience of the idealistic college-bred married couple hoping for happiness in the Big City. Professor Carver's philosophy of optimism sounded attractive in Radcliffe, but in New York it could not withstand the basic realities. No fat royalty checks come to Peter for his stories. The only opening is in an advertising agency. Joan supplements the meager income by working as a stenographer. Although they had not desired to have a child until they felt financially able to care for it, Nature and God, with a sublime disrespect for Dr. Stopes, Dr. Von Der Velde and Havelock Ellis, presented Joan with a still-born child. Joan's health is permanently injured and Peter rapidly loses his faith in Professor Carver's way of living.

Nathan's first novel was well received, but he never returned to that type. His second venture in fiction came from a man who could scarcely be identified with the author of *Peter Kindred*. *Autumn* (1921) is akin to the works of Thomas Hardy, A. E. Coppard, Dorothy Canfield Fisher, Maristan Chapman, and all other lovers of the countryside. No cigarette smoke, no city dust contaminate the clear, invigorating rustic atmosphere. One could hardly guess that a city-dweller would write so tenderly and sympathetically of the simple ways of simple folk. *Autumn* is the first of a bucolic trilogy which deserves recognition as one of the most significant studies of the open country in American literature. *The Fiddler in Barly* (1926) and *The Woodcutter's House* (1927) are the other volumes in the series. Nathan closes his "Nature" period with the last work. Beginning with *The Bishop's Wife* (1928) he returns again to the City and treats of its problems. Yet his love for the open country breaks through in his descriptions of the *flora* of Central Park in *One More Spring* (1933) and of the eastern seaboard in *Enchanted Voyage* (1936).

That Nathan should describe with fidelity and deep love the New England countryside is not surprising in view of his attendance at one of the well-known private schools prior to his admission to Harvard. In the beginning of *Peter Kindred* the country around Exeter, New Hampshire, is pictured with the poet's pen and fond affection. Although no definite geographical area is indicated in *Autumn,* it resembles New England very closely and was probably intended to supplement the early passages in *Peter Kindred.* The language of the inhabitants, which Nathan has recorded with artistic selection, is of New Hampshire or thereabouts. Such idioms as "I don't aim to," "You're too easy satisfied," "This, is the best cooked beans I ever eat," "It's a grief to me," and "My Uncle Henry is a power with vegetables" are in the best New England linguistic tradition.

Nathan's selection of characters might be explained by his epigram:

> Give me no more than homely words
> And kindly thoughts to build my house;
> No more than what is given birds
> Or less than might be loaned a mouse.[5]

These four lines might well serve as an introduction to his complete creative output.

Knowing the insignificance of mere magnitude, unsupported

by spiritual greatness, the novelist prefers characters who are humble, sincere, failures as far as material possessions go, but bright successes as concerns their humanity and nobility of soul. Thus Dr. Pembauer and Professor Wutheridge and Mr. Otkar would never be rewarded with statues in the cities of their birth, but they exhibit qualities which make them true Nature's noblemen.

Nathan's love is for the failures in life. His second novel, written in his late twenties showed that his hero was not the conventional kind. Jeminry, the old schoolmaster, who was about to be retired, was an American Mr. Chips, who unfortunately did not gain the respect and admiration of his students, such as comforted the later years of his British colleague. He never harmed anyone and took his pleasures in simple things. Thrown out of his position which he held for over thirty years, he became a farmer's helper, still uncomplaining.

Mr. Jeminry had once dreamed of better things. Like Professor Pembauer and Papa Jonas, he had hoped to scale the heights of his profession, but as the years passed he resigned himself to the simple pleasures in life.

This affection for "noble failures" on the part of Robert Nathan reveals the quality of the man himself. The author has been called ironical because he writes with criticism and irony of such "material successes" as Julian Heavenstreet, the steel magnate in *The Orchid*, The Reverend Dr. Brougham in *The Bishop's Wife*, Hiram the Phoenician merchant in *Jonah*, and Adam Barly, the prosperous farmer, in *The Fiddler in Barly*. Nathan dislikes the Babbit type as Sinclair Lewis and Theodore Dreiser and Sherwood Anderson dislike him. At all times, however, he preserves his good manners. One does not find any long tirades against this or that hypocritical pillar of society, but one finds these representatives of big business, religion, and agriculture speaking and acting as their natural selves, which is enough to condemn them.

Nathan always controls his temper. His eyes are keen, his

understanding is profound, yet his tongue is not bitter. Even his most fatuous creations win more of our sympathy and pity than our disgust. Nathan has not created a villain. Thus one can read all of his thirteen novels with mild amusement, but not with indignation. Nathan refuses to become excited. He does not believe that the novelist should descend to the low levels of the demagogue or the politician and release his baser emotions. Even such crises as the depression and the persecution of the Jews fail to destroy his even disposition. About these tragic experiences he writes with restrained emotion, never raucously or blatantly.

In a world of novelists screaming their incoherent messages from their several housetops, Nathan speaks gently, sincerely, with that touch of understatement which is the essence of irony. He reminds one at times of Cabell, though his language is much simpler and his characters more human. Perhaps he would be more at home among the novel writers of the eighteenth century with their code of urbanity, skepticism and perfection of form and language.

Why does one not tire of the same group of Nathanesque derelicts, but reads ahead with sustained interest? After all, the musician in *One More Spring*, the poet in *The Puppet Master*, the dentist in *Enchanted Voyage*, David in *Road of Ages* are all youths who have failed in their respective arts or professions. Is it because the failures in life so outnumber the successes that we almost instinctively feel a kinship with them in Nathan's novels?

The novels of Nathan are read quickly because the plot is always simple and the characters come to life with a minimum of description. Using the selectivity which is the badge of the artist in prose fiction, Nathan loses no time in drawing a lasting pen-portrait which quickly reveals character. He describes the special quality of Mr. Frye, the store-keeper at Hillsboro, which is the cataloguing of all his neighbors in terms of the commodities in his store. People were seen by Mr. Frye

in the form of fruits, vegetables, stick-pins, and pieces of calico. Of

ROBERT NATHAN

Mr. Jeminry he used to say: "Sweet apples, but small, very small, small and sweet."[6]

Today critics grow almost hysterical in their praise of writers who represent the speech of their characters with revealing fidelity. Thus the dialogue of Clifford Odets has been called the best in contemporary drama for its suggestiveness by Stark Young, drama critic of the *New Republic*. Writing of John Steinbeck's dramatization of his own novel, *Of Mice and Men*, Richard Watts, Jr., drama critic of the *New York Herald Tribune* (November 24, 1937) said:

What must strike one above all things in "Of Mice and Men" is the economy and truth of the dialogue. Not even Clifford Odets at his best can present the believable and yet dramatic talk of plain people with more wisdom than the author brings to the new play.

Robert Nathan has long been a master of dialogue that was revelatory of character and drama. The following is from *Autumn:*

Mr. Crabbe spat into the stubble. "The way I look at it," he said, "it's like this: first there's me; and then there's you. That's the way I look at it, Mr. B." And he went home to repeat to his wife what he had said to Farmer Barly. "I gave it to him," he declared.[7]

The expression "eternal verities" has come into vogue in recent years. Though thoroughly worn-down by too frequent usage, it is useful. To Nathan certain experiences in life are terribly important. They are found in almost each novel. The experience of true love is one of them. One might say with little chance of dispute that a novel by him is a love-story nourished by some beneficent older person who is a catalytic agent in hastening the physico-chemical reaction and bringing it to its climax. The novel, *Enchanted Voyage* (1936), is the story of Dr. Williams, the unemployed dentist, and Mary Kelly, the waitress.

In *Road of Ages* (1935) Raoul Perez and Leah supply the love interest. In *The Orchid* (1931) Mr. Gambrino and Mrs. Connor learn the bliss of happy union. In *The Puppet Master* another poet and a writer are finally joined. Love, then, to Mr. Nathan is one of the eternal verities. His ingenuity in varying the scene in which the couple discover that they are in love and try to communicate to each other their rapture is amazing. In his resourceful hands such scenes never grow old, and they capture that sense of being the "one big moment" in the life of the two lovers which such an experience is in actual life. To a pair of lovers, their love is the newest, greatest, most lasting, most ecstatic experience in the whole world. Nathan writes of it in a way that gives his readers that sense of overpowering magnitude. Sometimes the course of true love does not run smooth. In *Autumn* Tom Frye is in love with the daughter of Farmer Barly, but she cannot force herself to love him. She had her romantic dreams which never seemed realized in the person of Tom Frye. Nature, which forced an unwanted still-born child on Joan and Peter, now repeats the performance and the couple are forced into marriage.

Autumn furnishes us, too, with the first full-length portrait of the cultured man who has been a material failure, in the person of Mr. Jeminry, the schoolmaster. Here, too, Nathan reveals his touch of irony with which he contemplates the foibles of our civilization. He reflects over the rationalization of greed in the mind of a minnow:

One, larger than the rest, found a piece of bread which had fallen into the water. "This is my bread," he said, and gazed angrily at his friends, who were trying to bite him. "I deserve this bread," he added.[8]

Nathan has the ironic temper. It is his way of describing faults while not condemning them. It is his gentle way to expose the imperfection of the human soul. It represents his mind's disapproval of things which his heart refuses to hate. A gentleman of culture can display the ironic temperament. Among Jewish men-of-letters in America today S. N. Behrman and Robert Nathan are the two outstanding representatives, one in pure comedy, the other in the novel.

ROBERT NATHAN

In *Jonah* (1925) irony has been developed into a fine art. The literary atmosphere of the time was charged with it. John Erskine wrote *The Private Life of Helen of Troy* that year. Other writers were treating the past with irreverence. Idols, literary and historical, were being given feet of clay. They were being modernized, streamlined, colloquialized. Edwin Justus Mayer wrote *The Firebrand* in which Benvenuto Cellini became all Don Juan and lost his identity as an artist. *And So to Bed* gave us Samuel Pepys, not as a member of the Admiralty Board, but as a gallant. *The Road to Rome* made Hannibal into more of a lover than a conqueror. Nathan went back to the Bible for his story. Today with Thomas Mann's trilogy on Joseph, Marc Connelly's *Green Pastures,* Andre Obey's *Noah,* James Bridie's *Susannah and the Elders,* we have become accustomed to psychological and fictional treatments of biblical episodes. Nathan's was one of the first. Irony and humor are distributed generously. Jonah is a young prophet who tires of life in the caves and returns to the city of his birth. Falling in love with the daughter of the richest prince in the neighborhood, he is thwarted by his poverty. His place is taken by Hiram, a Phoenician merchant, a Babbitt of the biblical era. God wishes to re-establish Jonah's faith and arranges for the whale episode. At the end the Prophet returns to his solitary existence, denied the comforts of love because he was "different."

Nathan displays his ironic attitude toward religious institutionalism as contrasted with true religion. In *The Bishop's Wife* and *There Is Another Heaven* he again gently punctures the inflated personalities of those who consider themselves God's representatives on earth.

In *Jonah* the High Priest is portrayed as an executive of religious administration, rather than a man of true religion. He argues badly, but impressively. He has all the trimmings appertaining to administration. He is a good compromiser, as he declares pompously: "Let us all be right—or at least as many of us as possible." Only high-priestly vanity would be responsible for such words as: "Is it likely that God in his infinite wisdom should see this any less clearly than I do?" A splendid example of a *non sequitur* is his argument in support of monotheism: "Moreover, there is a regularity about the seasons that would be impossible in the case of a number of Gods."

Nathan's sympathy for the materially unsuccessful man is apparent in his portrait of Jonah, who like Mr. Jeminry and Papa Jonas, the puppet-master, is the third in the series of "noble failures." He has no money nor any profession. The world even in biblical times was a practical one. In words that would do credit to a contemporary matron intent on a fortunate marriage for her daughter, Miriam, the object of Jonah's love, is told: "What would people think of you if you were to marry for nothing? You would be ruined socially." Those were the days before the cinema fed love-hungry millions the sagas of marriages between heiresses and starving musicians and heirs and pure stenographers.

Naaman is one of Nathan's grand old men in the company of Pembauer, Otkar, Jeminry and Wutheridge. To him Jonah comes for comfort and wisdom. The love of nature which is both Naaman's and Nathan's is shown in this passage:

I do not need to travel; here in this quiet garden the sun sets and the moon rises; the breeze of evening whispers through the leaves of my acacia tree, and I see through the branches the stars, which have not changed; I hear the voices of cicada, shrill and sad, *as when I was a boy,* I heard the herds winding down the hills. All is as it was and as it will be; and my heart overflows with love and peace.[9]

Robert Nathan in writing *Jonah* was not trying to be irreverent. For of his faith in religion and especially in the religion of Israel there can be no doubt.

Although the Hitler regime galvanized Nathan as well as other Jewish novelists in this and other lands to re-examine their religious heritage, Nathan had expressed certain phenomena of American-Jewish life as early as 1928 in his *The Bishop's Wife*. It is an ingenious fantasy of the visitation of the Archangel Michael to the household of the Reverend Dr. Brougham, minister of the fashionable St. Timothy's, which he is trying to rebuild. One of the most characteristic passages in all of Nathan's novels is the account of the interview of the angel Michael and Mr. Cohen.

In *There Is Another Heaven* (1929) Nathan presents another Jewish problem of our time—conversion to Christianity. Mr. Lewis, born Levy, has been baptized, was a good churchman, used to lend his pictures to the charities, and is now on his way to heaven, accompanied by Professor Wutheridge, first introduced in *The Bishop's Wife,* and William Meiggs, son of the distinguished reformer, Emma Meiggs. Nathan was rushing in where angels feared to tread. Having written of religion in biblical times and in Herbert Hoover's times, he now crossed the boundary between heaven and earth. Few writers have fictionalized the celestial regions. Lord Dunsany in *The Gate* represented heaven as mere black emptiness punctuated by stars. Shaw in *The Simpleton of the Unexpected Isles* introduced an angel from heaven. Charles E. S. Wood's *Heavenly Discourse* is perhaps the closest parallel to Nathan's novel, although it appeared two years earlier. Marc Connelly's *Green Pastures* is another treatment.

To write of heaven amusingly, yet not irreverently is no simple task. Nathan, as his essay *On Being a Jew* shows, is not irreligious or atheistic. As an ironist, however, he can reveal the absurdities and hypocrisies that beset little minds. Nathan is not amused at a heaven, but at the Calvinistic-democratic heaven which has been built by dogma and personal prejudice. Professor Wutheridge, the sane man, who is a usual character in a Nathan novel, discusses with Lewis this heaven:

. . . this is a city made to receive in beatitude those who have gone regularly to church and have not sinned too much. The citizenry numbers many important people, but not the great archangels of the Thebald, the Kerubs of Safed, or the saints of Rome; and not, so far as I know, the most mystic of all figures, Jesus, the Son of Man . . . Of course, I had forgotten that you belong to the race of the psalmists, of the prophets, of Hillel of Jerusalem, of Philo of Alexandria, of Loria of Safed, of Jochai, of Akiba, of Eliezer of Worms. Now you find yourself among such men as Oliver Cromwell and W. J. Bryan.[10]

Lewis and Wutheridge see strange sights in this heaven. Professor Wutheridge finds his perennially youthful mother maintaining a *ménage à trois,* with perfect ease and impunity, since there is no sin involved. In heaven, one is reminded, there is no sin. William Meiggs finds his erstwhile frigid mother enjoying the demonstrativeness of her spouse, since in heaven she has lost her sense of the sinfulness of such behaviour. Another entertaining episode is the swimming exhibition of Wutheridge Senior and "Uncle" Adolph. The final chapter represents Nathan at his best as Jew and critic. Lewis has found existence unendurable in this heaven. After bequeathing his collection of gold pieces to the Museum, he plunges into a stream, hoping thus to end everything. Strange voices come to him, recalling his past, his Jewish household, the insults which he suffered, the indignations endured by his parents who were afraid to strike back, his determination to break away from his own people and be like the Gentiles, his failure to find love even after conversion. Finally, Lewis finds words:

See father, I am not afraid any more. I can even pity you now; I am sorry for you, that is all. You were you and I was I; but I was afraid I would be you all over again. Well, I am simply myself now. A man, a Jew—what does it matter? What did it ever matter? To live, that is what matters; to be myself again. I did not have to weep because you wept. I did not have to be afraid of you. I did not have to run away from you. I could have loved you.[11]

Nathan's latest treatment of the Jewish problem is *Road of Ages* (1935). The Nazi régime aroused him to protest against the reversion to medieval barbarism.

Road of Ages is a sad tale of the expulsion of all Jews into the Gobi desert. Plagued by enemies without, who robbed and pillaged and slew those who were unprotected, torn apart by personal prejudices among Communist Jews and capitalists, among

American and Polish, among German and Levantine Jews, the epic journey is one of the saddest in contemporary literature. Here and there, Nathan throws the incandescent beam of his ironic eye on the frailties of his own people, which saves the book from being all tears and no laughter. Throughout his sympathy is displayed, now to the Christian wife of Dr. Kohn, the athletic young surgeon, now to the couple in love, Raoul Perez and Leah, daughter of a Polish rabbi. One recognizes at times old friends with new names, but with the same personalities. David the poet we have met in *The Puppet Master*. Raoul in love resembles Nathan's other young men in love: Dr. Williams, Peter, Jonah.

An artist in fiction is often praised for his powers of selecting details which illuminate character and plot. In *Road of Ages* Nathan is at his best. At least twenty characters are made to live by some significant remark. There is Lord Steyne, who leads the protective unit, who has become so anglicized that he has developed Great Britain's favorite policy of intervening in a quarrel only when both factions have exhausted themselves. Thus he settles the quarrel between the socialists and communists after they have practically annihilated each other, with the characteristic phrase of British foreign policy, "Now we shall have peace."

Equally brilliant is the portrait of the French banker M. Perez, who joins the caravan in his limousine. He can hardly wait to begin to raise capital for its development. He is certain that he can raise Christian money in Paris. The conversations of Perez, Baron Wertheim, the Viennese banker, and other former tycoons, on this tragic exodus contain some of Nathan's cleverest satire.

Throughout the book is perceived the author's sympathy for these misguided people. Nathan does not write to express his hatred, but his injuries of mind and spirit. He writes from love rather than hate. Hate changes the man of intelligence into the brute. It clouds the understanding and destroys faith in living. Lewis was saved because he regained his faith in himself, in living. Professor Pembauer says to himself when he has little else left, "One must have faith if one is to be an artist."

ROBERT NATHAN

Faith in romantic love may have been destroyed by our material world, but in the universe of Nathan's creation it is still supreme. *The Orchid* (1931) has two variations on the theme of love. It is one of his gentlest books. Professor Pembauer is an old friend of ours. A failure in life, he has descended from his dreams of a career as a concert pianist to the reality of a life as a piano-teacher. Yet in his domain he is his own master. One love story concerns the affair of the prominent steel magnate, Mr. Julian Heavenstreet, and Miss Grogarty, a prominent actress. The other is in a humbler environment, between Miss Grogarty's servant, Mrs. Connor, and Mr. Gambrino, owner of the carousel in Central Park. The Professor is the connecting link between the two strata of society represented. The carousel serves as the medium which finally solves both problems. Gambrino has sung at La Scala (in the chorus) and has never given up his plans to sing again. Encouraged by Professor Pembauer and warmed by the love of Mrs. Connor, he modernizes his carousel and invites many of his prominent patrons to the opening. On that occasion Miss Grogarty realized that love could not be bought and definitely refused Mr. Heavenstreet's offer to go to Europe with him. Mrs. Heavenstreet on the same occasion learned that the way to win back her husband was to show him that she was attractive to other men. The novel is the second in a series of three in which New York's Central Park usurps the place held by the New England countryside in his trilogy *Autumn, The Fiddler in Barly,* and *The Woodcutter's House.* Nathan has left the New England of his adolescence and has come to New York. Green grass and tall trees, birds and flowers are still important elements in life to him.

Nature is so alive that in *The Woodcutter's House* Nathan has dogs and horses and a little man of the forest engage in delightful conversation. In *The Puppet Master* the puppets speak like human beings. Such practices have earned for Nathan the title of writer of fantasy. Nature is so alive to him and dull people so dead that it is not surprising that he chooses to make animals and marionettes speak, especially when they are entertaining.

ROBERT NATHAN

One More Spring (1935) and *Enchanted Voyage* (1936) were inspired by the Great Depression. One notices again the characteristic trio. In the former there are Mr. Otkar, bankrupt antique dealer, Mr. Morris Rosenberg, unemployed musician, and Elizabeth Cheney, starving lady of the streets. In the latter we have Mr. Peckett, carpenter who builds a boat never meant for sailing, Miss Mary Kelly, waitress, and Dr. Williams, graduate dentist with nothing to fill but his spare time.

Nathan has enjoyed a good musical education, which culminated in several published musical compositions. His interest in music is shown in his portrayal of the fiddler in *The Fiddler in Barly,* of Mr. Gambrino in *The Orchid,* of Dr. Pembauer in the same, of Mr. Rosenberg in *One More Spring* and in *Road of Ages.* In this the child prodigy, Sonia, gives a violin recital as soloist under the direction of a German-Jewish conductor, who has formed an orchestra out of the exiles.

One obtains in Nathan's novels not only his attitude toward music but observations on the function and spirit of all the arts. It would be hazardous to insist that the views expressed are the author's since frequently they are spoken by characters of the novel. Typical is this opinion of Mr. Otkar in *One More Spring* on the effect of poverty on art:

Besides, what is there left to make music about? The artist cannot forget that he is starving, and that the entire world is probably coming to an end. Should he try to overlook such things? That is not very good for the artist. Or should he try, on the contrary, to express in art his anxiety and his indignation? That is not very good for art.[12]

One More Spring is an idyll of the depression in New York City. The characters besides the familiar trio include Mr. Sheridan, former head of a large bank, and Mr. Sweeney, who works in Central Park, and Mrs. Sweeney. An unused toolshed is the *locus operandi* for this tale which Hollywood found attractive enough to translate on the screen. Nathan has achieved the enviable distinction of preserving in artistic form some of the familiar experiences of those days. Thus when the banker helps himself to Rosenberg's meager savings, he defends his investment by saying as General Hugh Johnson said so often and so distinctly, "This is no time for hoarding." Like the bankers who were the pillars of society in 1929, he said of the 1933 election, "I intend to vote for the Republicans in the Fall, because with the Democrats you can never tell what to expect."

The book opens with a page of description which is so characteristic of Nathan's lucid, crisp style that it merits quotation in full. What more need be added about the effects of the depression upon America in the Spring of 1933:

> That was the year business failed, and many families, investors, and business houses were ruined. In the country, farmers plowed their fields under, rather than harvest the wheat or cotton they were unable to sell; and in the cities, people starved, or sold apples on the street. Everywhere was misery and apathy, for no one could see any hope for the future.
> As a result, a tragic calm, induced by surprise, by despair, and aided by the weather, filled everyone's heart. It was autumn, a season of skies as blue as cornflowers, of yellow sunlight, of warm, unmoving air. The poor stood in lines, waiting for their cup of soup and piece of bread; they sat on the park benches and, warming themselves in the last sun of summer, or breathing the cool, kind air of autumn, turned their faces with a certain trust to the sky, in which were the sun and the stars, just as always.
> Their fate was of interest to no one but themselves. Even the poets did not write about them, because the poets also were poor, and their nature made them indignant. They no longer wished to write poetry; on the contrary, they wished to fight; they threw themselves into the coal wars in the south, and were sent home with broken heads, like the heroes of antiquity.
> Their foes wasted no time in calling them atheists, hypocrites, and communists. And they replied by silence, or in prose which did not cause anyone's heart to beat any faster.
> In the larger cities, there was not a street without its auction, or clearance sale in some little shop which was obliged to go out of busi-

ness. As a result, each day there were more poor people than before, and each day the bread-lines grew longer.[13]

Enchanted Voyage represents the familiar triad no longer confined to a toolshed, but traveling on the highways in a boat which Simon Peckett, Bronx carpenter, had built in his spare time. It was not meant for the ocean, though Skipper Peckett had hoped to make it seaworthy. Mrs. Peckett, however, was more practical. She had sold it to Schultz the butcher. In order to transport the clumsy vehicle she had attached wheels. A providential storm, which tore the boat from its moorings on the night Simon Peckett refused to sleep indoors, started it on the enchanted journey which ended in its sinking the moment it reached the ocean. Skipper Peckett was almost drowned, but he had been on his journey and he was ready for the return to the Bronx.

This novel is typical of Nathan's work at its best. All the qualities which have made him a favorite with discriminating readers are discovered here. His style, which is that of a prose-poet, is a rarity in these days of all sorts of verbal cacophonies and linguistic monstrosities. His ironic temper leads him to discriminate between the sham and the genuine article, whether the commodity be religion as in *Jonah* and *The Bishop's Wife* or love as in almost all his novels. His technique and plot structure are simple, yet logical. Rather than supply an endless chain of cause and effect, Nathan has character B meet character A and continues the story from that point on. In *One More Spring* this technique is excellently displayed. Rosenberg simply enters the empty store of Mr. Otkar and decides to stay. In *Enchanted Voyage* Mary Kelly is waiting for a "ride" when Skipper Peckett navigates his boat down a Bronx highway and invites her in. In *The Bishop's Wife* Dr. Brougham wishes for an angel and Michael appears. One questions the necessity of ponderous 1,000-paged novels in view of the wisdom, artistry and story element which Nathan includes in a novel of two hundred pages. Throughout his works there emanates his personal temperament, which has in it the qualities of charm, tolerance, understanding, and benevolence. He

ROBERT NATHAN

represents the finest elements of the literary tradition in demonstrating those excellent auctorial virtues of which Branch Cabell speaks so much in *Beyond Life*. Nathan has never forgotten his racial and religious heritage. He has written of Jewish problems as frankly as he wrote of the depression, rustic love, and metropolitan life. He might well be describing himself in his quatrain on the poet:

> He lives on pain,
> And sells his utter
> Grief for roses,
> Bread and butter.

11. BEN HECHT:

THE RE-DISCOVERY OF THE ARTIST

Ben Hecht, like Heine, Börne, Brandes, Wassermann, Toller, Zangwill, and Edmond Fleg, is a typical Jewish man of letters. Their points of difference may seem numerous and disturbing, but their core is Jewish. Their medium of expression may be German, Danish, French or English but their soul is Jewish. All write keenly, bitterly, ironically, precisely, and cleverly. All fought against oppression, injustice, ignorance, Philistinism, and dull conventionality. Just as J. W. Krutch has written an illuminating study entitled *From Ibsen to Odets,* describing the development of the drama of ideas from the Norwegian master to the thirty-year-old author of *Awake and Sing,* so one could easily write a companion volume with the name *From the Reisebilder to To Quito and Back.*

What a galaxy of Jewish authors of sharp tongues and stout hearts would be found in the pages of such a volume! Alfred Kerr and Maximilian Harden making of German dramatic and political criticism a thing of terrible power as well as burning truth! How close they came to that "hard gem-like flame" of which Walter Pater spoke in his enunciation of the effect of a true love of art upon sincere devotees. When Dr. Bodenheimer's Aryan mistress in Sholem Asch's *The War Goes On* complains about the cruel Jewish critic who ridiculed her histrionic pretensions, she must have echoed the sentiments of many an Aryan who had met with scorn at the hands of such brilliant critics as Alfred Kerr, of the *Berliner Tageblatt*. Maximilian Harden's courage as a journalist, despite his Jewish origin, would make Walter Lippmann's attacks on the New Deal seem like so many pin pricks. In his younger days Léon Blum, former Premier of France, was the outstanding dramatic critic of his country, known for his fearlessness and sincerity.

It would be dull repetition to list the characteristics which make authors of such diverse social origins and localities write with a pen that seems to be dipped in the same inkwell. Some pages in Edmond Fleg might easily have been written by Ben Hecht, and Schnitzler's *Reigen* claims a close kinship to Hecht's *A Jew in Love*. It is as a Jew, therefore, as much as a Bohemian and a Mid-Westerner that Hecht claims our attention as we attempt to evaluate his literary significance. For Hecht chose a Jew, Erik Dorn, as his hero in his first novel, and a Jew is the central character in *A Jew in Love*. Jews of various ages and social strata live in the works of Israel Zangwill or Abraham Cahan. Hecht may be writing in the idiom of the descendants of the *Mayflower*, but his words have about them the aura of the heroes of the Book.

When *Erik Dorn* appeared in 1921 to startle a war-weary and peace-treaty-disillusioned world, Ben Hecht was only twenty-eight years old. The world has been accustomed to works of enduring merit and even genius from artists under thirty, to be sure, but the critical-minded usually view with indulgence the faults of genius still in its twenties. Thus all the deficiencies of Hecht's first novel could be excused in an initial production. Though the inclusion of Erik Dorn in the *Modern Library* added a certain permanence to its circulation, it could not remove the indications of artistic carelessness and youthful indiscretions in the book.

It must be admitted that Burton Rascoe said of Hecht that he was "our first great epithetician," and that "the verbal patterns, the pungently evocative word-combinations, the strange richness of metaphor cause it, for no other reason, to stand out as a distinct new model in the mechanics of expression." Other critics were not so kind. A writer in the *London Times* described the book as "an intolerable scurry of noise and jar and strain, a roaring mechanism of existence in which the soul of man is ground and ground until it becomes no more than a bundle of twitching nerves."

Provocative the novel undoubtedly was. The stir caused by Hecht was comparable to the excitement aroused in 1934 by another young writer of twenty-eight, Clifford Odets, who startled the theatre-goers of New York with *Waiting for Lefty* and *Awake and Sing*. Hecht's talent was in need of restraint, of polish, of less subjectivity and more objectivity, but of its presence there was no doubt. It is appropriate, therefore, to evaluate the development of his literary skill as exemplified in his most recent work, *To Quito and Back,* which was presented by the New York Theatre Guild on October 6, 1937.

Hecht appears as the sole author in a form of literature in which he formerly achieved distinction as a collaborator, with Kenneth Sawyer Goodman and Charles MacArthur. When we discover, therefore, certain similarities of expression, of characterization, of plot construction and of philosophy in these two works spaced sixteen years apart, we are tempted to deduce that in these similarities we can discover the "essential" Hecht. Critics have toyed endlessly with speculations concerning the identity of the author and his literary creations. Unless such speculations lead to a more intelligent appreciation of the artistic accomplishments, they seem of slight consequence.

Ben Hecht lends himself easily to identification. His idiosyncrasies as an individual are well known. His gift of words convinces one that he, like O. Henry, also considered Webster's *Unabridged Dictionary* as the most useful of all books. His pranks are supposed to have inspired the Spewacks in their delineation of the dramatists in *Boy Meets Girl*. He has long been known as an incessant, fascinating, cynical, and iconoclastic conversationalist.

BEN HECHT

It is not surprising that the heroes of *Erik Dorn* and of *To Quito and Back* are both writers, that they both exude epigrams as easily as the average person exudes banalities, that they are both restless, both escaping from unwanted wives, both incapable of making firm decisions, both capable of attracting the opposite sex, and both extremely unhappy. Why does Hecht seem so preoccupied with epigrammatic speech, with the minutiae of sex, with escaping from one's first wife, with indecision? These elements are not confined to the first and last work. In *Gargoyles* (1922) the sensuality of the hero George Basine is given an almost case-history presentation. In *A Jew in Love* (1931) the sexual equipment, experience and conquests of the Jewish publisher, Jo Boshere, are catalogued with a verisimilitude more frequently found in the numbered cases of Krafft-Ebing.

Sixteen years, however, of world changes have made a difference. Erik Dorn lived through the German revolution and the founding of the Bavarian Soviet Republic, but returned to America unmoved by the impact of the social upheavals in Europe. Alexander Sterns of *To Quito and Back* dies fighting in the cause of social revolution. Hecht and his hero have realized that in the world of today one cannot stand by calmly without taking sides. Although Sterns says "We're always on the right side in discussions but never on any side of the barricades," he finally stops talking and fights for his ideals.

In the evolution of Hecht's heroes, one perceives the evolution of Ben Hecht. His first novel, and his short stories written at the beginning of his career, reveal a talent astoundingly rich in language, unrestrained as to artistic form, emotional, attuned to the miseries of the world and intensely subjective. Thus one finds in his early collections of short stories, *Tales of Chicago Streets* (1924) and *Broken Necks* (1924), narratives that abound in treatments of the sordidness, the material and spiritual decay of the poverty-stricken areas of Chicago. We note also the strivings for a meaning in life, for some philosophy of existence which will make life significant and hence endurable. The story "Life," for example, deals with Moisse the dramatist's musings on the emptiness of life.

At times as one witnesses the performance of *To Quito and Back,* one can hear the words of Moisse the dramatist coming from the mouth of Alexander Sterns.

The early Hechtian hero would stop at the confession of his helplessness in the face of action, but Sterns finds a way out. As if symbolic of the dilemma of the contemporary liberal writer who realizes that he cannot remain aloof from the turmoils of our time, cannot long remain free from the necessity of choosing sides, Sterns goes over to the revolutionary party, first as Minister of Education and finally as a machine-gunner in a forlorn hope. Hecht and his heroes were always sympathetic, but they were also cynical and impatient with the foibles and stupidities of the ignorant masses. Now there is a change. Sterns is tired of pretending and takes action.

In the end Alex Sterns breaks with his past and dies for the future. One can hear prophecies in his final words, adumbrations of a world to come, premonitions of dangers leading ultimately to a better life.

As one heard Stearns enunciate his credo, one could not help recalling other credos in the theatre and the difference in environment which gave them birth. One recalls the dying artist Dubedat in Bernard Shaw's *Doctor's Dilemma:*

> I believe in Michael Angelo, Velasquez, and Rembrandt; in the might of design, the mystery of color, the redemption of all things by Beauty everlasting, and the message of Art that has made these hands blessed.

Such a belief seemed proper in 1906, in those halcyon days when everything seemed settled with finality and art was one of the escapes which gorged materialists indulged in. A certain hypocritical sanctity was ascribed to art and artists, and money-weary Americans went to Rome, to breathe the purer air of St. Paul's and the Sistine Chapel.

BEN HECHT

How changed is the world today! Franco's cannon destroyed Madrid block by block, wiping out monument after monument. Priceless paintings of the Prado Museum had to be transported hastily to vaults in France or kept in subterranean chambers in Madrid at the risk of deterioration or final destruction. In China, treasures of art thousands of years old are destroyed by Japanese bombs. Can one die with his trust in art these days?

There was a time in Ben Hecht's literary career when his faith, too, was in art, and in himself as the artist. Like Dr. Stockmann in Ibsen's *An Enemy of the People* he could say "He is most strong who stands alone." Ibsen was no lover of the common folk and the aforementioned play is as rich in contempt for the masses as any play in all literature. There was a time in Hecht's career when the masses, the "great unwashed," were not to his liking. He sympathized with them, but he would not take sides with them. He was too much of an egotist.

The Ben Hecht of today realized the impossibility of remaining aloof from the turbulent life-and-death struggle of nations. He has cast his lot with the common people. He has given us one hero who was willing to die for them. He will give us more heroes who will fight for them and lead them into their Land of Promise. Hecht, like Shelley, like Zola, like Brandes, like Heine, has realized that a writer's noblest task is not self-glorification but dedication to the elevation of mankind. As Maxwell Anderson so wisely expressed it in his speech in October, 1937 before the Carnegie Institute,

> The dream of the race is that it may make itself better and wiser than it is, and every great philosopher or artist who has ever appeared among us has turned his face away from what man is toward whatever seems to him most godlike that man may become.

Ben Hecht has joined that noble fraternity of artistic legislators of mankind, the spiritual descendants of Prometheus, bringing to their era the torch of enlightenment and truth. His new literary career has only just begun.

12. JEWISH POETS IN AMERICA

IN THE NINETEENTH CENTURY

"No other American woman has surpassed her in passion, in genuineness of emotion, in pure lyric effect." One would not be surprised to hear these words spoken of Emily Dickinson or Edna St. Vincent Millay, but they are used by Fred Lewis Pattee in his *History of American Literature Since* 1870 to characterize the poetry of Emma Lazarus, the oustanding Jewish poetess in America of the nineteenth century.[1]

Jewish women have participated in American literature for over a hundred years and their contributions have been significant both as American literature and as expressions of the Jewish spirit in America.

Many men of Jewish extraction have written in America with hardly a trace of their ancestry indicated in their writings, but Jewesses seem less capable of subduing their racial pride or their racial pity. From Penina Moise (1797-1880) to Jessie Sampter, over a span of a century we can learn the feelings and thoughts of sensitive Jewesses viewing America as individuals and as representatives of their religion and race.

To the historian of American literature the reactions of Emma Lazarus to the Jewish massacres of 1879 and Jessie Sampter's condemnation of the Nazi persecutions form links in one chain. The preoccupation of Jewish writers with the plight of their people exists not only in America but wherever they have suffered. The historian of the reactions of the sensitive immigrant to American freedom can read the glowing pages of Anzia Yezierska and Mary Antin. The observations of an American-born Jewess of American ghetto life can be read in Fannie Hurst's *Humoresque* and *Lummox*. It would be too narrow-minded a point of view, however, to consider the literature of American Jewesses exclusively as an expression of their feelings toward the problems of their own people in the new land.

It cannot be denied that Penina Moise was as conscious of her Spanish-Jewish ancestry as of her American birth. In a most interesting novel about the Sephardic-Jewish community in Charleston, S. C., *Storm Beach* (1933), Virginia Hersch writes of Miss Moise as one of the distinguished members of that community.

"Well, I know a little of Miss Penina's history," says Jacob Jacobs. Everyone admires her, and everybody pities her for being an old maid and gives various reasons, but no one can come anywhere near the truth without saying, to begin with, that her mother is a vixen."

"What do you know about her mother?", Sarah (the mother of the Carvalho family described in this novel) said. "She was my friend n Santo Domingo as well as here. Do you think it is easy to go from wealth to poverty, to change your land, to change your customs?"

"Why not call it," David (one of Sarah Carvalho's sons) asked, "Miss Penina's great devotion to her mother? They say she never leaves the house."

Judith (daughter of Sarah Carvalho):
"They say her mother will not let her. All the exercise she has is walking up and down the porch while her mother watches from the window and counts the trips." [2]

This passage indicates the kind of life Penina Moise led and her reputation among the members of her community. In 1830, when thirty-three, she published many of her poems, which had appeared occasionally in the local newspapers and magazines, in *Fancy's Sketch Book,* perhaps a tribute to Irving's *Sketch Book,* which appeared in 1820. She was also a contributor to the *Occi-*

dent and *American Jewish Advocate, Godey's Lady's Book, Home Journal,* and the *Boston Daily Times.*

Proud of her membership in the Sephardic community, she wrote in 1856 *Hymns Written for the Use of Hebrew Congregations,* which contains her best work. Her long life extended almost from the beginnings of America as a nation, including within its span America's development through foreign and domestic wars, the Reconstruction period in the South and the great expansion of the post-Civil War period. Although her poems are more in the classical vein of the eighteenth century, they have at times a passion and verbal beauty which reveal the sensitive and yet independent soul of the recluse of Charleston.

Emma Lazarus was a representative of the cultured northern American Jewry of the mid-nineteenth century as Penina Moise was of the South. What an interesting exchange of letters there might have been between Emma Lazarus and Penina Moise! Miss Lazarus was born in New York City on July 22, 1849 in a home characterized by its refinement and culture. She was a precocious child, showed an early inclination to seriousness and to preoccupation with literature rather than social relations. In 1866 she published *Poems and Translations,* which was marked by its unusual melancholy even for poems written by women. Professor Pattee is perhaps too cruel in his criticism of this volume as "valueless utterly." [3]

At twenty-one she published *Admetus, and Other Poems* (1871), which she inscribed to "My Friend Ralph Waldo Emerson." The Sage of Concord was so delighted with the poems, which he called "Greek in its chaste beauty" that he invited her to his Concord home and corresponded with her often. Having read the literature of the Greeks as well as the Bible, she had much of the classical Greek spirit in her sensitivity to pure beauty, a sensitivity which was later to extend to the cries of her own people in their sufferings.

In *Storm Beach,* the novel mentioned earlier, Judith Carvalho, its heroine, has a similar division of loyalty. Though a proud

Sephardic Jewess, she fell in love with a handsome Gentile. Her mother bluntly told this scion of one of the aristocratic families of the South that she would never permit her daughter to marry out of her faith. In the end Judith remains unmarried, since she was prevented from marrying Roger Lavenden and refused to marry Jacob Jacobs, whom her mother thought eligible. Yet for a time, Judith Carvalho permitted herself to love Roger and to wish to be loved by him. She was almost willing to separate herself from her people and worship a strange beauty, an alien god, though he came to her in the form of Roger.

Such a conflict of emotions must have disturbed Emma Lazarus, as she beheld the Venus in the Louvre. In a sonnet, which has been called "a miracle among modern sonnets," she wrote:

> I saw not her alone,
> Serenely poised on her world-worshiped throne,
> As when she guided once her dove-drawn car,
> But at her feet a pale, death-stricken Jew,
> Her life adorer, sobbed farewell to love.
> Here *Heine* wept! Here still he weeps anew,
> Nor ever shall his shadow lift or move,
> While mourns one ardent heart, one poet-brain
> For vanished Hellas and Hebraic pain.

In 1874 she published *Alide: a Romance*; two years later she wrote *The Spagnoletto,* a poetic drama with a setting in Italy of the seventeenth century. In this play there were foreshadowed the passionate denunciation against Jewish oppression, which characterized *Songs of a Semite.* In 1879 news reached America of the massacres of Jews in Russia. Such poems as "The Crowing of the Red Cock," "In Exile," "The New Ezekiel," and "The Valley of Baca" contain her reactions to the Russian atrocities.

In "The Banner of the Jew" she is most characteristic of her new mood. Gone is the melancholy and bookish little Miss of *Poems and Translations.* The Glory that was Greece is forgotten while she remembers the sufferings of Israel:

> Oh, for Jerusalem's trumpet now,
> To blow a blast of shattering power
> To wake the sleepers high and low
> And rouse them to the urgent hour.
> No hand for vengeance—but to save,
> A million naked swords should wave.

She translated her words into definite action. Relief work was organized and assistance was quickly offered to the refugees that came to America in that great wave of immigration of the 1880's. The intensity of her emotions and the strenuousness of her efforts proved too great a strain on her frail body. In 1887 she died at the early age of thirty-eight.

"No more impetuous and Hebraic lines in the literature of the period than hers," writes Pattee. "Often she achieved a distinction of phrase and an inevitability of word and rhythm denied to all but the truest of poets." [4] Her verses are inscribed on the pedestal of Bartholdi's Statue of Liberty in New York harbor.

Another Jewish poetess, but one who was also among the most distinguished American actresses of the nineteenth century, was Adah Isaacs Menken. She was born on June 15, 1835 in the village of Milneburg, a suburb of New Orleans. Her theatrical career is part of the vivid history of the American theatre of the last century. Before she died in Paris, on August 10, 1868, she had gained the friendship of Swinburne, Dickens, Dumas, Longfellow and many other literary celebrities of two continents.

Only a few days after her death her thin volume of poetry, entitled *Infelicia,* was published, with a dedication to Charles Dickens.[5] Although this volume is left unmentioned in Herbert Stuart Stone's *First Editions of American Authors* (1893), and her name is merely noted by Professor Pattee in his *History of American Literature,* her book created a marked impression upon European critics. The situation is somewhat similar to the popularity of Walt Whitman's poetry in Europe at the time when he was being assailed in America.

Dante Gabriel Rossetti wrote to his brother William, who in

1871 was compiling an anthology of American poems, your American Selections ought certainly, I think, to contain some specimens of poor Menken. I have her book, which is really remarkable.

Even Oscar Wilde, years after Adah Menken's death saw a resemblance between Salome's words "I will kiss thy mouth, Iokanon!" and certain lines in her poem "Judith." In America, Clement Wood in his *Poets of America* gives her unstinted praise and presents generous quotations of her poetry.

It was at the age of twenty-two, after she had married Mr. Alexander Isaac Menken, of a wealthy Jewish family in Cincinnati, and had taken to professional dramatic performances after her husband had lost his fortune in the depression of 1857, that her first poems were published. The organ was *The Israelite,* a weekly which had been founded by Rabbi Isaac M. Wise in 1854.

Her poems, mostly autobiographical, are marked by the struggles in her own soul, and her feeling of kinship with the members of her own race. Just as the Russian massacres of 1879 had definitely turned Emma Lazarus from her sweet songs about Greece and post-Renaissance Italy, so the massacres of the Jews in Turkey stimulated the Muse of Adah Menken. In "At Spes Non Fracta," she begs for the Messiah to come:

> Will He never come! Will the Jew,
> In exile eternally pine?
> By the idolaters scorned, pitied only by a few,
> Will he never his vows to Jehovah renew,
> Beneath his own olive and vine?

When she came to Cincinnati in June, 1858, she was made even more conscious of her racial heritage. In her adolescent years, at an age when Emma Lazarus was concerned with books, Adah Menken had already dreamed of power to restore the Jew to the position in the world which she believed was justly his.

In Cincinnati she intensified her call to action. Respectable Jewish pillars of society were somewhat disturbed by the impetuosity of her emotions in "Light for the Soul":

> Do we not live in those blest days,
>   So long foretold,
> When Thou shouldst come to bring us light?
> And yet I sit in darkness as of old,
>   Pining to see
> That light, but thou art still far from me.
> If thus in darkness ever left
>   Can I fulfil
> The works of light, while of light bereft?
> How shall I learn in love and gentleness still,
>   To follow thee?
> And all the sinful works of darkness flee?

It is amazing that at a time when the Jews in America were trying to adopt the folk-ways of their American neighbors and to forget that Jews in other parts of the world were still living in ghettos and were being massacred, this young Jewess should speak up against any indignities that might be heaped upon Jews whereever they might live. When Baron Rothschild was engaged in the controversy over the wording of his oath of office in the British Parliament, "on the faith of a Christian," Adah's voice was one of the few in America to be raised in protest in her poem, "The Jew in Parliament."

When she was informed of the infamous kidnapping of Edgar Mortara, the young son of a Jew of Bologna, by members of the Holy Inquisition, she became enraged and wrote one of her most intense poems. After she left Cincinnati for New York her reputation as a poetess of her people was established. In 1860 the editor of the *New York Sunday Mercury* wrote of her, "the lady is a Jewess, and almost insane in her eagerness to behold her people restored once more to their ancient power and glory."

Adah Menken was proud of her religion to the extent of publicly denying the allegation that she had adopted Judaism after her marriage to Menken. This marriage ended unhappily and her second matrimonial adventure with John Carmel Heenan, heavyweight boxing champion of America, was even more disastrous. Critics have marvelled at the concentrated emotional content of Emily Dickinson's poetry, written as the result of her tragic love story. Adah Menken's poems, which flowed from a heart twice disappointed and humiliated by love, are eloquent testimony to her sufferings.

It was about this time that she met Walt Whitman. Poet felt kinship to poet and she was among the first in America to appreciate his greatness. Her appreciation of his poetry developed into the adoption of his poetic form, and her poems written after her meeting with Whitman represent perhaps the best that were written in his surging rhythms by any of his contemporaries. In "Hear, O Israel" she demonstrates her skill in the new verse-form, to which she adds her individual fervor, as she assumes the role of a spokesman of her people:

> Hear, O Israel, and plead, and plead my cause against the ungodly nation!
> 'Midst the terrible conflict, of Love and Peace, I departed from thee, my people, and spread my tent of many colors in the land of Egypt.
> In their crimson and fine linen I girded my white form.
> Sapphires gleamed their purple light from out the darkness of my hair.
> The silver folds of their temple foot-cloth was spread beneath my sandal'd feet.
> Thus I slumbered through the daylight.
>   Slumbered 'midst the vapor of sin,
>   Slumbered 'midst the battle and din,
>   Wakened 'midst the strangle of breath,
>   Wakened 'midst the struggle of death!

When she married Robert Henry Newell, the literary editor of the *Sunday Mercury,* in 1862, she was now fortunate in having a husband who understood and encouraged her in her literary efforts. Many of her poems in *Infelicia* appeared originally in the *Sunday Mercury.* Even the prose of her letters is charged with emotional vitality. In the depths of her despair, after Heenan had publicly denied that he had ever married her, she wrote:

God forgive those who hate me and bless all who have one kind thought left for a poor reckless loving woman who cast her soul out upon the broad ocean of human love, where it was the sport of the happy waves for a few short hours, and then was left to drift helpless against the cold rocks, until she learned to love death better than life.

Adah Menken was able to shake off the melancholy which produced this letter in 1860. She startled the theatre-goers of America and England in her daring performances as Mazeppa. She was admired in England by Swinburne, who persuaded his publisher, John Camden Hotten, to print a volume of her selected poems. Charles Dickens and Charles Reade were her friends. When she was suffering from her fatal illness, Henry Wadsworth Longfellow visited her and inscribed her album. Thomas Buchanan Read was with her until her tragic end.

These three remarkable American Jewesses of the nineteenth century combined a sensitivity to beauty with a pride in their racial and religious heritage. When Jewish men-of-letters preserved a dignified silence in the face of massacres and humiliations of their co-religionists in other parts of the world, these three women cried out in fervent verses. They may not have been blessed with the characteristics of the model Jewish housewife as enumerated in the Thirty-first Chapter of Proverbs, but they were in truth daughters of Deborah.

The Anglo-Jewish magazines during the latter half of the nineteenth century printed the poems of scores of poets. Most of the output was of distinctly Jewish interest. Translations of the Psalms, songs of protest and indignation whenever any new oppression of Jews in Europe came to the attention of these writers in America, paeans of praise to leading figures in Jewish biblical and post-biblical history, expressions of the Jewish spirit in its various manifestations—this was the poetic output offered to the readers of *The American Israelite, Menorah,* and similar periodicals.[6] Although many of these names are unknown to the students of American poetry, such truly significant figures as Adah Isaacs Menken and Emma Lazarus published a considerable number of their poems in these magazines.

These poets deserve at least a brief mention. *The American Israelite* printed since its beginning in 1854 the poems of the following:

Jacob Bamberger, Nathan Bernstein, Hannchen Bonnheim, William Goldsmith Brown, B. Castello, Henry Cohen, Sylvie D'Avigdor, Nathan Haskell Dole, A. B. Franklin, Eugene Furstner, Felix N. Gerson, Milton Goldsmith, Mrs. Hartog (editor of the *Jewish Sabbath Journal*), Isabella R. Hess, George Horton, Ruth Ward Kahn, Hermann Kuhn, Mrs. Levitas, I. Levy, Jr., Robert Loveman, Isaac N. Lowenstein, Arthur Mayer, Nathan Mayer (also the author of several novels published in the *Israelite*), R. C. V. Meyers, H. M. Moos (also a novelist), Charles Newburgh, Richard Realf, "Shira-shirim," Debbie H. Silver, Leopold Stern, Helen K. Weil, Edward Youl.

These and other Jewish poets did not exert any important influence on the great body of American poetry, yet they kept alive the creative lyrical spirit, which has always expressed itself wherever Jews have lived.

13. CONTEMPORARY JEWISH

POETS IN AMERICA

Contemporary American poetry can hardly be mentioned today without bringing to mind several outstanding Jewish poets. No one has done more to make poetry interesting to and popular with school-children than Louis Untermeyer. Franklin P. Adams, Arthur Guiterman, Samuel Hoffenstein, Newman Levy are among the most skilful authors of light verse living. Joseph Auslander's translations of the sonnets of Petrarch are among the few great translations in contemporary English literature. Hardly an anthology of contemporary American poetry appears without poems by Maxwell Bodenheim, James Oppenheim, Babette Deutsch, Nathalia Crane, and Dorothy Parker. In some instances leaders of new schools of poetry number among their ranks Jewish poets. Louis Zukofsky has edited An "Objectivist's" Anthology,[1] and has been prominent in the movement.

Many coveted awards for American poetry have been made to Jewish poets. *The Nation's* annual prize was won by Martin Feinstein in 1922 for "In Memoriam"; in 1925 by Eli Siegel for "Hot Afternoons Have Been in Montana"; in 1926 by Babette Deutsch for "Thoughts at the Year's End." To Charles A. Wagner, editor of the anthology, *Prize poems*, 1913-1929, was given *Poetry Magazine's* prize for 1929. *Palms* similarly honored Joseph Auslander in 1929 for his "Letter to Emily Dickinson."

CONTEMPORARY JEWISH POETS

The number of American Jewish poets whose published volumes have earned high praise from the critics must run into scores and the printed output includes hundreds of volumes. Arthur Guiterman alone has published sixteen books of poetry since 1907; Franklin P. Adams accounts for twelve; Louis Untermeyer has published seven collections of original verse. How can one organize the tremendous body of American verse of Jewish poets into some systematic order? Are there any recognizable tendencies or characteristics in the output of poets of Jewish origin? How is the Jew and Judaism treated? These are some of the interesting questions which deserve answers.

Certain obvious distinctions can be made with comparative ease. For example, some of these poets treat subject-matter of Jewish interest exclusively; some, occasionally; some, never. Jessie Sampter and Philip Raskin are almost exclusively concerned with Jewish subjects. Franklin P. Adams, Arthur Guiterman and Dorothy Parker have hardly mentioned a Jew in their poems. As was the case in the nineteenth century, the Anglo-Jewish periodicals have encouraged many Jewish poets, who might not otherwise have seen their works in print. It will be illuminating to list the Jewish poets whose work, almost always of Jewish interest, appeared in several representative magazines. To the *Menorah Journal,* since its beginning in 1915, the following poets have been contributors:

Louis K. Anspacher, Sydney Appelbaum, David P. Berenberg, Joseph M. Bernstein, Walter Hart Blumenthal, Maxwell Bodenheim, Alter Brody, Stanley Burnshaw, Simon Chasen, Kenneth F. Fearing, James Feibelman, Martin Feinstein, Hortense Flexner, Florence Kiper Frank, Don Gordon, David N. Grokowsky, Julius S. Hoffman, Isaac Heber, Alan Kanfer, Abraham M. Klein, I. M. Lask, Marvin Lowenthal, A. B. Magil, Abel Meeropol, Gerald P. Meyer, Rebekah ha Levi-Mordeki, Louis I. Newman, Harry Alan Potamkin, Alice Raphael, Charles Reznikoff, Edward Robbin, David Ross, Maurice Samuel, Edward Sapir, Isidor Schneider, Edwin Seaver, Eugene Silverman, Thelma Spear, Jean Starr Untermeyer, Louis Untermeyer, Lucy Weinstein, Morris Weisenthal, Walter B. Wolfe.

Opinion, founded in 1932, has presented works of the following Jewish poets, not listed above:

Mildred Barish, Max Berman, Babette Deutsch, Diane Farber, Johanna Frada, Philip Freund, Louis Ginsberg, Alice Ginsburg, Shirley Bliss Goldberg, Minnie Goodfriend, Ethel Fleming Guttman, Vivian Heyerdahl, James I. Jacobs, L. Jaffe, Alexander Javits, Dorothy Ruth Kahn, Sholom J. Kahn, Ben Kelson, Lucy Kent, Douglas B. Krantzor, Fania Kruger, Manuel Laderman, William Grant Lewi, Jr., Ludwig Lewisohn, Theodore R. Nathan, Gertrude Stewart Phillips, Victor E. Reichert, Sara Adler Rosalsky, Sidney Rosen, Jessie E. Sampter, Miriam Joyce Selker, Lillian Turner, Leonard Twynham, Hilda Ziegler, Gremin Zorn.

This list by no means exhausts the number of American poets of Jewish origin who have written on Jewish subjects. Many other magazines in all parts of the country print verse, and the total annual output numbers hundreds of poems a year.

It is the contribution to American poetry as a whole, rather than to Jewish poetry written in English, which compels attention. Even in this broader field, with the very best of American poetry to serve as comparison, the output of Jewish poets has assumed a unique position. Sometimes a poem like Isidor Schneider's "The Temptation of Anthony," which appeared in a large anthology of American prose and poetry, *The American Caravan* (1927), stands out as the most promising contribution of the book. In another instance, a poem like Louis Untermeyer's "Caliban in the Coal Mines" becomes almost a classic. Occasionally a book of poems by a Jewish poet becomes a national best-seller, as was the case with Samuel Hoffenstein's *Poems in Praise of Practically Nothing* (1928). Many Jewish poets have been "socially conscious." Some have written carefully planned and exquisitely polished sonnets like those of Robert Nathan. Others like James Oppenheim have preferred the Whitmanesque form. Morris Abel Beer has interpreted the life of the city.

CONTEMPORARY JEWISH POETS

James Oppenheim has tried to wed poetry and psychoanalysis. Samuel Roth has castigated a devastated, world-weary Europe. Almost every form and school of poetry has its adherents among the Jewish poets of America.

Among the scores of these poets the dozen of highest rank may now be examined for their individual excellences. Around them can be gathered the many other secondary figures who have not yet reached their prime. Louis Untermeyer in his anthology, *Modern American Poetry,* fifth edition, 1936, includes the works of Franklin P. Adams, James Oppenheim, Jean Starr Untermeyer, Maxwell Bodenheim, Robert Nathan, Joseph Auslander, Nathalia Crane, and his own. The fourth edition, 1930, included Alter Brody, Babette Deutsch, Louis Ginsberg, and Horace Traubel.

Robert Nathan, whose achievements as a novelist are discussed in another chapter, has especial significance. As a craftsman of almost infallible taste and precision, and as an author definitely concerned with Jewish problems, he holds the attention of the students of both subjects. His poetical output is confined to three small volumes: *Youth Grows Old* (1922), *The Cedar Box* (1929), and *Selected Poems* (1935).

Percy Hutchinson, reviewing the last volume in the *New York Times,* concludes his criticism with:

> The future of American poetry is safe as long as we have poets to turn out work so accomplished as this sonnet ("Ethiopia").

Nathan has obliged the many admirers of his poetry with an introduction to *Selected Poems,* which explains his preoccupation with the sonnet form. "When I was young," he says, "I believed that music was song, and poetry music. This book is small (38 pages), but in so far as it is able it sings.... I have never believed that size and art were one. Within the walls of the sonnet, as in the body of the violin, there is room for everything. It has its own music, perfect and inviolate." As he reveals in his series of three novels, published collectively as *The Barly Fields,* Nathan's love for nature places him in the category with such a poet as Wordsworth and such a prose artist as Thoreau. His poem "Mountain Interval" is typical. In the past few years the outbursts of savagery all over Europe, attacking his co-religionists as well as all men of good will, have stimulated him to the expression of the part which poets must play in preserving our civilization. His sonnet "Ethiopia" is typical of the new, prophetic strain, which has animated his poems and novels. He has written several poems on Hitlerite Germany and the Spanish Civil War.

Nathan's sensitive spirit is evident in the many lines expressing his sadness. Such lines are found: "Sorrow is the best thing, I've ever had," "See how the city in her lonely light puts out like lanterns one by one our hopes," "I am no stranger in the house of pain."

The afflictions of Jewry throughout the world have left their mark on the poet and have re-echoed in his poems. He has been disillusioned and discouraged but undaunted. To his co-religionists, in the sonnet "These are the chosen people," he gives the hopeful message:

> It is for them the honey and the gall
> To be the wakeful, the abiding race,
> And guard the wells of pity of the heart.

Throughout his poetry there is revealed a sensitive mind, a sympathetic heart, a distaste for violence and ugliness in any form, and a keen ear for verbal music which makes of his prose as well as of his poetry rare delights.

In direct contrast to Robert Nathan's perfection of poetic form is James Oppenheim's rhapsodic style. He has left a much larger body of poetry than Nathan's, his single volume *The Sea* containing 557 pages. His books of poetry include: *Monday Morning, and Other Poems* (1909), *Wild Oats* (1910), *Songs for the New Age* (1914), *War and Laughter* (1916), *The Book of Self* (1917), *Solitary* (1919), *The Mystic Warrior* (1921) and *The Sea* (1924).

Oppenheim is a spiritual descendant of Whitman, whom he imitated in his first book, and whose "surging rhythms" have animated his own poetry. "The Slave" and "The Runner in the Skies" are included in the anthology of Untermeyer and in *The New Poetry*, edited by Harriet Monroe and Alice Corbin Henderson (1923).

In the introduction to *The Sea,* he explains his sources of inspiration for his earlier volumes. Of *Songs for the New Age* he writes, "He plundered the Old Testament and *Leaves of Grass* and his own depths, and a book of a hundred songs came as an inundation, a confused glory, so that now it was the poet singing, and now the prophetical preacher denouncing."[2]

Oppenheim's *The Sea* is really the poetical autobiography of a courageous rebel and liberator of mankind. He writes of his first poetical strivings that "he pulled out of the mire in which the American was stuck, and in breaking many of his own chains, struck like a new Prometheus against the chains binding others."[3] His later volumes expressed his vision of a new world which he, as well as many other artists, projected after the Great War. Deeply read in the new psychoanalysis, he probed the most secret recesses of his mind and heart. Throughout, he remembers his Hebrew heritage. As Louis Untermeyer writes:

Oppenheim is a throw-back to the ancient Hebrew singers; the music of the Psalms rolls through his lines, the fire of Isaiah kindles his spirit. This poetry, with its obvious reminders of Whitman, is biblical in its inflection, Oriental in its heat. It runs through forgotten centuries and brings Asia to busy America; it carries to the Western world the color of the East.[4]

Although a great deal of his poetry which seemed so rich in meaning and language may not seem so significant today, Oppenheim has not lost in stature as one of the great rebels and prophets in American poetry during the decade, 1914-1924.

Maxwell Bodenheim is represented not only in the anthologies of Louis Untermeyer and Monroe and Henderson, but in Conrad Aiken's *Modern American Poets* (1927). His published volumes include: *Minna and Myself* (1918), *Advice* (1920), *Introducing Irony* (1922), *Against This Age* (1923), *The Sardonic Arm* (1923), *Returning to Emotion* (1927), *King of Spain* (1928), and *Bringing Jazz* (1930).

His first volume, published when he was twenty-six, revealed his unusual power of words. "Words, under his hands, have unexpected growths; placid nouns and sober adjectives bear fantastic fruit."[5] The poems in *Minna and Myself* are represented in Untermeyer's anthology by "Poet to His Love" and "Old Age." Conrad Aiken in his anthology has several others. Joseph Kling's *Pagan Anthology* prints four: "Soldiers," "The Walk," "Intrusion," and "To a Man." Written at the period in American poetry when Imagism was most popular, it is not surprising that many of Bodenheim's early poems are elaborated images.

In "Poet to His Love," the variation is upon the theme, "An old silver church in a forest is my love for you." "Soldiers" is a vivid picture of

> Dead soldiers, in a moon-dipped crescent,
> Whose faces form a gravely mocking sentence.

In "Intrusion" a comparison is made between "your silence and the mist of soft words breaking it" and the lilies and the young breeze. "Old Age" is a clear-cut image of the poet's thoughts represented as old men living in his mind. In later collections of poetry this imagist tendency is applied to more familiar objects: "The Interne" who exclaims "Oh, the agony of having too much power"; "The Old Jew," another picture of a patient in a hospital, whose austerity made even the doctors bow in respect; "The Miner," who says so vividly:

> Those on the top say they know you, Earth—they are liars.
> You are my father, and the silence I work in is my mother.

Other poems in similar style are "The Rear-Porches of an Apartment-Building," "To an Enemy," "To a Discarded Steel Rail," "Love," "Songs to a Woman," "Death," and "Impulsive Dialogue." In *Advice* (1920) Bodenheim is more interested in getting at the inner significance of things than in finding words with which to make brilliant images. Certain outstanding poems in the collection are: "Advice to a Street Pavement," "Advice to a Buttercup," "Foundry Workers," "Rattlesnake," "Mountain Fable," "Advice to a Butterfly," "Fifth Avenue," "Boarding House Episode," "Steel Mills," and "South Chicago."

Introducing Irony (1922) continued Bodenheim's preoccupations with cerebral rather than emotional poetry. Not especially interested in melody or in verse form, Bodenheim strove to express the unusual ideas which the various simple objects of daily life suggested to him. Few poets might have seen in a discarded steel rail the subjects for a poem, yet Bodenheim could see that

> Straight strength pitched into the surliness of the ditch,
> A soul you have—strength has always delicate secret reasons.
> Your soul is a dull question.
> I do not care for your strength, but for your stiff smile at
>   Time—
> A smile which men call rust.

In *The Sardonic Arm* (1923) Bodenheim continued his probings for the essence of things. His irony, hinted at in early volumes, is more obvious now. The disillusionment is stronger. In *Returning to Emotion* (1927) he answered his critics who had found his poetry lacking in emotion. *King of Spain* (1928) is a brilliant attempt at a long narrative poem. *Bringing Jazz* (1930) was in an entirely new style. The subjects pertain to city life in Greenwich Village, Broadway, Harlem, and Chicago's South Side. All of these are written in a rhythm equivalent to jazz in music. The preoccupation with words has yielded to an interest in rhythms. The old preference for the quickly assimilated image is still conspicuous.

Reviewing Bodenheim's eight volumes of verse, one concludes that here is a poetic talent that is rich verbally, illuminated by a brilliant intellect which reveals with uncanny intuition, essences and truths, but a talent strikingly individualistic, subjective, and egotistic. Such was the general picture of American poetry during the War years, which led to such critiques as Amy Lowell's *Tendencies in Modern American Poetry* (1917), and to the corrosive criticism of these tendencies in John L. Lowes' *Convention and Revolt in Poetry* (1917).

Louis Untermeyer is the best-known anthologist in America and has done more to make poetry an integral part of the English curriculum than any other author. He has written seven volumes of original verse, five volumes of parodies, a book of travel, four books of criticism, two novels, and a definitive biography of Heinrich Heine together with a volume of brilliant translations of the poet and in addition has compiled six anthologies. Untermeyer in his *Modern British and American Poetry* has given his own criticism of his works.

Untermeyer's first volume was *The Younger Quire* (1911), a twenty-four-page burlesque of an anthology (*The Younger Choir*). It was issued anonymously and only one hundred copies were printed. Later in the same year, he published a sequence of some seventy lyrics entitled *First Love* (1911). With the exception of about five of these songs, the volume is devoid of character and, in spite of a certain technical facility, wholly undistinguished.

Untermeyer then discusses *Challenge* (1914), in which he speaks in his own idiom. "Caliban in the Coal Mines" has become as popular to contemporary school-children as Gray's "Elegy" or Goldsmith's "The Deserted Village" was a generation ago. In this volume Untermeyer spoke for social justice before most of the "propaganda" dramatists, novelists and poets were out of child's clothes. Untermeyer was called a "radical" by one of his reviewers—"a radical, but an affirmative radical; he is angry at certain traditions but (like all true poets) he knows the greatness of faith. Love and democracy are his favorite themes, and few living poets are worthier to sing them."

In *These Times* (1917) Untermeyer varied his subject-matter.

He arranged his poems in groups: the wave, thirteen portraits, havens, Dick (six poems for a child), battle-cries, youth moralizes, two rebels.

The New Adam (1920) is devoted to poetry of love. In an introductory note to the book, the author states that the love poetry of the preceding age has been artificial, and that in our time there is a tendency to return "to the upright vigor, the wide and healthy curiosity of our earlier ancestors, the Elizabethans." Representative poems include "The New Adam," "Hands," "Asleep," "Summer Storm," "A Marriage," "Wrangle," "Equals," "Supplications," "The Eternal Masculine," "Windy Days," "The Embarrassed Amorist," "Words for a Jig," "Disillusion," and "The Prodigal."

Untermeyer's contributions to Jewish poetry are found mainly in his next volume, *Roast Leviathan* (1923). He has entertained certain definite ideas on Jewish poetry and has expressed them in his critical volumes and in such essays as "The Jewish Spirit in Modern American Poetry," in *The Menorah Journal* for August 1921. To Untermeyer there are definitely perceivable and describable qualities like "Semitic fantasy," and "that strange blend of irony and imagery" which constitute for him the literary heritage of the Jews. In the foreword to *Roast Leviathan,* Untermeyer expresses in detail his theories on this much debated topic. His poems are designed as illustrations of his views. Among them "He Goads Himself," "Lenox Avenue Express," "Boy and Tadpoles" are typical. The volume belongs definitely to that specific body of American poetry of Jewish interest, together with the *Songs of a Semite* of Emma Lazarus, *Infelicia* of Adah I. Menken, and *Brand Plucked from the Fire* of Jessie Sampter.

Burning Bush (1928) and *Food and Drink* (1932) represent his maturest work. The latter is divided into four sections: "Yes and No" consisting of dramatic lyrics; "A Country Year," a cycle of modern bucolics; "With the Left Hand," a set of brief satires; and "Against Time," containing the more metaphysical poems.

Untermeyer ranks with the leading American parodists, his volumes including *The Younger Quire* (1911), *And Other Poets* (1916), *Including Horace* (1919), *Heavens* (1922), and *Collected Parodies* (1926). His reputation as a critic is firmly established as a result of such volumes as *American Poetry since 1900* (1923), *The Forms of Poetry* (1926), and *Poetry: Its Appreciation and Enjoyment* (1934).

He represents a truly rare personality in literature—the creative artist who is also a critic. English and American literature can boast of very few such literary dual personalities. Jewish authors in America have often combined these apparently irreconcilable traits. One has but to recall Ludwig Lewisohn, Paul Rosenfeld, Joseph Auslander, Babette Deutsch, Benjamin De Casseres, Waldo Frank, Simeon Strunsky, all of whom have achieved reputations as novelists or poets and as critics.

Evaluating Untermeyer's contributions to American poetry, we notice first his sincere interest in social justice, in the welfare of the common man. He has managed to preserve a balance between his subjective poems, concerned with his personal experiences, and his poems of outer experience. He has been proud of his Hebraic heritage, which he has attempted to analyze in critical terms. He has preferred the poetry of form to the experimental styles of the past three decades. Imitating, as all poets must, his favorites, Heine, Housman, Horace and others, he has managed to find his own expression and stamped his own individuality on his later verses.

Babette Deutsch has been extremely versatile. She has produced four volumes of original poetry, three novels, two anthologies, and two books of criticism. She is extremely well acquainted with Hebrew poetry and the Hebraic spirit in poetry. Her poem, "Thoughts at the Year's End," which won the Poetry Prize awarded by the *Nation* magazine in 1926, is definitely an expression of the Hebraic spirit. She has contributed frequently to the Anglo-Jewish press. In the *Menorah Journal* have appeared "Maariv," "The Meeting of Jacob and Joseph," "Sun

Bath," "Saffron Flower," and "Despair Rejoices." To *Opinion* she contributed "Psalm: 1933." *Reflex* printed "Faith" and "Pithecanthrope."

Her first volume of poetry, *Banners* (1918), won immediate critical acclaim. The title poem was written in 1917 in honor of the beginning of the Russian revolution, and is the most stirring in the book. The poems are arranged in five groups: The dancers, Ephemeris, songs and silences, sonnets, and Banners. In verse form she runs the gamut from strict sonnets to *vers libre*. Her pictures of Isadora Duncan's dancers are unique in their attempt to capture a dynamic art in terms of another art. Her poems "Anna," "The Death of a Child," "Distance," and "The Undelivered" are among the more distinguished in this first volume. Miss Deutsch revealed at once a sharp intensity of feeling and even sharper sensitivity. Richly endowed emotionally, merciless in her search for precise expression, her poems left clear-cut impressions and vivid pictures.

Her second volume, *Honey out of the Rock* (1925), was divided into four sections: wind and iron, time's fuel, sonnets, and for Adam. Her carefully wrought lines, permeated by her glowing intensity made this book a decided advance over her first. *Fire for the Night* (1930) is dominated throughout by the bleak figure of Time. Loving the world with a poet's fire, she cannot escape the sadness upon the realization of the evanescence of all things. She tries to gather up in the treasure-house of her senses as many sensuous impressions as her brief existence will permit her. For she realizes that

> Let the saint forego the world,
> Let the martyr tear his flesh,
> Only death shall wrench from me
> The treasures in the sensual mesh.

Epistle to Prometheus (1931) is a long philosophical poem, mostly in free verse, in which Miss Deutsch addresses the mythical creator of man and giver of fire. Seeking the Promethean spirit, she glimpses it in Socrates, Christ, Voltaire, Lenin, and Gandhi. The imagination of the poet has been moved by the wrongs and degradations of human life and by the contrasting vision of what it might have become.

Not all Jewish poets in America are seriously inclined or are entirely occupied with the woes of their fellow men. Among the most accomplished authors of light verse in America are to be included Franklin P. Adams, Arthur Guiterman, Dorothy Parker, Newman Levy, Samuel Hoffenstein, Edward Anthony, and Arthur L. Lippman. Most of the poems constituting the twelve volumes by Franklin P. Adams have appeared in his famous column, "The Conning Tower," in various New York newspapers. His first volume, *Tobogganing on Parnassus*, was published in 1910. For the past three decades Adams has proven himself a worthy successor of Eugene Field and other early columnists. Although his poems are rarely devoted to specifically Jewish subjects, now and then he will be aroused by some new indignity or persecution to an expression of melancholy or bitter irony.

Arthur Guiterman's first volume of light verse appeared in 1907. Since then fifteen other collections have given him the reputation of being one of the most skilful craftsmen in the field. He originated the "rhymed reviews" in *Life* magazine, when it was a comic weekly. When asked to contribute a few biographical facts to an anthology published in 1918, he wrote:

> For the past nine years I have been the principal contributor of verse to Life, and I suppose that I am popularly known, as the originator of Rhymed Reviews and other humorous metrical stunts in that paper. But don't try to pigeon-hole me in any compartment, or I'll fool you; because I have always written, and shall continue to write, on any theme that interests me or fills me with enthusiasm, and in whatever style happens.

With the publication of *Ballads of Old New York* (1920), Guiterman revealed new talents in the narrative form. Some of his best known ballads are: "The Call to the Colors," "The Rush of the Oregon," "Quivira," "Storm Ship," "Sleepy Hollow," "Harlem Heights," "The Ballad of John Paul Jones," "The Quest of the Ribband," "The Legend of the First Cam-u-e-l" and "This Is She."

Arthur Guiterman has gone his merry way writing his own kind of verse through the last four decades, hardly affected by the many poetical currents and tendencies of that period. Imagism, objectivism, cerebralism, proletarianism have all passed him by and he has remained, as the title of his last book so aptly indicates, *Gaily the Troubadour.*

Specializing in a different variety of comic verse, Newman Levy in *Opera Guyed* (1923) and *Theatre Guyed* (1933) has burlesqued popular operas and plays to the obvious delight of his many admirers. Writing under the pseudonym of Flaccus in F. P. A.'s "Conning Tower," Newman Levy has been awarded more than one prize for the best comic poem submitted by the contributors. In the first volume, fourteen operas are burlesqued, including *Tannhauser, Tosca, Carmen, Samson and Delilah,* and *Thais.* In the second collection the plots of the following plays are retold in humorous verse: *The Merchant of Venice, Strange Interlude, Rain, Faust, Othello, Oedipus Rex, The Second Mrs. Tanqueray, East Lynne, The Belle of the Balkans, Cyrano, Uncle Tom's Cabin, Trilby, A Doll's House, The Three Cherry Sisters Karamazov.* Levy has written various other ballads and burlesques, which have been collected in *Gay But Wistful* (1925), *Saturday to Monday* (1931).

One of the best-selling books of poetry in recent years was Samuel Hoffenstein's *Poems in Praise of Practically Nothing* (1928), which indicated new possibilities for comic verse. Burton Rascoe's encomium sums up adequately the general consensus of critical acclaim which greeted the volume:

. . . he has fashioned some fine and beautiful verses out of his heart and intellect . . . they are technically perfect . . . they are original as far as originality in poetry can go . . . they are in the main line of the Heinesque tradition, and . . . they are the epitome of lyrical wit and musical sardonic laughter.[6]

Some of the titles demonstrate the wide range of subject matter upon which Hoffenstein has bestowed his felicity of phrasing, wit, technical brilliance, and sardonic lyricism. Some of these topics have probably never before been treated in poetry: "To Break the Tedium of Riding a Bicycle, Seeing One's Friends, or Heartbreak," "Verses Demonstrating That No Man Can Be Unhappy Amid the Infinite Variety of the World, and Giving the Reader the Choice of Several Titles, the Author's Favorite Being 'Some Play Golf and Some Do Not'," "Poems Carefully Restrained So as to Offend Nobody," "Poems Intended to Excite the Utmost Depression," "Songs of Fairly Utter Despair."

Hoffenstein has many of the sentiments of his fellow poets in serious vein, but he has less patience and a more practical approach. He writes:

> Lady, to whose feet I'd bring
> The world, if I could win it,
> Are you sure of anything
> For a single minute?

Another typical love poem is

> When love, at last, had left me quiet,
> And my heart was clear of pain,
> Toxins, due to faulty diet,
> Broke it right in two again.

The beauties of nature, sources of inspiration to so many poets, inspire Hoffenstein also,—to complain:

> When the wind is in the tree
> It makes a noise just like the sea,
> As if there were not noise enough
> To bother one, without that stuff.

Hoffenstein's later volume, *Year In, You're Out* (1930), consolidated his position as a poet in the brilliant, satirical, pessi-

CONTEMPORARY JEWISH POETS

mistic strain of Heine, Crashaw, Herrick, Donne, and Suckling.

Dorothy Parker was for a time one of the most-quoted among New York's *literati* of that gay Prohibition Era, reflected so brilliantly in the early volumes of *The New Yorker,* the plays of Philip Barry and S. N. Behrman, and the essays of Alexander Woollcott. Her poetic output is confined to four small collections: *Enough Rope* (1927), *Sunset Gun* (1928), *Death and Taxes* (1931), *Collected Poems* (1936).

Characteristic of Miss Parker's attitude to love, which is the theme of so many of her poems is "Two-volume Novel":

> The sun's gone dim, and
>   The moon's turned black;
> For I loved him, and
>   He didn't love back.

Her poem, "To a Lady, Who Must Write Verse," is an admonition against revealing the secrets of love's disillusionments and closes with the quatrain:

> Never print, poor child, a lay on
> Love and blood and anguishing,
> Lest a cooled, benignant Phaon
> Murmur, "Foolish little thing!"

Brilliant, easily bored with people less gifted than herself, Miss Parker has written caustically of the many pretentious people in the Era of Prosperity. Some of her most vicious thrusts have punctured the flatulent egos of her fellow-artists. The poem "Bohemia" after cataloguing the authors, actors, sculptors, and singers who have bored her, ends with:

> People Who Do Things exceed my endurance;
> God, for a man who solicits insurance!

Dorothy Parker is in the same class of gifted, emotionally rich Jewesses who have expressed in poetry and in prose, such as Tess Slesinger's *The Unpossessed* and Aline Bernstein's *The Journey Down,* their reactions to a world full of enervating, boring, third-rate personalities. Miss Parker is not vicious and, on the contrary, was a favorite of the literary set with which she associated.

Another Jewish contributor of comic verse to F. P. A.'s "Conning Tower" is Edward Anthony, whose *Merry-go-Roundelays* (1921) contain his best efforts. He is expert in the ballad, rondeau, and triolet forms, and his subjects range from barber shops to Mexican generals.

The remaining Jewish poets in America may be classified as follows:

Singers of social significance: Benjamin Appel, Alter Brody, Benjamin De Casseres, Martin Feinstein, Samuel Roth, and Charles A. Wagner.

Lyricists: Joseph Auslander, Nathalia Crane, Gustav Davidson, Hortense Flexner, Louis Ginsberg, Rebekah ha Levi-Mordeki, Lincoln Kirstein, Robert Loveman, Debbie H. Silver, Thelma Spear.

Narrative Poets: David P. Berenberg, Isidor Schneider, Stanley Burnshaw, Stanton A. Coblentz, Evaleen Stein.

Singers of the Jewish Spirit and Subject Matter: Mildred Barish, Walter Hart Blumenthal, John Cournos, Edward Doro, James K. Feibelman, Florence Kiper Frank, Fania Kruger, Louis I. Newman, Philip Raskin, Charles Reznikoff, Jessie Sampter.

Interpreters of City Life: Morris Abel Beer, Kenneth Fearing, Elias Lieberman, Charles Recht.

Balladists: Herman Hagedorn, George S. Hellman.

The works pertaining to Jewish subject-matter deserve particular mention. David P. Berenberg has written in *The Kid* (1931) a long narrative poem about a Jewish prize-fighter. The poet manages to present the environment which made The Kid conscious of his Jewish origin, his fears, his sensitivity, and even his Jewish distaste for struggle. The poem is an unusual revelation of a Jewish character, much the same way as a novel or play about a Jewish scientist or lawyer reveals insights heretofore neglected in literature.

Charles Reznikoff came to America with boyhood memories of

Russia. In his novel *By the Waters of Manhattan* and frequently in his poems he contrasts the two civilizations. Jessie Sampter was an active Zionist who lived and worked in Palestine. Her collected poems, *Brand Plucked from the Fire* (1937), are divided into five sections: Land of Israel, Little Songs of Big and Little Things, Coming of Peace, Psalms in Struggle, and Diaspora. Florence Kiper Frank's *The Jew to Jesus, and Other Poems* (1915) was the expression of a poet keenly alive to the tragedies and ironies to which Jews throughout the world were subjected. Her poems, "The Jewish Conscript," "The Movies," "You," and "Sleep the Mother" are included by Harriet Monroe in her anthology, *The New Poetry*. John Cournos has created Jewish characters in several novels and in his poems expresses the loneliness and sensitivity of one who is between two worlds and is fashioning a new world of his own. Edward Doro's *Shiloh* (1936) consists of episodes in the life of Jesus. Philip Raskin has confined all his poetry to meditations and reflections of a sensitive Jew.

Joseph Auslander's eight volumes of original verse, his history of poetry, *The Winged Horse* (with Frank E. Hill), and his translations from La Fontaine and Petrarch have shown him to possess a rich knowledge of world poetry, an acute ear for verbal melody, a true poet's sense of beauty, and a gift of words with which to express it.

Jean Starr Untermeyer, Hortense Flexner, Rebekah ha Levi-Mordeki, Debbie H. Sliver, and Thelma Spear have wrought exquisite songs of lyrics, much in the classical tradition.

Decidedly urban in their interests have been the singers of New York, Morris Abel Beer, Kenneth Fearing, Elias Lieberman, and Charles Recht. This note of preoccupation with the multitudinous sights and sounds of ordinary daily life in the great Metropolis is a decidedly new note in contemporary poetry. While Amy Lowell sang of her "Patterns" and T. S. Eliot of "The Waste Land," these singers of the symphony of seven million saw all the beauties in their native city.

Since the Great Depression, which began to afflict America in

1929, many creative artists have written works of social significance. When Louis Untermeyer's *Challenge* appeared in 1914, he too was called a fighter for social justice. Yet his flaming verses are mild compared to those of his successors of today. Critics now call representatives of this school "Proletarians" or "Propagandists," but their aims are much the same as those of Shelley, Heine, and Wordsworth, when they castigated their age for permitting the miserable conditions which existed. Samuel Roth's *Europe* (1919) was only one of hundreds of books of disillusioned artists inspired by the Great War. Roth lashes vehemently against the cruel inhumanity which inundated Europe during 1914-1918 and later. The sufferings of Jews do not escape his attention. He writes:

> God, how will it all end?
> Are we who saw Egypt, Babylon and Assyria to bed
> And witnessed the last fires of Rome on
>   the shores of the Mediterranean,
> Are we at last to fall at the hands of the Poles?

Martin Feinstein served in the Great War and has written of that catastrophe as a Jew, to whom the lust for battle was distasteful. His songs constitute some of the authentic reactions of Jews in the different armies. Isaac Rosenberg's English poems offer an interesting comparison.

The contemplation of the vast amount of American poetry written by poets of Jewish origin strikes the student with awe and amazement. The differences in style and language, the richness of thought, the definite influence of the Hebraic traditions and culture, the exceptional command of the language, verse forms, and technique—all these confront the critic who would like to perceive some order out of this generous output of creative talent. Perhaps order is neither perceptible, nor necessary. It is sufficient that these poets, each a distinct personality, yet each stemming from Israel, has enriched American poetry in its various manifestations.

PART II

The Jew As Portrayed In American Literature

14. A SURVEY OF

THREE CENTURIES

The Jew has been a subject of discussion in American literature since 1640. Every type of creative expression—novel, drama, poem, essay, and theological tract—has been used to characterize, explain, defend or criticize him. In fiction and in drama hundreds of Jews of various capacities and classes have been portrayed. Many poems have treated of his experiences through the ages, and a most interesting anthology could be collected of such writings. Longfellow, Whittier, Emerson, Adah Isaacs Menken, and Emma Lazarus are but a few of the poets of the nineteenth century who have sung the glories of Israel's past and the trials of more recent times. American poets of the present century who have chosen Jewish subjects are even more numerous.

Almost every major personality in American letters has expressed his sentiments about the Jews. There exists consequently a rich literature pertaining to the Jews in America, a literature which for the first two centuries came almost entirely from the pens of non-Jewish writers. These writings offer a most illuminating insight into the impressions made upon our foremost literary figures by the Jews of America.

The first book published in the English settlements of America was the *Bay Psalm Book* (1640), which was translated directly from the Hebrew text. In the preface Richard Mather wrote the first dissertation on the language and poetry of the Hebrews to be published in America. In this book Hebrew type was used for the first time in the Western hemisphere.

The first of the hundred and fifty publications of the Puritan preacher, Increase Mather, was *The Mystery of Israel's Salvation*, published in 1669. The great minister, quoting from a host of authorities to the extent of almost two hundred pages, attempted to prove that mass conversion was the only hope of the Jews.

In the early eighteenth century the conversion of the Jews was the subject of many theological discussions. Some of the more important examples included Increase Mather's *Dissertation concerning the future conversion of the Jewish Nation* (1709), Samuel Willard's *The Fountains Opened, or the blessings plentifully to be dispersed at the national conversion of the Jews* (1722), John Beach's *Three discourses, showing the reason and propriety of rejoicing at the dissolution of the Jewish State,* and Robert Sandeman's *Some Thoughts on Christianity* (1764).

Whenever a conversion occurred in other countries these authors lost no time in giving an account of it. Cotton Mather wrote one of a British Jew in 1699 and of three Jewish children in Berlin in 1718. Perhaps the most publicized conversion in America of the eighteenth century was that of Judah Monis, the first Jewish teacher in Harvard and the first Jew to obtain a degree from that college before 1800. On March 27, 1722 he was publicly baptized in the College-Hall at Cambridge. The Reverend B. Colman delivered a discourse, *A Witness to Our Lord,* and Monis gave three discourses, *The Truth, The Whole Truth, Nothing but the Truth.*

Monis became instructor in Hebrew at Harvard and taught for almost forty years. In 1734 he published a *Grammar of the Hebrew Tongue,* the first of its kind in America. The following year there was an advertisement of a *Dissertation upon the 49th Chapter of Genesis,* but the book was probably never printed. He died April 25, 1764. His epitaph is interesting:

> Here lies buried the remains of

A SURVEY OF THREE CENTURIES

> Rabbi Judah Monis, M.A.
> Late Hebrew Instructor,
> at Harvard College in Cambridge,
> In which office he continued forty years,
> He was by birth and religion, a Jew
> But embraced the Christian faith,
> And was publicly baptized,
> At Cambridge, A. D. 1722,
> And departed this life,
> April 25th, 1764
> Aged 81 yrs, 2 m, 21 d.

The baptism of Monis evidently aroused much discussion, since extended accounts were given in the newspapers.[1] His three discourses, published in 1722, constitute the first work in English written by a Jew in America. Increase Mather, ever alert for new conversions, whether they occurred in London or in Frankfort or in Cambridge, wrote the preface. One statement is clearly indicative of Mather's attitude toward the Jews:

> The miraculous manner of God's preserving the Jewish Nation is an invincible Proof hereof; for it is an unpresidented (*sic*) and incomprehensible thing, that God should for two thousand years preserve this People dispersed among other Nations, without being confounded with them in their Religions and Customs, as is usual among all dispersed People; this clearly Demonstrates that God has preserved them for some great Design, which what can it be but their Conversion.[2]

The Jews in America were not long in replying to these pleas, and occasionally these commands, to abandon their ancient faith. Since the Christian ministers at times made erroneous statements, it is not surprising that forms of prayer and other elements of the Hebrew faith were printed. In 1760 there appeared the *Form of Prayer Performed at Jews Synagogue for the Incorporation of Canada to the Colonies,* composed by D. R. Joseph Jesurun Pinto in Hebrew and translated into English. The first volume of prayers in English for use on Rosh Hashonah and Yom Kippur appeared in 1761 from the hand of Isaac Pinto, who made use of Isaac Nieto's Spanish rendering of 1740.[3]

Samuel Langdon in 1764 attacked Sandeman's book in his *Impartial examination of Robert Sandeman's Letters*. In 1788 he preached and published the sermon *The Republic of the Israelites*.

Joseph Priestley, the English chemist and philosopher, had written in 1794 *Letters to the Jews inviting them to an Amicable discussion of the evidences of Christianity*. He was answered in that same year by David Levi in his *Letters to Dr. Priestley*. The conversion and "friendly discussion literature" was kept up by J. Bicheno in his *Friendly Address to the Jews* (1795), Richard Brothers in his *Revealed Knowledge of the Prophecies of Our Times* (1795), and Antoine Guénée's *Letters of Certain Jews to M. Voltaire* (1795). Although these authors were not Americans, their works were printed here and were widely circulated.

Another obsession of the early writers on Jews in America was the identification of the Indians with the lost tribes of Israel, Jonathan Edwards in his *Language of the Muhhekaneew Indians* cited analogies between this Indian dialect and Hebrew and hoped to prove by this means that the Indians belonged to the Chosen People. On July 4, 1777 William Gordon preached a sermon on *The Separation of the Jewish Tribes after the Death of Solomon accounted for and applied to the present day*. Other writings on this subject included John Eliot's *A tract to prove that Indians are descendants of the Jews,* Abiel Abbot's *Traits of Resemblance in the People of America to Ancient Israel,* and Elias Boudinot's *Star in the West* (1816). As late as 1827 Mordecai M. Noah delivered an address on the *Evidences of the American Indians Being the Descendants of the Lost Tribes of Israel*.

The Jewish colony at Newport, Rhode Island, received considerable attention in literature. On May 28, 1773 Rabbi Haim Isaac Karigal preached a sermon in Spanish on *The Salvation of Israel,* which was translated into English by Abraham Lopez and printed in the same year. Longfellow's poem on the *Jewish Cemetery at*

Newport (1852), is a characteristic tribute to the greatness of Israel by one who wrote of Jews on several occasions.

Ezra Stiles, a President of Harvard College and friend of Rabbi Haim Isaac Karigal, left in his diary and manuscript papers the most complete records of Jews in Colonial America. He described their communities in Newport, New Haven, Philadelphia, and elsewhere.[4] Stiles offers keen observations on the religion, customs, beliefs, and lore of the Jews. He knew many Jews and left vivid portraits of them, particularly of their attitude during the Revolution. His descriptions of the colonial synagogues and their services are among the most reliable extant.

One of the first non-theological authors to describe his experiences with Jews of America was Washington Irving. His friendship with Rebecca Gratz of Philadelphia accounts for the character of Rebecca in *Ivanhoe*. While Scott was working on the novel, Irving visited him in Abbotsford. His description of the gifted Miss Gratz induced Scott to ascribe her traits to his heroine. When *Ivanhoe* was published he sent a copy to Irving asking, "How do you like your Rebecca? Does the Rebecca I have pictured compare well with the pattern given?"

Sir Walter took a particular interest in the character of the beautiful Jewess. On one occasion when some admirer praised him for his success in a portion of the novel already completed, he replied, "Well, I think I shall make something of my Jewess."[5]

Longfellow indicated a sympathetic attitude to the Jews and an admiration for their qualities. Even while traveling in Europe in 1835 he liked to visit the old bookshops owned by Jews and to chat with the owners. On July 9, 1852 he visited the Jewish cemetery at Newport, R. I., and wrote in his diary:

Went this morning into the Jewish burying-ground, with a polite old gentleman who keeps the key. There are few graves; nearly all are low tombstones of marble, with Hebrew inscriptions and a few words added in English or Portuguese. At the foot of each the letters S. A. D. G. It is a shady nook, at the corner of the two dusty streets, with an iron fence and a granite gateway, erected at the expense of Mr. Tauro of New Orleans. Over one of the graves grows a weeping willow—a grandchild of the willow over Napoleon's grave in St. Helena.[6]

In the same year he wrote his poem on the cemetery, already mentioned. "Sandalphon," which he wrote in 1857, was based on passages from J. P. Stehelin's *The Traditions of the Jews.* Longfellow begins:

> Have you read in the Talmud of old,
> In the Legends the Rabbins have told
>   Of the limitless realms of the air,
> Have you read it,—the marvellous story
> Of Sandalphon, the Angel of Glory,
>   Sandalphon, the Angel of Prayer?

In 1852 Longfellow wrote "The Legend of Rabbi Ben Levi." He relates the Rabbi's encounter with the Angel of Death, from whom he extracts the promise that he will remain invisible to his future victims. Said the Rabbi:

> "Swear
> No human eye shall look on it again;
> But when thou takest away the souls of men,
> Thyself unseen, and with an unseen sword,
> Thou wilt perform the bidding of the Lord."
> The Angel took the sword again, and swore,
> And walks on earth unseen forevermore.

It is believed that Longfellow was indebted for this story to his friend Emmanuel Vitalis Scherb.

Longfellow's *Tales of a Wayside Inn* is the only American parallel to Chaucer's far greater *Canterbury Tales,* just as his *Hiawatha* is the earliest American epic. One of the travellers is a Spanish Jew, whose living prototype was Israel Edrehi, a Moroccan Jew, whom Longfellow met on his travels.

This favorable portrait of the Spanish Jew is one of the earliest of its kind in American literature:

A SURVEY OF THREE CENTURIES

> A Spanish Jew from Alicant
> With aspect grand and grave was there;
> Vender of silks and fabrics rare,
> And attar of rose from the Levant.
> Like an old Patriarch he appeared,
> Abraham or Isaac, or at least
> Some later Prophet or High-Priest;
> With lustrous eyes, and olive skin,
> And, wildly tossed from cheeks and chin,
> The tumbling cataract of his beard.
> His garments breathed a spicy scent
> Of cinnamon and sandal blent,
> Like the soft aromatic gales
> That meet the mariner, who sails
> Through the Moluccas, and the seas
> That wash the shores of Celebes.
> All stories that recorded are
> Pierre Alphonse he knew by heart,
> And it was rumored he could say
> The Parables of Sandabar,
> And all the Fables of Pilpay,
> Or if not all, the greater part!
> Well versed was he in Hebrew books,
> Talmud and Targum, and the lore
> Of Kabala; and evermore
> There was a mystery in his looks;
> His eyes seemed gazing far away,
> As if in vision or in trance
> He heard the solemn sackbut play,
> And saw the Jewish maidens dance.

In view of the fact that not before 1875, in Milton Nobles' *The Phoenix* was a Jew portrayed on the American stage who was not a villain, Longfellow's truly appreciative portrait stands out as a tribute to his own sincerity and friendship. His Jewish friends included the famous actress-poet, Adah Isaacs Menken, whom he visited in Paris while she lay dying and in whose album he wrote a short poem. Longfellow's five-act tragedy, *Judas Macca-*

baeus (1872), is one of the noblest treatments of the great leader.

The poet Whittier wrote four poems of Jewish interest, although none of them mentioned the Jews of his own day. These were: "Judith at the Tent of Holofernes," "Rabbi Ishmael," "The Two Rabbins," and "King Solomon and the Ants." He revealed in these poems considerable knowledge of the *Apocrypha* and of Rabbinical Lore.

Emerson in his essays, poems, and *Journal* refers to Jews several times. In his essay on *Fate* he writes: "The sufferance which is the badge of the Jew has made him in these days (1853) the ruler of the rulers of the earth." Emerson knew personally the distinguished American Jewish poet, Emma Lazarus, from whom he received a copy of her book of poems *Admetus* (1871). When he was in England he had the opportunity to see both Disraeli and one of the English Rothschilds. Of Disraeli's novels he writes in his *Journal:*

> Disraeli is well worth reading, quite a grand student of his English world, and a very clever expounder of its wisdom and craft: never quite a master.

Of Rothschild he wrote, "a round, young comfortable-looking man."

James Russell Lowell in his *Address on Democracy* (1886) paid his tribute to the people of Israel thus:

> One of the most curious of these frenzies of exclusion was that against the emancipation of the Jews. All share in the government of the world was denied for centuries to perhaps the ablest, certainly the most tenacious, race that ever lived in it—the race to whom we owed our religion and the purest spiritual stimulus and consolation to be found in all literature—a race in which ability seems as natural and hereditary as the curve of their noses, and whose blood, furtively mingling with the bluest bloods in Europe, has quickened them with its own indomitable impulsion.

The wise and genial Oliver Wendell Holmes in *The Professor at the Breakfast Table* (1859) comments:

A SURVEY OF THREE CENTURIES

I suspect the story of sweating gold was one of the many fables got up to make the Jews odious and afford a pretext for plundering them.

Years later in *Over the Teacups* (1891), replying to a series of questions pertinent to racial prejudice, he writes that from his own personal experience he finds no justification for prejudice towards Jews.

Mark Twain expressed his sentiments toward Jews in an article entitled "Concerning the Jews" (1898). He stresses his belief that anti-Semitism antedates Christianity, was existent among the nations of antiquity, and that "religious issues are responsible to only a very small extent for prejudice toward Jews."

Jewish persecution he calls a "trade-union boycott in religious disguise." Bread and economic determination, he goes on to say, lie closer to the desires of mankind than religion, and economic factors are the primary impulse behind such prejudice. He states that he has arrived at these conclusions with an "open mind." Professing to be entirely free of racial prejudice of any kind, he conveys in his analysis a sense of admiration and sympathy for the Jews. He praises particularly their efficient organization of charities and Jewish philanthropy in general. He finds that Jews have been slow to organize and make their influence felt politically, and advises them to strengthen their position. One biographer writes in this connection:

> The Jews he did consistently admire as a people and considered the most gifted race in the world.[6a]

Lafcadio Hearn, who wrote of places so far apart as Tokyo and New Orleans, and of personalities of many countries, left four sketches of Jewish interest in his book *Occidental Gleanings* (1886). One is an essay on Ferdinand Lassalle. The others include *A Peep between Leaves of the Talmud, Note on a Hebrew Funeral,* and *The Jew upon the Stage.* The last essay is characteristic of the nobility and sense of justice of the author, who expresses his disapproval of the stock indignities and villainies that were foisted upon and have stuck to the character of the Jew in the tradition of the European theatre.[7]

James Huneker, critic of many arts, who knew many prominent Jewish artists, expresses in his essay, "Eili, Eili, Lomo Asovtoni" in the book *Variations* (1921) his admiration for the "sublimities" of Hebrew poetry and the Jewish liturgy. In his short story *The Shofar Blew at Sunset* he criticizes Jews for succumbing to the influence of contemporary materialism and the consequent loss of Jewish idealism.

H. L. Mencken in his *Treatise on the Gods* (1930) notes his respect for the Jews as the "chief dreamers of the human race and beyond all comparison its greatest poets."

The literature about the Jews during the twentieth century has grown to vast proportions. The annual bibliographies compiled for the *American Jewish Yearbook* for 1905-1911 testified to the great interest displayed by Jewish and Christian authors in the many problems which faced the American Jew and his co-religionists throughout the world. With the coming of such extraordinary matters of Jewish interest as the Kishineff pogrom of 1905, the pogroms after the Great War, the government-inspired anti-Semitism following the emergence of the Hitler régime, there has appeared a vast literature, historical, sociological, and polemical, bearing on the Jew. Leading periodicals, including the *Atlantic, Harper's, Forum,* and *Scribner's,* have discussed the Jewish question on many occasions in recent years.

Three hundred years of American-Jewish literary history cannot be adequately treated in an essay, or even in a single volume. From Increase Mather to John Haynes Holmes there exists a long and noble tradition, in which great personalities have attempted to understand, evaluate, and pay respect to the American Jew, not only for his remarkable spiritual heritage, which has enriched the entire world, but for his personal attributes, his patriotism, industry, integrity, and genius.

The fiction of non-Jewish authors of the twentieth century is extremely rich in Jewish portraits. Jewish characters as portrayed in American drama and as described by Jewish novelists are subjects of special chapters. It is interesting to observe the impression made upon non-Jewish writers by the various types of Jews with whom they came in contact. Sometimes the delineation indicates careful observation and sincere appreciation. Occasionally the author reveals a faint touch of prejudice. The novels and short stories mentioned in this essay are representative of the various attitudes and lines of interest and do not constitute an exhaustive list.

The Jew has appeared in American fiction in many capacities and in many environments. In Robert W. Chambers' romantic novel of the American Revolution, *Cardigan* (1901), Saul Shemuel is a peddler who shares many perilous experiences with the hero. The participation of prominent American Jews in the Revolution is well known and the letters and journals of the time contain many references to them.[8] The relationship between the gifted Rebecca Gratz and the Rebecca of Scott's *Ivanhoe* has already been mentioned.

The experiences of a Southern Jewish family as a result of General Grant's notorious expulsion order are related by Evelyn Scott in her novel *The Wave* (1929).

In Margaret Hill McCarter's *Winning of the Wilderness* (1914), the participation of a Jew, Joseph Jacobs, in the pioneer life of Kansas is described. By his foresight and uprightness he contributes to the success of the venture. The portrait is wholly complimentary.

Many non-Jewish novelists and short story writers have written with genuine sympathy and tenderness of the poor Jews who came to America to escape persecutions abroad. Myra Kelly concentrated on depicting the life of Jewish youngsters in the schoolroom on New York's East Side. Her stories have been included in many collections and have a charm and excellence which, coupled with her tenderness for the young people she describes, place them in the front rank of the fictional treatment of the Jew. Her volumes include: *Little Citizens* (1904), *Wards of Liberty* (1909), and *Little Aliens* (1910).

Jacob Riis, himself an immigrant from the Netherlands, was well equipped to treat of the life on New York's East Side. In *Children of the Tenements* (1905), and *Neighbors* (1914) he portrays the home life of the Russian-Jewish immigrants with a verisimilitude found in few non-Jewish authors. Another sympathetic treatment of Jews is in Harold Frederic's *The New Exodus* (1892), which depicts the Russian persecutions. Frederic was European representative of the *New York Times* and was famous as an international correspondent. His observations were evidently first-hand.

Jews of humble occupations, as well as successful public figures and representatives of the learned professions, have been characters in American fiction. F. Hopkinson Smith in *Peter* (1909) describes Isaac Cohen, a tailor, who is introduced to illustrate a still existing prejudice, which his friendly personality does much to dispel. Another portrait of a tailor is found in Edward King's *Joseph Zalmonah* (1893). A poor Jewish peddler is pictured in Hypkin Brown's *Farmer Bibbins* (1914).

The Jewish intellectual has interested a number of American novelists. Sinclair Lewis in *Arrowsmith* (1925) has portrayed one of the most convincing characters in the fiction of the Jew, the scientist, Dr. Gottlieb. Although an American only by adoption, Dr. Gottlieb must be considered in any integrated study of the American Jew. He remains one of Lewis' greatest characterizations, a noble example of devotion to science, to the exclusion of all personal interests. Together with Arthur Schnitzler's Professor Bernhardi, Sidney Kingsley's Dr. Hochberg in *Men in White* (1933), and Friedrich Wolf's Dr. Mamlock, in *Professor Mamlock* (1936), he represents a new type of Jew in world literature, the Jew as Scientist.

In his novel *Elmer Gantry* (1927), Lewis presents two rabbis, and in *It Can't Happen Here* (1936) he introduces other Jewish characters. A rabbi is portrayed by Floyd Dell in *Moon Calf* (1920).

The Jewish college student has appeared in the American novel, most often as an admirable person. Thomas Nelson Page in *John Marvel, Assistant* (1909) relates the experiences of three friends, all students in a Southern college. The crude mountaineer, the brilliant Jew, and the aristocratic planter's son form a lasting friendship, which enables them in later years to collaborate in fighting for reform in their newly-adopted city. Ernest Hemingway in *The Sun Also Rises* (1926) projects a critical portrait of Robert Cohen, the brilliant scholar-pugilist of Princeton. As a representative of the post-war Lost Generation, Cohen is afflicted with the *malaise* and instability which afflicted so many intellectuals, Jews and Gentiles.

Another type of Jewish intellectual is one of the important characters in James Huneker's novel, *Painted Veils* (1920). Alfred Stone is a music critic—disillusioned, cynical, and coldly contemptuous of the uneducated classes.

John Dos Passos in *Three Soldiers* (1921) delineates two different Jewish types. In "Wild Dan" Cohen the War has produced an irresponsibility and a forsaking of normal values. Eisenstein is a Socialist and is court-martialed for airing his sentiments regarding the purpose of the War. In his novel "1919" (1932) there is a portrait of Compton, a Jew who embraces the cause of the working-class, one of the few characters in the book who preserve their integrity in an opportunistic post-war world.

Not all the Jews in the novels of non-Jewish authors have been admirable. Edith Wharton in her *House of Mirth* (1905) makes no effort to conceal her dislike for Simon Rosedale, who has accumulated a fortune and tries to break into society. Her first description of him is illuminating:

He was a plump rosy man of the blond Jewish type, with smart London clothes fitting him like upholstery, and small sidelong eyes which gave him the air of appraising people as if they were bric-a-brac.

Numerous American short stories have presented vivid sketches of certain types of Jews. O. Henry in his *Love Philtre of Ikey Shonstein* offers his most complete Jewish character. He has also described Ziegler, an Armenian Jewish peddler; Isaacstein, another peddler; and Policeman Kohen in *Vanity and Some Sables*. Although O. Henry lived in New York City and wrote extensively of the "Four Million," he apparently made no serious effort to study Jewish life or character.

Fitz-James O'Brien, in his famous short story *The Diamond Lens* (1858) introduces Jules Simon, a diamond merchant, whom he supposes to be a Jew. Jack London in *The Benefit of the Doubt* sketches a Jewish magistrate. Harry Leon Wilson in *Two Black Sheep* delineates a Jewish proprietress of a fashion shop. Barry Benefield in *Up Bayou Dubac* has the story turn on intermarriage between a local boy and a Sephardic Jewess.

Hundreds of American short stories by non-Jewish authors have depicted Jews of all types and capabilities. Although occasionally a note of criticism is evident, most often the Jews portrayed are honorable representatives of their communities or professions. Literary anti-Semitism has been attempted in such polemics as *The International Jew,* reprinted from the *Dearborn Independent* in 1921, seldom in creative literature. Hence, the Jew in contemporary American fiction is most often a character to be admired and honored.

After a long and unfortunate tradition in world literature, lasting for almost two thousand years, the Jew in fiction, like the Jew in drama, has taken his place with the great and the noble in the land of the creative imagination.

The general impression gained from a perusal of the considerable literature on Jews in America by non-Jews is that almost all of it is fair, sympathetic, and indicative of a willingness to understand strange ways and customs. Hospitality, rather than hostility, is the keynote of these writings. More stories have been written about the Jews in America by non-Jews than about any other large immigrant stock. This indicates a genuine curiosity and interest. Although many of the portraits are superficial, yet some of the stories like those of Myra Kelly, Jacob Riis and I. A. R. Wylie go deep into the racial and religious heritage of the Jews. A statistical summary may prove helpful. Writing in 1916, Miss Rebecca

A SURVEY OF THREE CENTURIES

Schneider in her *Bibliography of Jewish Life in the Fiction of America and England* listed the fictional treatments of Jews by countries as follows:

General, 4; Austria-Hungary, 9; Biblical, 43; Post-biblical, 12; Byzantine Empire, 1; Life and Times of Christ, 11; Crusades, 1; England, 60; France, 3; Germany, 6; Italy, 1; Jerusalem, 13; Mexico, 1; Morocco, 1; Netherlands, 1; Modern Palestine, 2; Persia, 1; Poland, 5; Russia, 23; Spain, 4; United States, 55.

It is seen that the Jew in America up to 1916 received almost the greatest attention of English-writing novelists. Since the Great War more studies of American Jewish life have appeared than of the Jews of any other country. Just as there has been an evolution in the treatment of the American Jew by Jewish novelists, so the non-Jewish authors have seen him in various changed situations. In the early part of the twentieth century the immigrant Jew was distinguished by his speech, poverty, and tendency to live with his own people. The stories about him would either sympathize with his plight or, as was the case in the works of Edith Wharton, Willa Cather, and Robert Herrick, would present certain generalized traits which displeased the authors.

The depression of the late twenties and the persecution of the German, Austrian, Polish, and Roumanian Jews of the early thirties have given rise to a most sympathetic series of studies in fiction and non-fiction which is really the traditional treatment of Jews in America. The next great wave of literature of Jews in America will probably be concerned with the brilliant exiles from hate-ridden Europe who have found a haven in America.

15. THE AMERICAN DRAMA

PRESENTS THE JEW

The portrayal of Jewish characters in drama can often serve as an index of a nation's attitude to its Jewish population. The medieval Miracle and Mystery plays reveal only too clearly the popular dislike for the Jews living at the time. The earliest English plays of the Elizabethan era in which a Jewish character appeared continued the tradition of theatrical Jew-baiting which lasted almost two hundred years, before Lessing in his *Die Juden* (1749) painted a favorable portrait of a Jew. How much damage this anti-Semitic tradition in the theatre has done, it is impossible, of course, to calculate. That it added fuel to the fires of hatred and prejudice is undeniable. It constitutes one of the more tragic aspects of the concept, "art for man's sake," for here we observe a form of art that was anything but contributory to the enrichment and elevation of mankind.

A study of the portraits of Jewish characters in recent drama illustrates as few other phenomena can the position of the Jew in our contemporary civilization. If we accept the statement that the purpose of the drama is, in the words of Hamlet, "to hold the mirror up to nature," then the reproductions in the mirror become important for the student of society. The portraits of Jews in drama and in fiction challenge our attention not only because they express an author's personal opinion, but because they are based upon the predilections and the prejudices of the audiences. The intolerance and misrepresentation observed in the handling of Shylock by Shakespeare, and Barrabas by Marlowe are not due so much to the bigotry of the dramatists as to the demands made upon them by their audiences. A "good Jew" could not be portrayed by Chaucer or by Shakespeare because their respective audiences would not have accepted him.

The popular hatred stirred up against Dr. Roderigo Lopez, the Portuguese-Jewish physician of Queen Elizabeth because of his alleged participation in a plot to poison her, was echoed in the contemporary British theatre.

Henslowe records in his famous diary that between May and the end of the year 1594, there were twenty theatrical representations in which a Jew was the subject. Marlowe's *The Jew of Malta,* and *The Merchant of Venice,* are the more famous survivors of these plays.

The traditional portrayal of Jews in drama and fiction until the middle of the eighteenth century is unfavorable. The treatment of Shylock was only one of the early libels which have had their modern descendants. On the American stage, from 1752-1821 when twenty-eight plays with Jewish characters were presented, most of them portrayed him as a villain. Tradition was so powerful that the Jewish dramatists of America of the early nineteenth century, M. M. Noah, Isaac Harby, Samuel B. H. Judah, and Jonas B. Phillips, have no Jewish characters in their plays. As one scholar has expressed it, ". . . to present him (a Jew) as a villain would have meant self-stultification, and to picture him as decent and human would have been in defiance of the centuries-old tradition that in the drama the Jew must be the villain or the subject of derision."[1]

The first play by an American to portray a Jew, Mrs. Susanna Rawson's *Slaves in Algiers* (1794), presented him as a thorough scoundrel.

In the late eighteenth century, Lessing wrote his *Nathan der Weise* as a plea for a more tolerant attitude toward Jews in Germany—an attitude that had its brightest exemplification in the high esteem in which Moses Mendelssohn was held.

It was the first major play in the world's dramatic literature to present a noble portrait of a Jew. The first favorable dramatic treatment by an English dramatist was by Richard Cumberland in *The Jew* (1793). Other plays appeared in which the Jewish characters were dealt with honorably. Charles Dibdin's *The Jew and the Doctor* and *The School for Prejudice* were produced in America after their success in England.

As soon as the traditional defamation of the Jew in drama lost its appeal, more numerous and more varied portraits of Jews appeared on the American stage.

In the last few years, especially, there have been numerous portrayals of individual Jews or groups of Jews. The research student of the future will have a rich field for speculation when he delves into the theatrical record of our time. Jewish characters have been created by first-rate dramatists, as well as by the ever-present hack-writers. No one, for instance, could attach much literary significance to the interpretation of Jewish character as revealed in Montague Glass's *Potash and Perlmutter* series or in Anne Nichols' *Abie's Irish Rose,* for these plays are hardly in the category of enduring literature.

Although an occasional Shylock-type still appears, the presentment of the Jew in contemporary American drama is the most varied as well as the most appreciative in the history of dramatic literature. The early dramatizations of Jewish content were confined to biblical stories, as in the early Miracle and Mystery plays from the twelfth to the fifteenth centuries. When a modern Jew was mentioned he was delineated as a merchant or a money-lender because only in those occupations was he permitted to survive. When the emancipation of the Jew gained for him the right to enter any profession and occupation, he appeared on the stage in other capacities than those associated with commerce and finance. The Jew as teacher, scientist, creative artist, and farmer became dramatic material.

THE JEW IN AMERICAN DRAMA

Among the new capacities of the Jew in American drama are those listed below:

1. Teacher; 2. Attorney; 3. Physician; 4. A Purveyor of Entertainment; 5. Labor Leader; 6. Man of Courage; 7. Philosopher; 8. The Jewish Mother.

As economic difficulties arose after the depression of 1929, the old hostilities to Jews were revived once again. Dramatists, keen in their perception of the dignity of human character and the indignities to which it might be subjected in times of economic distress and emotional disturbance, set down the results of their observations in plays of power and insight. Today we can point to a series of portraits of Jews who have had to contend with practically all the problems which Israel has had to face in its long history.

1. DISCRIMINATION IN EDUCATIONAL INSTITUTIONS

Among the many unforgettable characterizations in Clifford Odets' *Waiting for Lefty* (1934) is Dr. Benjamin, who was dropped from his hospital appointment as the first victim of a retrenchment drive. Dr. Benjamin's arraignment of the "rich Gentiles" as pillars of a society who are utterly callous to human rights is a cry of our own times. It is significant for the present and will be equally so for the future historian.

In 1932 Elmer Rice, after having written two remarkably successful plays primarily concerned with local color—*Street Scene* and *Counsellor-at-Law*—turned to the drama of social protest in *We, the People*. He was one of the pioneers in this field, and consequently *We, the People* did not receive the attention showered upon much inferior plays a few years later. Rice attacked many of the ills then afflicting the country—all in the last months of the expiring Hoover regime. He did not omit the plight of the Jewish instructor, discharged from his university because he was unfortunate enough to lead a delegation of protesting citizens to the senator's office. A poignant scene is the one in which he confronts his dean and is informed that his services are no longer required. "Are you dismissing me because I'm a liberal economist or because I'm a Jew?" he asks, only to receive a non-committal answer.

2. THE SUCCESSFUL JEWISH ATTORNEY

The Jew as a successful attorney has appeared in at least two significant plays in recent years: Elmer Rice's *Counsellor-at-Law* (1931) and John Wexley's *They Shall Not Die* (1932). The playwrights were fortunate in having such outstanding artists as Paul Muni and Claude Rains to play the parts of their respective heroes. A third successful Jewish attorney, but one portrayed in a most unfavorable light, is Meyer Hirsch in Samuel Ornitz's *Haunch, Paunch and Jowl,* presented in Yiddish in 1936 by the New York Artef Players. Elmer Rice's Mr. Simon represents an idealization of the many traits of the successful Jewish attorney: humble beginnings (usually East Side or immigrant), helpful political contacts, mental superiority, a yearning for social advancement, marriage out of his own people with its consequent disillusionment.

John Wexley is a much younger playwright who showed great promise in his first play, *The Last Mile* (1929). He fulfilled the expectations of his many admirers with *They Shall Not Die* (1932), a plea for justice to the nine Scottsboro Negroes, whose case aroused national interest. His Jewish attorney, Rubin, was played unforgettably by Claude Rains. Omitting this time the humble origin and the climb to success, Wexley concentrated on Rubin's power as a crusader for justice and wrote in the last act one of the most moving pleas in recent drama. Plays set in courtrooms appear every season. Rarely, however, does a dramatist provide a speech of such emotional power as was Rubin's summation to the jury. In *Counsellor-at-Law,* Rice described another Jewish attorney of somewhat different background and culture, Mr. Weinberg, graduate of Harvard Law School. He is more interested in the arts than his brilliant employer, is much more reserved and at all times observant of the social amenities. Like the many other characters of the play, Weinberg is another example of Rice's remarkably acute powers of observation.

3. THE JEWISH PHYSICIAN

Many American plays have portrayed the Jewish physician. In 1911 Augustus Thomas wrote *As a Man Thinks* in which the relationship of cultured Jews and Gentiles is candidly and sympathetically discussed. Dr. Silber, a successful physician, is the hero of the play. Sidney Kingsley's *Men in White* (1933) presented Dr. Hochberg, who made a remarkable impression upon the audience because of his refusal to compromise with his code as a scientist. John Howard Lawson's *Gentlewoman* (1933) showed us Dr. Lewis Golden, a Jewish psychoanalyst. He was shrewd, ironic, unmoved by the impending collapse of the economic and social order which was feared by many in the dark days of 1933.

The Jewish physician in contemporary American drama is most often a man of dignity, a follower of the Hippocratic oath in his professional life and a man of wide culture and wordly wisdom.

4. THE JEW AS A PURVEYOR OF ENTERTAINMENT

The stage has its own way of dealing with motion picture magnates. Most often they speak with foreign accents, gesticulate wildly, and show bad taste. In *Three Waltzes* (1937) an American producer was portrayed according to the stage type. He was obviously pictured for his comic effects, and bore little resemblance to actuality. No more convincing was the composer, Sidney Cohen, in the musical comedy *On Your Toes* (1936). He possessed unbounded self-confidence, bad manners, and many of the traits which anti-Semites attribute to artistic Jews. George S. Kaufman in *Merrily We Roll Along* (1934) gave a none too favorable picture of a successful Jewish composer-pianist, whose egotism is completely unbelievable. The same author in *Once in a Lifetime* (1930) delineated perhaps the typical Jewish movie magnate in drama, Mr. Glogauer. It is interesting to speculate on the priority of such portraits in the minds of the audiences or the minds of the dramatists.

THE JEW IN AMERICAN DRAMA

Who created this peculiar mixture of comic misunderstanding and tragic bluntness—the Jewish movie producer so often found on stage and screen? If he serves only to provoke laughter, he stands as a living witness of the lack of ingenuity of his creators.

5. THE JEW AS RADICAL

To many ignorant or unprejudiced observers the terms *Red* and *Jew* are synonymous. On October 21, 1935 a pamphlet was issued by three Jewish organizations with the title, "A Public Statement on Communism and Jews." The authors of this pamphlet irrefutably challenged all the charges against German Jews for their alleged communistic leanings, and pointed out the historical basis for the liberal, democratic viewpoint of Jews throughout the ages. Their arguments cannot be denied and whole libraries of volumes equally unchallengeable in their denial of Jewish subversive tendencies in America would not eradicate from the minds of millions of ignorant Red-baiters the notion that all Jews are communists. In a one-act play by Albert Maltz, called *Private Hicks* (1936), the commander of the strike-breaking National Guardsmen asks a Guardsman who had refused to shoot at strikers: "Who was he (the man who distributed leaflets against the shooting)? Was he a Jew?" Hicks replied, "No. He had red hair."

At the beginning of the 1935 dramatic season, Jed Harris emerged from retirement to produce *Life's Too Short*, by John Whedon and Arthur Caplan. It was a rather inept attempt at an evaluation of the effect of the depression on a representative of the white-collar class. The radical point of view was presented by a stenographer named Esther Rosenberg. All the old *clichés*, from her father's pants-pressing for twelve hours a day, to his broken head for too violent picketing, were enumerated by Miss Rosenberg. The delineation of her character to include an East Side intonation, a rather unkempt appearance and a brazenness that would have caused resentment in even the most tolerant employer, was totally unnecessary and vicious.

THE JEW IN AMERICAN DRAMA

John Howard Lawson's *Marching Song* (1937) has the character Woody Rosenbloom, who speaks bitterly about company unions, wars to save democracy, and governments which protect big business men in their inhuman treatment of the workers. His courage and sincerity make his role prominent.

6. THE JEW AS A MAN OF COURAGE

Ludwig Lewisohn in *Israel* (1925) describes the banner of a Jewish fighting unit that participated in the Polish uprising of 1794. A few years ago, the magazine *Liberty* had as its leading article, "Sam Dreben, Fighting Jew," and the New York *Daily News* devoted an editorial to that same personage. The Jew's courage is rarely celebrated in song and story, and when playwrights present fighting Jews, one sits up and takes notice. In the last few years of the American dramatic renaissance, three portraits of young Jewish fighters have stood out. Sidney Howard's dramatization of a chapter from De Kruif's *Microbe Hunters* resulted in *Yellow Jack* (1934), a play which many critics thought one of the most novel productions of the 1933-34 season. Bush is a young Jewish soldier from Chicago, stationed in Cuba in 1900. Proud of his Jewish blood, ready to defend himself at any time against all comers, he has no hesitation about risking his life in an experiment to prove the carrier of yellow fever. After witnessing the ruthless strivings of Ginsberg in *Success Story,* the unenviable maneuverings of Simon in *Counsellor-at-Law,* the animal courage of Bush came as a refreshing reminder of the physical prowess of the Jew in time of need.

In the regrettably short-lived *Paths of Glory* (1935) Meyer, a French Jew, loses no time in informing us that he is Jewish, that he is a Frenchman, and fears no one. The Dreyfus case and the sensitivity of Jews are mentioned significantly in the conversation.

Physical courage however is far less interesting than the courage of one's convictions. Arthur Schnitzler's Professor Bernhardi, in the play of the same name, is an aristocrat among scientists. Risking the loss of his hospital, his reputation as a physician, and his dearest friends, he stands firm in his conviction that one of his decisions was in complete accord with professional ethics. Bernhardi is one of the noblest dramatic portraits of a Jewish man of intellect in modern times. One cannot read it today without a sensation of pain from a touching of the old wounds, but one cannot finish it without a feeling of satisfaction that such courageous scientists exist.

The young Jewish intellectual girding himself to fight the battles of oppressed humanity is exemplified in Ralph Berger of Odets' *Awake and Sing*. Inheriting all the idealism of his maternal grandfather, he adds to it the strength and optimism of youth and the self-confidence still untarnished by the disillusionment of years. Where Meyer of *Paths of Glory* and Bush of *Yellow Jack* revealed mere physical strength, not particularly interesting except to boxing fans, Ralph realized that brute strength was not enough to fight the powerfully entrenched forces of reaction. Development of his intellectual forces and enrichment of his cultural heritage are Ralph's goals.

7. THE JEW AS PHILOSOPHER

Maxwell Anderson in *Winterset* (1935) made the most notable contribution to American drama of the 1935 season in the opinion of the seventeen critics of The Drama Critics' Circle of New York City. The character of Esdras, the father of the heroine, is truly one of the noblest portraits of the Jew as philosopher in the whole repertoire of English drama. Quoting the Scriptures, the Talmud, and other sources of Hebrew wisdom, and exemplifying their precepts in his own actions, he stands there—one of the grand old Jews in drama.

A bearded Jew immediately stirs up one's emotions. The ignorant may be inclined to ridicule because a beard is unusual and hence always laugh-provoking to the mentally undeveloped. The sensitive spectator is aroused to respect because the beard is the accompaniment of old age, and old age brings wisdom, and wisdom brings respect. As Esdras speaks his beautifully written lines, he expresses the crystallized wisdom of all the ages. His stoic calm in the face of threats of death, and death itself, his resignation to the inevitable, his own personal goodness, sum up a personality rare in life and rarer still on the stage. Anderson, with poetic genius, has created a character that takes its place among the great noble Jews in world literature—Lessing's Nathan, Browning's Rabbi Ben Ezra, and Cumberland's Sheva.

The dramatic portraits of Clifford Odets have assumed an importance rarely achieved by contemporary playwrights. Certain of the characters in *Awake and Sing* have already been mentioned. One cannot omit, however, Grandfather Berger. Here we have the idealist who hoped for the realization of his dreams in a new land. The faint music from *L'Africana* coming from Moe's bedroom is a most stirring exemplification of the *leit-motif* in recent American drama. When his daughter smashes the record of the song we realize without the need of words that for him the song has not only ended, but life itself has no longer any significance.

8. THE JEWISH MOTHER

A new note in the treatment of Jews is that of the "Yiddishe Mamma." The song by that title helped spread the sentiment, but such plays as Spewacks' *Spring Song* (1933) observed the formula to perfection. It resembled most closely the Yiddish plays of the Bowery. The mother is generally the proprietress of a tiny store or a pushcart and works day and night for the advancement of her children. Sometimes as the mother of Mr. Simon in *Counsellor-at-Law* she lives to derive "nachos." In the very same play another Yiddishe Mamma has the misfortune to have an agitator as her son and she derives little pleasure indeed from his activities. The Jewish mother was unknown in the plays about Jews until the present century. Much has been written about the reasons for Shakespeare's omission of Shylock's wife or Marlowe's neglect of Barrabas' wife. She was one Jewish character who could not be "typed." Whereas the traditional stage Jew could be given a long beaked nose and a red beard, there were no distinguishable characteristics that could be attributed to his wife; and thus, fortunately, the Jewish stage mother escaped the fate of the Jewish father. When she began to appear on the stage in the twentieth century, she was invariably a noble character. As Mrs. Silber in *As a Man Thinks* she is completely at ease, cultured, capable of managing any difficult situation. Most often she is the industrious, thrifty immigrant who takes pride in her children's success. Typical of this class are Mrs. Simon in *Counsellor-at-Law*, Mrs. Davis of Rita Wellman's *The Gentile Wife* (1919), the mothers in *Four Walls* (1927), and in Fannie Hurst's *It Is to Laugh* (1927), and the Spewacks' *Spring Song*. Mrs. Berger of Clifford Odets' *Awake and Sing* was the subject of considerable discussion as a result of her actions.

Most Jewish mothers in recent American drama are noble characters and inspire respect from all. One is tempted to wish that all portrayals of Jews were as honest and as respectful as are those of the mothers of Israel.

The history of the Jew on the recent American stage is truly one of emancipation. He is presented as doctor, lawyer, financier, teacher, soldier, agitator and in many other capacities. No longer is he the comic figure with red beard, hooked nose and gaberdine. His main interest is not his ducats or his bond. More often than not he is a character to admire. Now and then some dramatists, in their eagerness to stimulate untrained appetites to laughter, make use of foreign accent and marked gesticulation, but the practice is losing favor. Rothschild's words have come true of the Jew of the American stage, for he has learned to *live with dignity, to walk with dignity, to die with dignity.*

16. FAREWELL TO

SHYLOCKS AND FAGINS

In H. C. Engelbrecht's prize-winning essay on "How to Combat Anti-Semitism in America," printed in *Opinion* for April, 1937, there is an enumeration of the peculiar ideas about Jews which are held by people in the hinterland. Notions are still current, probably in the minds of thousands of Americans, that Jews have horns on their foreheads, that they have easily recognizable facial characteristics, and that they engage in all varieties of secret practices of evil intent. That such conceptions flourish is due partly to ignorance and partly to their perpetuation in the various media of artistic expression.

Shakespeare's *Merchant of Venice* will always, unfortunately, be on hand to acquaint new generations with the conduct of Shylock in demanding his pound of flesh; and Dickens with his Fagin will always do his little bit for the cause of ill-will. It is discouraging indeed that these authors have been responsible for creating incalculable hatred in non-Jewish minds which were willing to accept first impressions without weighing and considering them. All this, too, despite the fact that a large number of novels and plays have depicted, without any desire to exaggerate the truly estimable phases of Jewish life, have attempted to interpret Jewish culture to non-Jews.

Were the popularity of Israel Zangwill, Fannie Hurst, Anzia

Yezierska, Meyer Levin, Louis Golding, Sholem Asch and many other contemporary novelists as great as is that of Dickens, and did the memory of their scenes, characters, and sentiments remain as firmly fixed in the minds of readers as Dickens's pages, a great deal of prejudice might be avoided. Yet for one reader who remembers the name of the hero in *The Melting Pot,* a hundred readers know Fagin; and for each one who can identify Yezierska's Shenah Pessah, a thousand hate Shylock.

The contemporary stage has offered many pictures of Jewish domestic life which must have been revelations of completely strange ways of living to non-Jewish audiences. Even American Jews must be bewildered at such phases of Jewish life as are exemplified in Ansky's *The Dybbuk,* I. J. Singer's *Yoshe Kalb* and *The Water Carrier.* Strange as some of the customs appear to Jews who were born in America and whose knowledge of Judaism in other countries is confined to a few Sunday school lessons, how strange must seem some of the practices and ideas found in Odets' *Awake and Sing,* Bella and Samuel Spewacks' *Spring Song* and Anne Nichols' *Abie's Irish Rose?*

That the general public is interested in Jewish life seems indisputable in view of the many interpretations of it which can be found among the current plays. Franz Werfel's *The Eternal Road* (1937) won commendation from Christian critics, clergymen, and spectators which equalled in enthusiasm, to say the least, that of Jewish commentators. Perhaps the climax of encomium was reached with its recommendation as an appropriate play during the Lenten season of 1937.

Arthur Kober's *Having Wonderful Time* (1937) revealed what happens in a Jewish summer resort, a phase of life which is quite familiar to the Jew, but is always a mystery to others. The play, favored with the expert direction of Marc Connolly, enjoyed a prosperous run, during which it may have removed some of the persistent falsehoods relevant to young Jews at play.

Wherever the newest discrimination against Jews are discussed, one hears the old stories about Jews who had acted crudely, talked loudly and vulgarly, and in general, been public nuisances. Have we not all heard these same stories? The boisterousness of Jewish young men and women has been the subject of much criticism in colleges where Jews were very few. It was and is a current though false belief that Jewish students from New York could usually be distinguished from their more assimilated co-religionists, by their "New York accent," their aggressiveness, general disregard for the social amenities, and refusal to adopt the ways of the majority.

Sometimes this disapproval would take the form of articles in educational magazines. Sometimes, as in the case of Thomas Wolfe's *Of Time and The River,* it would be incorporated into a literary work which by its popularity could spread the accusations far and wide. All the criticisms of modern Jewish youth in America seem to be included in the following frank and unguarded attack of Thomas Wolfe. He introduces the character Abraham Jones with the description, "dreary, gray, and hopeless-looking Jew." The author continues with: "the whole flag and banner of his race was in the enormous putty-colored nose." Because Abraham changes his name to Alfred, he is accused of taking the new name "violently, by theft and rape." Alfred (née Abraham) does not grin as other mortals, but "with Kike delight." He has no ordinary countenance but "a cruel grinning Yiddish face." He is "gloomily engulfed in a great cloud of Yiddish murk"; he is a picture of Yiddish melancholy and discontent. Wolfe refers to "the faces, cruel, arrogant, and knowing of the beak-nosed Jews," to the hordes of beak-nosed shysters, poured out of the law school year by year.

Wolfe exhibits a similarly frank disapproval of the Jewish girls who attended the metropolitan college in which he served as instructor. The co-eds pressed on him "the sensual wave"; they annoyed him with "their swarming, shrieking, shouting tides of dark amber Jewish flesh." The class is described as a "horde of thirty or forty Jews and Jewesses, all laughing, shouting, screaming, thick with their hot and swarthy body-smells, their strong female odors of rut and crotch and arm-pit and cheap perfume."

It is obvious that Thomas Wolfe's experiences with Jewish students were not particularly happy. His indictment is not the only one in recent fiction. J. B. Priestley in his autobiographical *Midnight on the Desert* (1937) remarks that anti-Semitism is more wide-spread in America than in England, where he says it is practically non-existent. Yet a nation's authors are surely its spokesmen, and criticism expressed in novels generally represent what many readers think but are incapable of expressing. Thus Robert Briffault in his enormously successful *Europa* painted as unpleasant a picture as can be found in English literature of a Jewess in Baroness Rubinstein, and her flagellations must have created intense disgust in the minds of thousands of excited readers. No one would be so rash as to accuse either Wolfe or Briffault of being wilfully anti-Semitic, yet, because of the enormous popularity of their novels, the old charges are given new life and the minds of millions may be poisoned against the Jews. Another English novelist who has expressed a kind of aesthetic disapproval of the Jew is Aldous Huxley, who in *Eyeless in Gaza* comments bitingly about the sentimental approach of Jewish virtuosi to their art.

Yet this is only one side of the contemporary picture. A goodly number of novelists and dramatists have tried to write honestly about Jewish life and have been generally acclaimed. Kober's play mentioned above presents as much the idealism of the young Jews and Jewesses who save up all year for two weeks in the "country" as he describes their freedom from restraint, their Bronx idioms, and their simple enjoyment.

The tradition of the favorable presentation of Jewish family life on the stage goes back at least to the beginning of the present century. Many non-Jewish dramatists have tried to present admirable portraits of Jews who were noble and good and strangely different from the "Eastern Jew" so often occurring in caricatures. Again the tradition of Christian appreciation of Jewish achievements, so often illuminating the darkness of Jewish oppression with the light of tolerance, is observed.

Perhaps the most courageous treatment of Jewish-Gentile differences in this century is John Galsworthy's *Loyalties,* which was produced in 1922. Only a few years ago Basil Rathbone gave a truly inspiring performance of the Jew, Ferdy de Levis, in an English cinema version. In 1911 Augustus Thomas had presented in *As a Man Thinks* the Jewish professional who seems like a modern Maimonides with his devotion to science, his wisdom of life, his restraint, and withal his devout religious feelings. Jews outstanding in science have been created by Schnitzler in *Professor Bernhardi,* by Sinclair Lewis in *Arrowsmith* (Dr. Gottlieb), by Sidney Kingsley in *Men in White* (Dr. Hochberg), by Friedrich Wolf in *Professor Mamlock,* and by Irving Fineman in *Dr. Addams* (1939). The combination of benevolence and scientific achievement seems best portrayed by Augustus Thomas. For a similar portrait one must go back to the eighteenth century to Lessing's *Nathan der Weise.*

A most absorbing dramatic production with the scientific Jew as the central figure is *Professor Mamlock* (1937). The kinship between him and Professor Bernhardi, who was the subject of discussion at the beginning of the century, is closely established.

The devotion which a rabbi might feel to his chosen task as interpreter of God's way with the universe is echoed by these devotees of Nature, seeking to wrest her secrets for the benefit of mankind. Dr. Bernhardi, Dr. Seelig, Dr. Gottlieb, Dr. Hochberg, and Professor Mamlock allow nothing to stand in the way of their devotion to scientific truth. It seems as if all that firm ethical conviction which is in the heart of all the noblest of the spiritual leaders of Israel is now entrusted to these followers of science.

To many they appear as fanatics because of their refusal to compromise with the truth as they have discovered it after painful research. The students of Dr. Gottlieb, with the exception of Martin Arrowsmith, think he is far too much concerned with his idealism and his technique. Many internes in the hospital where Dr. Hochberg was stationed, think he has too little business acumen and too much concern over perfect sterilization of his instruments. In *Professor Mamlock* the same charge is directed, this time by Mrs. Mamlock, who is not Jewish. The speech is almost the final flowering in a long line of criticisms of Jewish men of science because they refuse to compromise with the truth:

MOTHER (*exploding*) Yes, you talked to him. Party or parents' home, right or left, either—or; oh, I know this cold absolute that calls itself logic, these lifeless slogans, these icy antitheses, this whole heartless fanaticism of yours.

MAMLOCK "Of yours?"

MOTHER (*letting herself go*) Yes, yours! yours! All people listen to others at some time, listen to one, another, have a spot where the other's words don't pass over the glacier of reason and freeze, but resound somewhere on the way, in the recesses of the heart. . . . But you, all of you, with you everything must be hot or cold, true or false, understood or not understood . . . brains, brains, brains, that is the heritage of your race!

"Brains, brains, brains, that is the heritage of your race!" Who has not heard the same accusation at some time in his scholastic, business, or professional career? All head and no heart! From Shylock to Mamlock the tradition, as far as the drama goes, is almost unbroken. Perhaps, because others are better statesmen and are willing to compromise more readily, this characteristic of Jews attracts attention. To the Jewish thinker a thing is either right or wrong; he is unaware of ethical hermaphroditism.

This, to the student of literature, is one of the most interesting phenomena—this persistence of the criticism of Jews because of their adherence to the strict, literal truth, whether expressed in a bond or in a code of medical ethics. What is the answer? Compromise? Adjusting the truth to fit the changing situation? Would the charges be dropped? It remains a field for interesting speculation.

17. RIGHTEOUSNESS ABOVE COMPROMISE:

NOBLE JEWISH LITERARY TYPES

Jews are exceptionally sensitive to any unfounded aspersions spread broadcast these troublous days, but they resent perhaps most strongly the insinuation that they do not habitually tell the truth.

Jews of culture and established position feel almost personally affected when the newspapers indicate new scandals and infractions in which men and women of Jewish extraction are the culprits. When the New York Prosecutor, Thomas E. Dewey, brought the loan sharks of New York to trial and effected their conviction in 1937, "good" Jews were embarrassed because some of the defendants were "bad" Jews.

Frequently, some dishonest or law-breaking Jew is mentioned in the newspaper headlines. No one in his complete senses would argue from these twenty or more instances that Jews are less honest, less respectable, or less trustworthy than representatives of other groups. But the circumstances in which Jews throughout the world find themselves today are so fraught with embarrassment, discomfort, and danger that one must reconsider and restate the Jewish ideals in general and the Jewish love for truth in particular.

The Jew is not a lover of compromise. When he sees the truth he will follow the gleam though its pursuit may bring torture and even death. Could not the history of the Jews be called the History of the Refusal to Compromise? The very phenomenon of the Jew's retention of his religious ideals, his customs, and his ethical code, after two thousand years of dispersion and persecution must seem to the impartial observer the most outstanding instance in world history of persistence in serving an ideal.

It is true that now and then Jews have adopted other faiths to save their lives, to advance politically and socially, and to demonstrate their patriotic love for their mother country. These compromisers have suffered. In Spain they were called pigs, "marranos"; in England Disraeli was always, in Bismarck's phase, "der alte Jude"; in Germany, Heine regretted his baptism. Compromise with the truth as dictated by their conscience did not win them peace and freedom and entrée into the aristocratic society which they sought.

These compromisers are untypical of the Jewish people. The great and good G. E. Lessing admired Moses Mendelssohn because he remained a Jew, although he had reformed his ancient faith. In the play *Nathan der Weise,* Nathan, the confidant of Saladin, is a Jew; and in one of the most noble of all monologues in dramatic literature, he relates the story of the three rings symbolic of the three religious faiths, Judaism, Protestantism, and Catholicism, which have so many tenets in common.

If a Jew is not liked for his intrinsic qualities or his usefulness to his community, he will not be liked any more because he adopts the Christian faith. Literary artists, who as a professional group, know man's soul most deeply, have had their say on the honesty and the ethical propensities of Jews throughout the course of literary history. The Jews in literature have not all been Shylocks and Fagins.

Unfortunately these baser personalities are impressed upon young readers and remain almost to the end of their lives. Not only are the qualities of Shylock firmly rooted in the minds of millions of young readers of *The Merchant of Venice,* but his appearance is a tradition. So long has he been portrayed on the stage with a white beard that when Maurice Moscovitch used a short black beard in his New York production in 1931 the spectators found it difficult to make adjustments. In America the production failed. A Parisian version of *The Merchant of Venice* in 1936 presented Shylock as a comic figure, with a red beard, a pathetic creature who ran down the aisles of the theatre screaming for his daughter and his ducats. Experienced theatre-goers found this version difficult to believe, so long had they been accustomed to a white-bearded Shylock.

If plays such as Augustus Thomas' *As a Man Thinks,* Sidney Kingsley's *Men in White,* Arthur Schnitzler's *Professor Bernhardi,* and Friedrich Wolf's *Professor Mamlock* were studied in our elementary schools, the portrait of a Jew that would remain in the minds of millions of readers would be quite different. For the four Jewish physicians who are the heroes in these dramas are so devoted to the truth that they are willing to suffer to defend it. Dr. Mamlock commits suicide rather than compromise with the brutal dictates of his nazi oppressors. Dr. Seelig, although hated as a Jew by the man whom he wishes to help, remains his calm, noble self in all crises, and eventually wins the respect of his former enemy.

Hollywood, although it is quite definitely represented by men of Jewish extraction, has done more than its share of preserving the notion of the deceit and loose code of ethics of the Jews it chooses to present on the screen. In its supposed answer to Hitler's charge against the Jews, *The House of Rothschild,* one of the first sequences shown is the first Rothschild cheating the tax-collector. Certainly one's estimation of the Jews could hardly go up after seeing that act. Why must Hollywood present an agent with a marked accent, with a multitude of gestures, which could be interpreted as only from the New York East Side; with a base code of business ethics, which includes lying, exaggeration, indelicacy, and bribery?

Respected members of other nationalities do not hesitate to protest to the producers when an Italian or a German is portrayed as dishonest or criminal, yet the Jewish producers go their blithe, unconcerned ways all for the sake of appealing to mass ignorance, which they euphemistically call "popular appeal."

Occasionally a Jewish social or fraternal order will voice its protest against falsifications of the position of the Jew. In 1935, when Clifford Odets' *Awake and Sing* presented a Jewish mother who rushed her pregnant daughter into marriage with the man who was not responsible for her condition, vigorous objections were raised to that characterization. The topic must have been discussed in many Jewish organizations, but no direct action was taken.

Other groups have not hesitated to demonstrate their displeasure with Hollywood's maltreatment of topics dear to them. Thus when *Red Salute,* a malicious attack on liberal students in the colleges, was released in 1936, student and labor groups all over the country so effectively boycotted the production that it failed miserably. Metrotone News was booed so often that its name was changed and its militaristic content diluted considerably.

No one would be so rash as to insist that Jews must always be presented as noble benefactors of humanity or as humble servants of the community, but it does not seem too much to ask that fair play be observed. Why should a whole people be condemned because of the infractions of a few of its members?

Enough anti-Semitic propaganda is being spread without the need of any additional contributions from Jewish movie producers, Jewish playwrights, and Jewish novelists. Not that these must confine their art and their vision to apologetics in behalf of their co-religionists. If they are truly great-souled—as all artists claim to be—they must surely recognize the fact that no greater crime can be committed than maligning their own race, and no greater contribution to spiritual sustenance, which is the heritage of great art, can be offered than the presentation of the truth.

G. K. Chesterton was never ashamed of promulgating the Catholic point of view in his writings. In America, the distinguished essayist Agnes Repplier has made no secret of her Catholicism.

RIGHTEOUSNESS ABOVE COMPROMISE

Catholic dramatists, like Ernest Lavery in his *First Legion,* poets like Joyce Kilmer, historians like Carleton J. Hayes, have never been ashamed of presenting the point of view of their faith. Yet in America today, perhaps the most scathing criticism of Jews comes from their own people. Perhaps they know the faults of their co-religionists best, but they must surely recognize their virtues as well.

Is it not time that we stopped looking for noble Jews in the works of Gentile authors, in Lessing's *Nathan der Weise,* in Thomas' *As a Man Thinks,* in Anderson's *Winterset,* in Lewis' *Arrowsmith?* We have enough of our Sons of Israel who have the talent and genius to portray to the world the admirable traits which they must have noted in Jews. Let us have more truth—about the Jews.

18. THE JEW IN WAR

AND PEACE

Inspired by occurrences in the Sino-Japanese War in 1937, Westbrook Pegler, columnist for the *New York World-Telegram,* commented that certain of the narratives of the Old Testament are just as gruesome and barbarous. Referring to passages which told of the complete annihilation of cities and the massacre of every human being within them, Mr. Pegler seemed to imply that the Jewish fighters in biblical history were as ruthless as they were courageous. It was both complimentary and subtly derogatory.

Generalizations about the Jewish attitude toward war are as frequent and as unreliable as the generalizations about the Jewish attitude toward any other thing. For one can prove almost anything about Jews depending upon the strength of one's prejudices and the credulity of one's audiences. For instance, an ancient generalization is that Jews are not brave fighters, that they are cowardly under fire and that they will try to use every means to escape battle. The person making this charge rarely stops to consider the goals which were set before the Jew when he was conscripted into a continental army. What makes Irving Fineman's novel, *Hear, Ye Sons* (1933), so powerful, is among other things, the description of the humiliations and physical and spiritual punishments which a Jewish recruit in the Czar's army was compelled to undergo. Fighting for a monarch who segregated and hounded one's people could hardly be expected of men even less justified in their resentment than were the Russian Jews under the Czar.

Yet Jews could be called upon to defend their ideals and freedom when the need came. Ludwig Lewisohn in *Israel* (1925) relates how in 1794 when Poland tried to free itself from Russian rule:

> Berek Joselewitz had raised a regiment of light cavalry among his fellow-Jews. The regiment fought under Kosciuszko and perished almost to a man in the defense of Warsaw. Again during the Polish uprising in 1830 a Jewish fighting unit in Central Poland carried its special ensign against the Russian tyrant. Men came from far villages, men unused to violence and blood. Upon their ensign they engraved in the middle of the shield held by the Polish eagle's claws the name of Jehovah in Hebrew. They studded the ensign with jewels and their women embroidered the rich silk that surrounds the glittering shield.

Jewish participation in the Spanish Civil War was revealed in an illuminating article by Herbert Burton in *Opinion* of October, 1937. The author, a member of the transport division, met a fellow Jew from Poland. It was discovered that the International Brigade contained Jews from Poland, Germany, New Zealand and more than three hundred from Palestine. One incident is told of a young Polish Jew who together with another comrade refused to retreat when the order was given, and inspired their fellow Loyalists to remain. "It was in that way that this young Jew," writes Mr. Burton, "had helped save the situation by holding off more than two thousand Fascists." One cannot help feeling proud of the achievements related in the article and of the many other acts of heroism which went unsung and unrecorded.

Individual bravery of the Jew has been the topic of endless discussions. When it appears in literature, it is doubly remarkable. Thus in Sholem Asch's *The War Goes On* one of the unforgettable pages describes Mischa Judkewitch's interviews with Russian émigrés in Berlin. As observed by Dr. Bodenheimer, the assimilated German Jew, Mischa's behavior opened his eyes to a new type of Jew, one who could wear a military uniform with poise and grace, one who could gaze unflinchingly at his former oppressors and command them. Such behavior in a Jew seemed impossible to the intellectual Dr. Bodenheimer, whose encounters in life were only of the verbal or literary variety. A Jew who stood on his own feet and gave orders—this was a new Jew indeed!

Our contemporary literature has many references and characterizations of this "new" Jew of courage in the battlefields of peace and of war. In Humphrey Cobb's terrifying novel of the French military blundering in the Great War, *Paths of Glory*, there is the character Meyer, a Jew of Marseilles, who loses no time in telling his fellow men that he is a Jew and that he is not afraid of any of them. Later on when men must be selected from each squad to be shot as punishment for the failure of the company to take its objective, the officers refuse to consider Meyer as a possible victim. First, his courage in action was well known and so he could not be accused of failing to advance with the command. Secondly, he was a Jew, and the officers feared repercussions in Jewish circles. The Dreyfus affair is mentioned as an example of official blundering and no repetition was desired.

The Dreyfus affair is of peculiar significance for two reasons. The memoirs of Dreyfus' son were published in 1938 and the cinema *Zola* (1937) presented this incredible miscarriage of Justice once more to the world. As portrayed by Joseph Schildkraut, who comes from a distinguished Jewish theatrical line, Dreyfus assumes an integrity and moral courage in the face of incredible odds which one can compare only with the behavior of some of the German-Jewish exiles and victims of the concentration camps. The spectacle of Ernst Toller, whose life reads more like the adventures of a knight of old than of a sensitive writer of our times, maintaining his artistic integrity in the face of exile from his native land, is awe-inspiring. He might well have been the living prototype of Hugo Willens, the refugee German-Jewish journalist in S. N. Behrman's play, *Rain from Heaven* (1935).'

Although Jews have not flinched from their duty when their nation required their services, they have been among the most bitter enemies of war and among the most sincere fighters for peace. The literature of Jewish writers on peace and war is vast and inspiring. With a clarity of vision, a freedom from chauvinism which may affect other nations with homelands, with a knowledge of history and economics which has its fruition in the works of a David Ricardo or of a Harold J. Laski and a Gustav Cassel, these writers have described with power and truth the horrors and futilities of settling international disputes by armed combats.

The literature of war is too vast to be discussed in an essay, but three recent dramatic productions written by young American Jewish dramatists deserve study, because they have their own intrinsic merits and because they are typical of a literature to which Jewish writers have given some of their best talents.

If one turns to the final pages of Ludwig Lewisohn's *Upstream* he will find there his recollection of the shattered ethics and morals in America brought on by the Great War. Young authors who were hardly aware of the tragic years of 1914-1918 now realize the horror and misery awaiting them in the not distant future. Thus we find Albert Maltz and George Sklar writing *Peace on Earth* (1933), which was remarkable for its prophetic vision of the present years. Irwin Shaw at twenty-three wrote *Bury the Dead,* which Brooks Atkinson, drama critic of the *New York Times,* described as "a grimly imaginative rebellion against warfare—a shattering bit of theatre magic that burrows under the skin of argument into the raw flesh of sensation." Robert Garland, drama critic of the *New York World-Telegram,* wrote: "Had I my way, *Bury the Dead* would be presented on every Memorial Day as long as men are sheep, war is hell and munition makers are licensed to ply their trade."

The World War has been attacked in many ways. Henri Barbusse in *Le Feu* gave a French soldier's view of it. Arnold Zweig in *The Case of Sergeant Grischa* and *Before Verdun* gave the cry of the ordinary German front-fighter. Who does not know Remarque's *All Quiet on the Western Front?* To strike at the war not through living characters but through dead soldiers who refuse to be buried—that was a stroke of imagination almost akin to genius, which critics praised in *Bury the Dead*. Here are the words of one of the corpses who refuses to be buried:

"Don't bury us—don't stay away—stay with us. We want to hear the sound of men talking. Don't be afraid of us. We're not really different from you. Are you afraid of six dead men, you who've lived with the dead?—Are we different from you? An ounce or so of lead in our hearts, and none in yours. A small difference between us. Tomorrow or the next day the lead will be in yours. Talk as equals—"

The American stage has never seen anything so moving in its plea against war. One might see this play and refuse to believe in the unorthodox resurrection, but one could never forget it.

In *Peace on Earth* Sklar and Maltz told the story of a liberal professor of psychology who refused to compromise with his ideals and eventually was imprisoned by the super-patriots in the Next War. Using the new expressionistic technique to indicate the ideas in the victim's mind as he stands behind his prison bars, the play leads up to an irresistible climax. Even more remarkable are the predictions made in the play, some of which, from loyalty oaths to dismissal of liberal professors, are part of our life today.

Another play about the World War was Sidney Kingsley's *Ten Million Ghosts,* which had its Broadway premiere October 23, 1936. As a financial venture it failed, but as a dramatization of the facts of history, it was perhaps the best of its kind. Contrasting vividly with the perfume and cigarette advertisements which usually adorn *The Playbill* were excerpts and quotations from books, magazines and newspapers, which supplied documentary proof for almost all of Kingsley's ten scenes. The play may have failed to convey any unity of emotion which a less factual production might have given, but it was perhaps the most completely documented play of modern times. It had the truth of a March of Time sequence plus the emotional richness of a tense drama.

Kingsley demonstrated a dramatic growth in *Ten Million Ghosts*. Advancing from the comparatively simple personal problem play, *Men in White,* which won the Pulitzer Prize in 1933, he turned his attention to the misery of the underprivileged in our slums, in *Dead End* (1935). From the misery of the submerged third to the tragedy of ten million men who gave their lives in vain, the step was natural.

The popular failure of *Ten Million Ghosts* could not detract from its significance, any more than the failure of Paul Green's *Johnny Johnson* (1937) prevented the Critics' Circle of New York from awarding it their annual prize. Plays which treat war seriously seldom fill the coffers of the box office. Notable failures in recent years despite the importance and interest of the plays include S. K. Lauren's *Men Must Fight,* John Haynes Holmes' *If This Be Treason,* and Humphrey Cobb's *Paths of Glory.* Such comic treatments as Robert E. Sherwood's *Idiot's Delight* are more easily digested by those who have no stomach for the blood and tears of war. But the box-office receipts have rarely been any criterion of the ultimate significance of any drama. Jewish dramatists and novelists will continue to write sincerely, fervently, burningly and movingly about war, just as they describe other injustices.

In the words of the Psalmist:

> "Oh, let the wickedness of the wicked be at an end;
> But establish the righteous." (*Psalms VII*)

Kingsley, Irwin Shaw, Maltz, Sklar, Schnitzler, Sassoon, and dozens of mighty names in world literature have testified to the courage of the Jewish man of letters and to the Jew fighting in peace and in war.

19. VICTIMS OF NAZISM AS

PORTRAYED IN AMERICAN DRAMA

The nazi régime in Germany has been responsible for several plays about Jewish characters, which may well merit a unified study. Political forces may leave certain creative artists unmoved, but upon others they make such marked impressions that historians of art never tire of repeating them. Thus every school child knows by this time that Beethoven's *Eroica* was originally dedicated to Napoleon but the dedication was changed when the composer heard that the Corsican had proclaimed himself Emperor. Likewise the fight for liberation from Russian control inspired Chopin, while Tchaikovsky's 1812 *Overture* celebrated the retreat of Napoleon from Moscow.

When the history of nazism will finally be written, several chapters will be devoted no doubt to its effect upon the arts not only of Germany but of the entire world. For Germany it meant the extirpation of some of its most original creative spirits of the time. Schönberg left for America; numerous writers, including Thomas Mann, Ernst Toller, Lion Feuchtwanger, Arnold Zweig and Heinz Liepmann, fled to the uncertain security of other lands; interpreters in the drama, in music, in the dance, were exiled from the land of their greatest successes.

It was not long before the specific problem of the relation of nazism to Jewry appeared on the American stage. Adolf Phillip, a German-Jewish dramatist who had written plays in German, Yiddish and English in America, translated Theodore Weachter's German play, *Kultur,* which was produced in September 1933. The plot revolved about the illness of the German Chancellor who could be saved only by Professor Koerner, whose grandfather was a Jew. Forgetting the oppression of his co-religionists and heeding the call to humanity, Koerner saves the Chancellor and becomes a national hero. The play ends with his fervent plea for liberty, equality and tolerance. Phillip later wrote a play in Yiddish on the Hitler régime.

Richard Maibaum's *Birthright* (1933) was based on a story which the playwright had heard from a German refugee in a park in London. A Jewish girl is loved by an Aryan. When the nazi régime sets in he is forced to join the National Socialist Party. He tries to save his beloved and her family. Her young communist brother is killed after shooting a nazi officer. The girl gives up her Aryan sweetheart.

Though the play was convincing and written with feeling, the New York audiences were evidently sufficiently acquainted with the horrors of the nazi régime and did not give the dramatist the same hearty response elicited from the critics. In spite of its brief run, it was considered worthy of publication and has the distinction of being the first play by an American Jew on the persecution of the Jews by the nazis.

In the spring of 1934 a play called *The Shatter'd Lamp* by Leslie Reade, an Englishman, met with considerable success in New York, thanks to moving performances by Effie Shannon, Guy Bates Post and Owen Davis, Jr. Strangely enough this indictment of the nazi régime was not permitted in England, where the censor felt that it was offensive to the head of another government. The story was a familiar one. The father was Professor of English Literature in a German University. The mother was a Jewess. One son had been killed in the Great War. Another son, hardly aware of his mother's ancestry, was associating with an officer of the Storm Troopers. This person is invited to the home and is entertained cordially. In the midst of the festivities he sings the "Horst Wessel" song, not knowing that his hostess is a Jewess. When informed of the fact, he apologizes for hurting her feelings and declares that he means to drive out only the "Eastern" Jews who came to Germany after the War.

In the course of the play we see dramatized all the excesses which characterized the nazi régime in its early stages. A little Marxist shoemaker is beaten and dragged through the streets. The theatre is filled with the screams of "radicals" who are rounded up one night and taken to concentration camps.

The Jewess commits suicide because she feels that she is causing trouble for her husband. The latter, after condemning the new government in the presence of several storm-troopers, is shot by one of them. The youngest son escapes to the British consulate.

Written so close to the event, the play was dramatically effective. Here was a crystallization of most of the indignities which people had read in newspapers and magazines. Moreover, the characters were living human beings, not mere spokesmen for the author's indignation. Yiddish newspapers in New York City marvelled at the verisimilitude of Effie Shannon's performance although she was not a Jewess, and Guy Bates Post was praised for his dignified performance. The late Moffat Johnson won acclaim for his excellent characterization of the middle-class German neighbor.

In September 1934, shortly after the Reichstag Fire Trial, Elmer Rice produced his own play, *Judgment Day*. The scene is the court-room in a Slavic country. The dictator's name is Vesnick, and the salute is at right angles to the line of the body; but the relationship to the Reichstag Trial is unmistakable. The half-witted scapegoat of the actual trial, Marinus Van der Lubbe, was represented, as well as an obvious imitation of Colonel Goering.

Rice, to be sure, did not bind himself to the literal truth, and his *dénouement* was indicative of wishful thinking; but his play was an exciting experience. The critics were somewhat disturbed by the shouting and the deviation from the actual events, and chided Rice for playing the soap-box orator. Rice, who was then owner of the Belasco Theatre, and had produced and directed the play himself, was annoyed. Burns Mantle, drama critic of the *New York Daily News,* put the critics' objections aptly in these words:

Even the frankest propaganda play must be believable to its audience. It matters very little that Mr. Rice can bring into court evidence to prove that he has not, either from bias or author's enthusiasm, overstated the case of Hitler, who is quite obviously the target of his wrath. The audience still does not believe it; still does not believe it humanly possible for so vicious and brazen a travesty of justice to have taken place in any civilized state, whatever its revolutionary adventures.

Rice, undaunted by the critics' disapproval, which had greeted him the year before with *We, the People,* turned to distinguished members of the audience for endorsement. Marc Connelly wrote: "It was a delight to join that audience cheering such a fine melodrama." Theodore Dreiser said: "A very intense and exciting dramatization of what most Americans assume Hitlerism to be like." Fannie Hurst declared: "A dramatist who can tear a ripping melodrama out of the marble subject of government is rare." Daniel Frohman added: "Your theme is big, strong, vital. . . . Your performance the most stirring I ever saw." Other recommendations came from Arthur Garfield Hays, Benjamin de Casseres, and Grace George. Burns Mantle admitted that the play was not to his liking, but paid Rice this tribute:

We need his courage, his independence, his fine dramatic sense, his determination to do those things he considers vitally worth doing in the theatre.

In September 1934 a translation of Otto Indig's European success *The Bride of Torozko* was presented in New York. Although it did not mention the Jewish persecution in Germany, it obviously was considered by its producers as pertinent to the entire Jewish problem which had been rendered more acute since January 1933. A young Roumanian girl is about to obtain a marriage license when she discovers that she is not a Catholic but a Jewess. Accepting her newly-discovered religion, she lives for a time with Hershkovitz, an innkeeper. He tries to instruct her in the history and traditions of his people, which she is eager to learn. In the end it is discovered that she is a Protestant, and she leaves her Jewish teacher. Commenting on the circumstances, Hershkovitz remarks that it would not do Jews any harm if all Gentiles learned something of the religious heritage of the Jews in such a manner. The play was extremely successful on the Continent, but was not well received in New York despite excellent portrayals by Helen Arthur as the girl and Sam Jaffe as Hershkovitz.

S. N. Behrman, the most successful writer of the comedy of manners on the American stage, wrote the first American play about a German-Jewish refugee. *Rain from Heaven* was produced on December 24, 1934 by the Theatre Guild. Like all of his plays, it was free from anger or indignation. It treated the refugee problem as a topic of drawing-room conversation in the home of the liberal Lady Violet Wyngate. Hugo Willens had only one Jewish grandparent, and was the son of a Lutheran minister, but he had aroused the ire of the régime by writing a satirical tale called *The Last Jew*.

Coming into a household where charm and good manners were usual, he nevertheless won the heart of Lady Wyngate, who was being courted by a wealthy American. The play represented the cultured German of Jewish ancestry, harassed by a régime unfriendly to culture. John Halliday made the part of Hugo Willens alive. His courage and unselfishness were with him to the end. Lady Wyngate, having dismissed her American suitor, begs Willens to stay in England where he can be free to continue his work. He refuses to live in ease and luxury while his dearest friends are still persecuted and imprisoned. He leaves England to join a group of exiles who are returning secretly to their native land to work for its liberation.

Early in 1935 the *New Masses* printed a translation of a German letter sent by a Communist to a friend in Prague. It told of the imprisonment of the writer's brother, his ousting from the Communist Party, and his suicide. Clifford Odets used this letter to fashion his play *Till the Day I Die.* Written in several tense scenes, with the crisp, revealing economical dialogue for which he is famous, the play made the events of the letter live. The cruel inhumanity of the nazi storm-troopers, the hounding of the Communist by spies as soon as he is released, the secret meetings of his comrades, under constant fear of detection, the final suicide as the only way out of the victim's present mode of living are all related succintly yet sharply.

Mention must be made of three plays by German authors which were produced in New York. Friedrich Wolf's *Dr. Mamlock* (1937) was based on an actual experience. The original Dr. Mamlock is now in America. In the play he is a prominent surgeon who had served notably in the War and was in charge of his own clinic. When the nazi régime came into power he was permitted to remain in his clinic as a special favor because of his service in the War, but his Jewish assistant is discharged. Dr. Mamlock cannot endure his humiliations and ends them by committing suicide.

Ernst Toller's *No More Peace* (1937) is a satire on the nazi dictatorship and its glorification of war. His dictator, originally a barber, is thrown out when it is learned that he himself has "Brazilian" blood, against which he had been carrying on his relentless campaign.

Franz Werfel in his *Eternal Road* (1937) tried to tell the glorious biblical history of the Jew to a congregation of frightened men and women who had fled to a synagogue to escape a pogrom. Max Reinhardt lavished upon the production all his genius and it resulted in a remarkable spectacle.

Another short-lived attempt to delineate the rulers of nazi Germany was made by Oliver H. P. Garrett in his *Waltz in Goose Step* (October 1938). The author used the "Blood Purge" of 1934 as his central theme and concentrated on the trickery and mutual hatred of the members of dictator's circle. The central character was an effeminate, musically-inclined associate of the dictator who is continually plotting to kill his leader but is trapped and killed in the end. Although the drama had many tense moments during which the audience witnessed actual experiences, and the portrayals of the leading characters left nothing to be desired, *Waltz in Goose Step,* in the words of Richard Watts, Jr., critic of the *New York Herald Tribune,* "proves once more how difficult it is to write a good play on the subject it has chosen."

Elmer Rice's *American Landscape* was a remarkable example of a play reflecting the occurrences of our own time, expressed in the language of powerful drama. Many of the newspaper readers who read about the attempt of a nazi organization to buy a tract of land in Connecticut in order to turn it into a training camp have long forgotten the incident, but those who saw the play will long remember the experience as it is stated by Elmer Rice, with all the skill of a dramatist who has written eighteen plays, some of them modern classics. Combining the realism of the daily newspapers with the fantasy of Lewis Carroll, Elmer Rice manages to convince the audience that the ghosts of Moll Flanders, Harriet Beecher Stowe, and veterans of the Revolutionary, Civil, and World Wars appear to guide the last surviving male of the Dale clan, who settled in America in 1620.

Captain Frank Dale, who was a distinguished officer in the Spanish-American War, is contemplating the selling of his once prosperous shoe-factory to a large corporation, and the disposal of his large estate to the *Deutsch-Amerikanischer Kulturgesellschaft.* Rice uses the plot as a vehicle to discuss the true American tradition, with its tolerance, its freedom, and to contrast this tradition with the fiendish nazi agency which seeks to destroy it. The play may be accepted both realistically and symbolically. It serves its purpose in holding the audience's attention to its excellences as a play, while at the same time stimulating all kinds of thoughts about democracy, totalitarianism and other vital issues of the day. Elmer Rice considers it his most important play, and critics generally shared his opinion.

The Yiddish Art Theatre's second production of its nineteenth season was H. Leivick's *Who Is Who,* perhaps the first drama to be produced about German refugees in America and the menace of nazism to them in their new haven. It comes as a significant contrast to such spectacular productions as *Three Cities, The Brothers Ashkenazi,* and *Yoshe Kalb,* which made earlier seasons noteworthy.

Professor Shelling is a world-famous mathematician who, after suffering five months in a nazi concentration camp, comes to America and is given a professorship in a small college in Connecticut. He has with him a son of college age and a paralyzed daughter. The increasing signs of anti-Semitism in America have been worrying Professor Shelling. He has hidden from his children the knowledge that he is a Jew and that their mother had been killed in a pogrom by the Petlura bandits of Russia.

Upon the occasion of the printing of a new edition of *Who's Who,* his Jewish origin is indicated. He tries to prevent the publication of the book by every means at his command in order to spare the children the shock and anguish of knowing that they are Jews. Professor Shelling fails in his attempt; his children learn of their Jewish origin and he is made to see the futility of his efforts to spare them the pangs of suffering from anti-Semitism by denying their origin. His friend, Judge Evans, is the spokesman of the truly American tradition of tolerance and respect for others, and under the guidance of the Judge, Professor Shelling goes back to his own people to help them in their fight against the forces of reaction.

Of all the plays about nazism, of which there have now been almost a dozen, this is one of the most moving in its delineation of the spiritual anguish caused by the unleashing of the barbarism of Hitlerland. While other plays have had more violent scenes and more heart-rending revelations of physical brutality, as in Clifford Odets' *Till The Day I Die* (1935) and Leslie

VICTIMS OF NAZISM

Reade's *The Shatter'd Lamp* (1933), *Who Is Who* is more memorable because it reveals the spiritual torture and mental anguish which will remain with the victims long after the physical evidences of the Hitlerian nightmare will have vanished.

Even in the snappy revue, Hitlerism and the evils of other totalitarian countries come in for their share of condemnation. The fabulous success of *Pins and Needles* (1937), the revue by Harold J. Rome and Charles Friedman, which was originally designed as a means of relaxation for members of the International Ladies Garment Workers Union, is a matter of theatrical history. Several of the numbers were anti-fascist, particularly the famous "Three Little Dictators Are We" in which Hirohito, Hitler, and Mussolini are caricatured. In the second revue by the same authors, *Sing Out the News* (1938), sponsored this time by one of the most respected producers on Broadway, Max Gordon, in association with George S. Kaufman and Moss Hart, there were more slaps at the great public enemies of our time. A ballet, "Peace and the Diplomat," reminded one of the famous Green Table number of the Jooss Ballet. The International Mountain Climbers satirized the Munich Pact. This was not the first musical to venture into criticism of international politics. In 1937 Ed Wynn played practically all year in *Hooray for What,* as hilarious an exposé of the munitions industry as the Nye Committee Report was serious.

BIBLIOGRAPHIES

1. *A List of Novels and Short Stories of Interest to Students of Jewish Life in America*

BERMAN, HENRY
    Worshippers. 1906.
BERNSTEIN, HERMAN
    In the Gates of Israel. 1902 (Short Stories).
    Contrite Hearts. 1906.
BRINIG, MYRON
    Singerman. 1929.
    The Sisters. 1937.
BROWN, HYPKIN
    Farmer Bibbins. 1914.
BRUDNO, EZRA SELIG
    The Fugitive. 1904.
    One of Us. 1905.
    The Little Conscript. 1905.
    The Tether. 1908.
BULLARD, ARTHUR
    Comrade Yetta. 1913.
BUTTERFIELD, J. A.
    Belshazzar.
CAHAN, ABRAHAM
    Yekel, a Tale of the New York Ghetto. 1896.
    The Imported Bridegroom and Other Stories of the New York Ghetto. 1898.
    The White Terror and the Red. 1905.

NOVELS AND SHORT STORIES

    The Rise of David Levinsky. 1917.
CHAMBERS, ROBERT W.
    Cardigan. 1901.
CLARKE, B.
    From Tent to Palace, or the Story of Joseph.
COHEN, LESTER
    Aaron Traum. 1930.
COOPER, SAMUEL W.
    Think and Thank, a Tale for the Young. 1890.
COURNOS, JOHN
    The Mask. 1919.
    The Wall. 1921.
    Babel. 1922.
CRAWFORD, FRANCIS MARION
    Zoroaster. 1894.
    The Witch of Prague. 1896.
DAVIS, WILLIAM STERN
    Belshazzar. 1902.
DRACHMAN, BERNARD
    From the Heart of Israel. 1905.
DRAKE, LAWRENCE
    Don't Call Me Clever. 1929.
EGAN, MAURICE FRANCIS
    The Ivy Hedge. 1914.
FERBER, EDNA
    Fanny Herself. 1917.
FERBER, NAT. J.
    The Sidewalks of New York. 1927.
    New York. 1928.
    Spawn. 1930.
    Women Are Devils. 1932.
    One Happy Jew. 1934.
FINEMAN, IRVING
    Hear, Ye Sons. 1933.
    Dr. Addams. 1939.
FRANK, WALDO
    The Life and Death of David Markand. 1934.

NOVELS AND SHORT STORIES

FRANKEL, A. H.
  In Gold We Trust.
FRIEDMAN, ISAAC K.
  The Lucky Number. 1896.
"FRIENDLY AUNT"
  The Jewish Twins.
FUCHS, DANIEL
  Summer in Williamsburg. 1935.
  Homage to Blenholt. 1936.
  Low Company. 1937.
GEORGE, W. L.
  Until the Day Break. 1913.
GERSON, EMILY.
  A Modern Esther, and Other Stories for Jewish Children. 1906.
GERSONI, HENRY
  The Metamorphosis of a Lithuanian Boy.
GILLMAN, NATHANIEL ISAIAH.
  Circumstantial Affection. 1901.
GLASS, MONTAGUE
  Potash and Perlmutter. 1910.
  Abe and Mawruss. 1911.
  Object: Matrimony. 1912.
  Elkan Lubliner, American. 1912.
  With the Best Intentions. 1914.
  The Competitive Nephew. 1915.
  Worrying Won't Win. 1918.
  Potash and Perlmutter Settle Things. 1919.
  Y' Understand. 1925.
  You Can't Learn 'em Nothin'. 1930.
GOLD, MICHAEL
  Jews Without Money. 1930.
GOLDSMITH, MILTON
  Rabbi and Priest. 1892.
  A Victim of Conscience. 1903.
GRATACUP, LOUIS D.
  Benjamin, the Jew. 1913.

NOVELS AND SHORT STORIES

HALPER, ALBERT
- Union Square. 1933.
- The Foundry. 1934.
- On the Shore. 1934 (Short Stories).
- The Chute. 1937.

HARDING, JOHN WILLIAM
- The Gate of the Kiss. 1902.

HARLAND, HENRY (Sidney Luska)
- As It Was Written, a Jewish Musician's Love Story. 1886.
- Mrs. Peixada. 1886.
- The Yoke of the Torah. 1887.
- My Uncle Florimond. 1888.
- Mr. Sonnenschein's Inheritance. 1889.
- A Latin Quartier Courtship and Other Stories.

HECHT, BEN
- Erik Dorn. 1921.
- A Jew in Love. 1931.
- Duke Herring. 1932.

HENLE, JAMES
- Sound and Fury. 1924.

HERSCH, VIRGINIA
- Storm Beach. 1933.

HESS, ISABELLA R.
- St. Cecelia of the Court. 1905.

HOMER, A. N.
- Hernani the Jew. 1898.

HURST, FANNIE
- Just Around the Corner. 1914 (Short Stories).
- Gaslight Sonatas. 1918 (Short Stories).
- Humoresque. 1918 (Short Stories).
- Lummox. 1923 (Short Stories).

ILIOWIZI, HENRY
- In the Pale. 1897.
- A Patriarch's Blessing.

INGRAHAM, J. H.
- The Prince of the House of David. 1896.

NOVELS AND SHORT STORIES

KANDEL, ABEN
    Black Sun. 1929.
KELLY, MYRA
    Little Citizens. 1904 (Short Stories).
    Wards of Liberty. 1909 (Short Stories).
    Little Aliens. 1910 (Short Stories).
KING, EDWARD
    Joseph Zalmonah. 1893.
LAUFERTY, LILLIAN
    The Street of Chains. 1929.
LAZARRE, JACOB
    Beating Sea and the Changeless Bar. 1905.
LEISER, JOSEPH
    Canaway and the Lustigs. 1909.
LESSING, BRUNO
    Children of Men. 1903 (Short Stories).
    With the Best Intentions. 1914.
LEVIN, MEYER
    Yehuda. 1931.
    The Old Bunch. 1937.
LEVY, MELVIN P.
    The Last Pioneers. 1934.
LEWISOHN, LUDWIG
    The Island Within. 1928.
    The Last Days of Shylock. 1933.
LUBIN, DAVID
    Let There Be Light. 1900.
LUDLOW, JAMES M.
    Deborah. 1901.
    A King of Tyre.
LUST, ADELINE C.
    A Tent of Grace. 1899.
McCARTER, MARGARET HILL
    Winning of the Wilderness. 1914.
MANHEIMER, LOUISE
    How Joe Learned to Darn Stockings. 1897.

NOVELS AND SHORT STORIES

MAYER, NATHAN
    Differences. 1867.

MENDES, H. PEREIRA
    In Old Egypt. 1903.

MILLER, ELIZABETH
    The Yoke. 1904.

MILLER, SARA
    Under the Eagle's Wing. 1899.

McLAWA, LAFAYETTE
    Jezebel. 1902.

MOSES, ADOLPH
    Luser, the Watchmaker.

MOSS, MARY
    Julian Meldola. 1903.
    Judith Lubestan.

NORRIS, FRANK
    McTeague. 1899.

NYBURG, SIDNEY L.
    The Chosen People. 1917.

OPPENHEIM, JAMES
    Doctor Rast. 1909.

ORNITZ, SAMUEL
    Haunch, Paunch and Jowl. 1924.

PAGE, THOMAS NELSON
    John Marvel, Assistant. 1909.

PARSONS, J. F.
    Bernstein and Firestein: A Musical Sketch. 1904.

PENDELTON, LOUIS
    Lost Prince Almon. 1898.
    In Assyrian Tents. 1904.

PHELPS, ELIZABETH STUART
    The Master of the Musicians. 1890.

RAY, ANNA CHAPIN
    Sheba. 1903.

RECHT, CHARLES
    Rue with a Difference. 1924.

NOVELS AND SHORT STORIES

REZNIKOFF, CHARLES
    By the Waters of Manhattan. 1929.
RICE, AURELIA
    Fortune Hunting. 1886.
RICHARDS, BERNARD G.
    Discourses of Keidansky. 1903.
RIIS, JACOB A.
    Children of the Tenements. 1905 (Short Stories).
    Neighbors. 1914 (Short Stories).
ROSENFELD, PAUL
    The Boy in the Sun. 1928.
ROTH, JOSEPH
    Call It Sleep. 1934.
ROYE, G. MONROE
    The Son of Amram. 1901.
ROWLAND, HENRY C.
    The Mountain of Fears. 1905.
RUPENS, OTTO
    The Peddler.
SCHNABEL, LOUIS
    Voegele's Marriage. 1892.
SCHNEIDER, ISIDOR
    From the Kingdom of Necessity. 1935.
SIDGWICK, MRS. CECILY
    Scene of Jewish Life. 1904.
SMITH, FRANCIS H.
    Peter. 1909.
SPITZER, MARION
    Who Would Be Free. 1924.
STEINER, EDWARD A.
    Broken Walls. 1911.
TILTON, DWIGHT
    Meyer and Son. 1908.
TOBENKIN, ELIAS
    Witte Arrives. 1916.
    The House of Conrad. 1918.

NOVELS AND SHORT STORIES

    The Road. 1922.
    God of Might. 1924.
    Lucky Numbers. 1927.
    In the Dark. 1931.
WADE, MARY H.
    Our Little Jewish Cousin. 1904.
WALLACE, LEW
    Ben Hur. 1880.
    The Prince of India. 1893.
WARD, MARY A.
    Marriage a la Mode. 1909.
WARD, JOSIAH H.
    Come with Me unto Babylon. 1902.
WARFIELD, DAVID
    Ghetto Silhouettes. 1902 (Short Stories).
WARNER, SUSAN
    The Walls of Jerusalem. 1879.
    The House of Israel. 1897.
WEIDMAN, JEROME
    I Can Get It for You Wholesale. 1937.
WHARTON, EDITH
    The House of Mirth. 1905.
WISE, ISAAC M.
    The Combat of the People.
    The First of the Maccabees.
WOLF, EMMA
    Other Things Being Equal. 1896.
    Heirs of Yesterday. 1900.
WOLFENSTEIN, MARTHA
    Idylls of the Gass. 1901.
    A Renegade and Other Tales. 1905 (Short Stories).
YEZIERSKA, ANZIA
    Hungry Hearts. 1920.
    Salome of the Tenements. 1922.
    Children of Loneliness. 1923 (Short Stories).
    Bread Givers. 1925.

2. *A List of Plays of Interest to Students of Jewish Life in America*

ANDERSON, MAXWELL. Winterset. New York, Anderson House, 1935.
In Esdras, Anderson portrays one of the noblest Jews in modern dramatic literature.

ATLAS, LEOPOLD. But for the Grace of God. New York, Samuel French, 1937.
Kababian, a Jewish petty manufacturer, has plenty of troubles trying to keep his small business going. He is killed by one of his boy-employees.

BEHRMAN, S. N. Wine of Choice. New York, 1938.
Binkie Niebuhr's family escaped massacre in a Russian pogrom because his mother was an excellent cook. He is a darling of the L. I. horsey set, whose problems he tries to solve.

BURNETT, DANA, and ABBOTT, GEORGE. Four Walls.
A psychological and sociological study of gangsterdom, in which one of the characters is of Jewish origin.

GLASS, MONTAGUE, and GOODMAN, JULES ECKERT. Potash and Perlmutter. New York, French, 1923.
Object Matrimony. New York, 1916.

GOODMAN, JULES ECKERT. His Honor, Abe Potash. New York, 1919.
Why Worry? New York, 1918.
Partners Again. New York, 1922.
Potash and Perlmutter, Detectives. New York, 1926.

PLAYS

HECHT, BEN, and MacARTHUR, CHARLES. Twentieth Century. New York.
   The uproarious story of the attempts of Oscar Jaffe, New York Jewish producer, to prevent his star actress from joining up with any other producer.
HOWARD, SIDNEY. Yellow Jack. New York, Harcourt, 1933.
   Busch, a young Chicago Jewish soldier in the Spanish American War, offers to assist in the experiment to discover the cause of yellow fever.
HURST, FANNIE. It Is To Laugh. New York.
KAUFMAN, GEORGE S., and HART, MOSS. Merrily We Roll Along. New York, Random House, 1934.
   Contains several Jewish characters of minor importance.
   Once in a Lifetime. New York, Samuel French, 1930.
   The Jewish movie magnate, Herman Glogauer, is one of the most characteristic portraits of the type.
KAUFMAN, GEORGE S., and RYSKIND, MORRIE. Of Thee I Sing. New York, Knopf, 1932.
   Several minor Jewish characters.
KINGSLEY, SIDNEY. Men in White. New York, Covici, 1933.
   Dr. Hochberg, like Schnitzler's Dr. Bernhardi and Wolf's Dr. Mamlock, is one of the distinguished Jewish scientists in modern drama.
KOBER, ARTHUR. Having Wonderful Time. New York, Random House, 1937.
   Jewish girls and boys on their vacation provide the material for this comedy.
LAWSON, JOHN HOWARD. Success Story. New York, Farrar, 1932.
   Ginsberg, a young man from New York's East Side, rises in his firm until he ousts his former employer. He is accidentally killed by his former sweetheart.
   Processional. New York, Boni, 1925.
   Includes Mr. Cohen, tailor, and Sadie Cohen, heroine.
   Marching Song. New York, Dramatists, 1937.
   One of the strikers is Woodrow Wilson Rosenbloom, whose father went to France to make the world safe for Democracy. The son is a disillusioned fighter for justice.

PLAYS

Gentlewoman. New York, Farrar, 1934.
Includes the Jewish psychoanalyst, Dr. Golden.

NICHOLS, ANNE. Abie's Irish Rose. New York, Samuel French.
The Levy's and the Murphy's are reconciled to the marriage of their children when twins are born.

ODETS, CLIFFORD. Golden Boy. New York, 1938.
Mr. Carp is an amusing philosopher. Roxy Gottlieb is a boxing promoter.
Awake and Sing. New York, Random House, 1935.
A Jewish family in the Bronx has its troubles in the Depression of the 1930's.
Waiting for Lefty. New York, Random House, 1935.
One of the striking taxicab drivers is Dr. Benjamin, whose father read Spinoza, but had to peddle neckties to make a living.

RICE, ELMER. Counsellor-at-Law. New York.
Mr. Simon, brilliant son of immigrants, climbs to dazzling heights professionally, but is a failure in his marriage with a Gentile of the upper classes.
Street Scene. New York, French, 1929.
We, the People. New York, Coward-McCann, 1933.
A play about the Depression. A Jewish professor is made to feel that anti-semitism may find a place in college administration.

SHAW, IRWIN. The Gentle People. New York, 1939.
The three Goodmans and Lammonowitz, are Jewish characters portrayed with sympathy, humor, and understanding.

SPEWACK, BELLA and SAMUEL. Spring Song. New York.
A Jewish mother struggling to support her family, cannot understand the modern ways of her daughters. Tragedy on New York's East Side.

THOMAS, AUGUSTA. As a Man Thinks. New York, Duffield, 1911.
The household of Dr. Seelig, eminent Jewish physician, is described and the relations with Christian neighbors are stressed. One of the first American plays about Jews who belong to the upper classes.

WELLMAN, RITA. The Gentile Wife. New York.
A study of inter-marriage which did not succeed.

PLAYS

WOLFSON, VICTOR. Excursion. New York, Random House, 1937.
A middle-class Jewish shop-keeper and his wife are among the occupants of a Coney Island steamboat whose captain takes them to an island in the Caribbean.

WEXLEY, JOHN. They Shall Not Die. New York, Knopf, 1934.
Rubin, Jewish attorney, goes South to defend a group of negroes who are wrongly accused of a crime. One of the important portraits of a Jew as a member of the legal profession.

ZANGWILL, ISRAEL. The Melting Pot. New York, French, 1909.
Expressive of the author's hopes that America will at last become the crucible in which all races of mankind could be fused into a single one.

3. Volumes of Poetry by Contemporary Jewish Poets in America

ADAMS, FRANKLIN PIERCE
    Tobogganing on Parnassus. 1910.
    In Other Words. 1912.
    By and Large. 1914.
    Weights and Measures. 1917.
    Something Else Again. 1920.
    Overset. 1922.
    So There. 1922.
    So Much Velvet. 1924.
    Half a Loaf. 1927.
    Column Book of F. P. A. 1928.
    Christopher Columbus. 1931.
    The Melancholy Lute. 1936.
ANTHONY, EDWARD
    Merry-go-Roundelays. 1921.
APPEL, BENJAMIN
    Mixed Vintage. 1929.
AUSLANDER, JOSEPH
    Sunrise Trumpets. 1924.
    Cyclops' Eye. 1926.
    Historia Amoris Mea. 1927.
    Hell in Harness. 1930.
    Letters to Women. 1930.
    No Traveller Returns. 1933.

Will Shakespeare. 1934.
More Than Bread. 1936.
Translations:
The Fables of La Fontaine. 1930.
The Sonnets of Petrarch. 1931.

BARISH, MILDRED
Songs for Somebody. 1931.

BEER, MORRIS ABEL
Songs of Manhattan. 1918.
Street Lamps. 1927.

BERENBERG, DAVID PAUL
Letters of Glaucon and Sarai. 1924.
The Kid. 1931.
Chants. 1935.

BLUMENTHAL, WALTER HART
Winepress. 1925.

BODENHEIM, MAXWELL
Minna and Myself. 1918.
Advice. 1920.
Introducing Irony. 1922.
Against This Age. 1923.
The Sardonic Arm. 1923.
Returning to Emotion. 1927.
King of Spain. 1928.
Bringing Jazz. 1930.

BRODY, ALTER
A Family Album. 1918.

BURNSHAW, STANLEY
The Iron Land. 1936.

COBLENTZ, STANTON ARTHUR
The Thinker and Other Poems. 1923.
The Lone Adventurer. 1927.
The Wonder Stick. 1929.
Shadows on a Wall. 1930.
The Enduring Flame. 1932.
Songs of the Redwoods. 1933.
The Merry Hunt and Other Poems. 1934.

The Pageant of Man. 1936.
COURNOS, JOHN
In Exile. 1923.
CRANE, NATHALIA
The Janitor's Boy. 1924.
Lava Lane. 1925.
The Singing Crow. 1926.
Venus Invisible. 1928.
Pocahontas. 1930.
Swear by the Night. 1936.
DAVIDSON, GUSTAV
Songs of Adoration. 1919.
Melmoth the Wanderer. 1919.
A Half Century of Sonnets. 1924.
Twenty Sonnets. 1926.
DeCASSERES, BENJAMIN
The Shadow Eater. 1915.
DEUTSCH, BABETTE
Banners. 1919.
Honey Out of the Rock. 1925.
Fire for the Night. 1930.
Epistle for Prometheus. 1931.
DORO, EDWARD
Alms for Oblivion. 1932.
The Boar and Shibboleth. 1933.
Shiloh. 1936.
EHRMANN, MAX
A Prayer. 1906.
Poems. 1906.
ELSHEMUS, LOUIS MICHAEL
Fragments and Flashes of Thought. 1907.
Mammon: A Dramatic Poem. 1907.
Moods of a Soul. 1907.
Elegiac Poems. 1907.
FEARING, KENNETH
Angel Arms. 1929.
Poems. 1935.

FEIBELMAN, JAMES
    Death of the God in Mexico. 1931.
FEINSTEIN, MARTIN
    In Memoriam. 1922.
FLEXNER, HORTENSE
    Clouds and Cobblestones. 1920.
    This Stubborn Root. 1930.
FRANK, FLORENCE KIPER
    The Jew to Jesus and Other Poems. 1915.
GINSBERG, LOUIS
    The Attic of the Past. 1920.
    Everlasting Minute and Other Lyrics. 1937.
GOELL, MILTON J.
    To All You Ladies. 1927.
GOLLOMB, JOSEPH
    Songs for Courage. 1917.
GORDON, DON
    Echoes of the South Seas. 1930.
GUITERMAN, ARTHUR
    Betel Nuts. 1907.
    Guest Book. 1908.
    Rubaiyat. 1909.
    Orestes. 1909.
    Laughing Muse. 1915.
    Mirthful Lyre. 1918.
    Ballads of Old New York. 1920.
    Chips of Jade. 1920.
    A Ballad Maker's Pack. 1921.
    Light Guitar. 1923.
    A Poet's Proverbs. 1924.
    I Sing the Pioneer. 1926.
    Wildwood Fables. 1927.
    Song and Laughter. 1929.
    Death of General Putnam. 1935.
    Gaily the Troubadour. 1936.
HAGEDORN, HERMAN
    Poems and Ballads. 1913.

Great Maze, and the Heart of Youth. 1916.
Ladders through the Blue. 1925.
Three Pharaohs; a Dramatic Poem. 1932.
HA LEVI-MORDEKI, REBEKAH
I Wish with a Rhythm of Song. 1936.
HELLMAN, GEORGE S.
Hudson and Other Poems. 1909.
HERTZBERG, H. R. R.
Lyrics of Love. 1906.
HEYERDAHL, VIVIAN
Poems; Coupled Bells. 1932.
HOFFENSTEIN, SAMUEL
Life Sings a Song. 1916.
Poems in Praise of Practically Nothing. 1928.
Year In, You're Out. 1930.
KIRSTEIN, LINCOLN
Low Ceiling. 1935.
KRUGER, FANIA
Cossack Laughter. 1937.
LEAVITT, EMANUEL
Songs of Grief and Gladness. 1907.
LEHMAN, RUDOLPH CHAMBERS
Selected Verse. 1929.
LEVY, NEWMAN
Opera Guyed. 1923.
Gay But Wistful. 1925.
Saturday to Monday. 1931.
Theatre Guyed. 1933.
LIEBERMAN, ELIAS
Paved Streets. 1917.
Hand Organ Man. 1930.
LIPPMAN, ARTHUR L.
Gay Matter: Good Natured Verse. 1927.
LONG, SOLOMON LEVY
Child Slaves and Other Poems. 1909.
LOVEMAN, ROBERT
Sonnets of Strife. 1918.

LOVEMAN, SAMUEL
    Hermaphrodite. 1926.
LOWENHEIM, GERTRUDE
    Goosie-Gander Rhymes. 1909.
NATHAN, ROBERT
    Youth Grows Old. 1922.
    The Cedar Box. 1929.
    Selected Poems. 1935.
NEWMAN, LOUIS I.
    Songs of Jewish Rebirth. 1921.
    Joyful Jeremiads. 1926.
OPPENHEIM, JAMES
    Monday Morning and Other Poems. 1909.
    War and Laughter. 1916.
    The Book of Self. 1917.
    The Solitary. 1919.
    The Sea. 1924.
PARKER, DOROTHY
    Enough Rope. 1927.
    Sunset Gun. 1928.
    Death and Taxes. 1931.
    Collected Poems. 1936.
PHILLIPS, MRS. GERTIE STEWART
    Blown Leaves and Petals. 1934.
PULITZER, WALTER
    A Cynic's Meditations. 1906.
RASKIN, PHILIP MAX
    Songs and Dreams. 1920.
    When a Soul Sings. 1922.
    Poems for Young Israel. 1928.
    Selected Poems. 1932.
    Lanterns in the Wind. 1937.
RECHT, CHARLES
    Manhattan Made. 1930.
REZNIKOFF, CHARLES
    Poems. 1920.
    Five Groups of Verse. 1927.

Jerusalem the Golden. 1934.
In Memoriam: 1933. 1934.
Separate Way. 1936.

ROTH, SAMUEL
Europe. 1919.

RYSKIND, MORRIE
Unaccustomed As I Am. 1921.

SAMPTER, JESSE
Around the Year in Rhymes. 1920.
Emek. 1927.
Brand Plucked from the Fire. 1937.

SCHNEIDER, ISIDOR
The Temptation of Anthony. 1928.
Comrade: Mister. 1934.

SILVER, DEBBIE H.
Scenario. 1925.

SILVERMAN, HIRSCH LAZAAR
In the Abysm of Time. 1938.

SPEAR, THELMA
First Fruits. 1927.

STEIN, EVALEEN
Child Songs of Cheer. 1918.
Troubadour Tales. 1929.

UNTERMEYER, JEAN STARR
Growing Pains. 1918.
Dreams Out of Darkness. 1922.
Steep Ascent. 1927.
The Winged Child. 1936.

UNTERMEYER, LOUIS
First Love. 1911.
Challenge. 1914.
These Times. 1917.
The New Adam. 1920.
Roast Leviathan. 1923.
Burning Bush. 1928.
Food and Drink. 1932.

Parodies:
The Younger Quire. 1911.
And Other Poets. 1916.
Including Horace. 1919.
Heavens. 1922.
Collected Parodies. 1926.

WAGNER, CHARLES A.
Poems of the Sea and Soil. 1930.

4. Autobiographies of American Jews

ANTIN, BENJAMIN
   The Gentleman from the 22nd. 1927.
ANTIN, MARY
   From Plotzk to Boston. 1899.
   The Promised Land. 1912.
BEIN, ALBERT
   Youth in Hell. 1930.
BOGEN, BORIS
   Born a Jew. 1930.
COWEN, PHILIP
   Memories of an American Jew. 1932.
COURNOS, JOHN
   Autobiography. 1935.
EDMAN, IRWIN
   A Philosopher's Holiday. 1938.
FERBER, EDNA
   A Peculiar Treasure. 1939.
FERBER, NAT JOSEPH
   Exclusive Story. 1937.
FREEMAN, JOSEPH
   An American Testament. 1936.
FROHMAN, DANIEL
   Encore. 1937.

AUTOBIOGRAPHIES

GESSNER, ROBERT
Some of My Best Friends Are Jews. 1936.
GOMPERS, SAMUEL
Seventy Years of Life and Labor. 1925.
HINDUS, MAURICE
Green Worlds. 1938.
HOROWITZ, LOUIS J.
The Towers of New York: the Memories of a Master Builder. 1937.
KLEIN, HENRY H.
My Last Fifty Years. 1935.
KOHUT, REBEKAH
My Portion. 1925.
LEVINGER, LEE J.
A Jewish Chaplain in France. 1921.
MAYER, EDWIN JUSTUS
A Preface to Life. 1925.
MENKEN, ALICE DAVIS
On the Side of Mercy. 1933.
MORGENTHAU, HENRY, SR.
All in a Lifetime. 1922.
My Trip around the World. 1928.
I Was Sent to Athens. 1929.
Ambassador Morgenthau's Story. 1938.
MORTON, LEAH
I Am a Woman and a Jew. 1926.
RAVAGE, MARCUS ELI
An American in the Making. 1917.
ROSENBACH, A. S. W.
A Book Hunter's Holiday. 1936.
SAMUEL, MAURICE
I, the Jew. 1927.
STERN, ELIZABETH G.
My Mother and I. 1917.
STRAUSS, OSCAR
Under Four Administrations. 1922.

AUTOBIOGRAPHIES

WALD, LILLIAN D.
   The House on Henry Street. 1915.
   Windows on Henry Street. 1934.
WOLF, SIMON
   The Presidents I Have Known from 1860-1918. 1918.

5. *Biographies Written by American Jews*

ADLER, CYRUS
    Jacob Schiff. 1926.
BERCOVICI, KONRAD
    Alexander. 1931.
    That Royal Lover: Carol of Rumania. 1931.
BERNSTEIN, HERMAN
    Herbert Hoover. 1928.
BROWNE, LEWIS
    That Man Heine. 1927.
COBLENTZ, STANTON A.
    Villains and Vigilantes. 1936.
COURNOS, JOHN
    A Modern Plutarch. 1928.
DAVIS, VIRGINIA H.
    The Youth of Chateaubriand. 1917.
    Bird of God: El Greco. 1929.
DE CASTRO, ADOLPHE D.
    Portrait of Ambrose Bierce. 1929.
DeCASSERES, BENJAMIN
    James Gibbon Huneker. 1925.
    Robinson Jeffers. 1928.
    Spinoza. 1932.
DEUTCH, HERMAN B.
    Incredible Yanqui. 1931.

BIOGRAPHIES

ENDORE, SAMUEL GUY
    Casanova. 1929.
    The Sword of God. 1931.

FERBER, NAT J.
    Rebels. 1920.

FRANKLIN, FABIAN
    The Life of Daniel Coit Gilman. 1910.

GABRIEL, GILBERT W.
    Famous Pianists and Composers. 1928.

GOLD, MICHAEL
    John Brown. 1928.

GOLDBERG, ISAAC
    Sir William S. Gilbert. 1913.
    The Man Mencken. 1925.
    The Theatre of George Jean Nathan. 1926.
    Havelock Ellis. 1926.
    George Gershwin. 1931.
    Queen of Hearts: The Life and Loves of Lola Montez. 1935.
    Major Noah. 1936.

HELLMAN, GEORGE S.
    The True Stevenson. 1925.
    Washington Irving, Esq. 1925.

JOSEPHSON, MATTHEW
    Zola and His Time. 1928.
    Jean Jacques Rousseau. 1931.
    The Robber Barons. 1934.
    The Politicos. 1938.

KAUN, ALEXANDER
    Leonid Andreyev. 1924.
    Maxim Gorky and His Russia. 1931.

KOHUT, REBEKAH
    As I Know Them. 1929.
    George Alexander Kohut. 1936.

LEVINE, ISAAC DON
    The Man Lenin. 1924.
    Stalin. 1931.

BIOGRAPHIES

MARCOSSON, ISAAC F.
    Charles Frohman, Manager and Man. 1917.
    David Graham Phillips and His Times. 1932.

MORDELL, ALBERT
    Quaker Militant: John Greenleaf Whittier. 1933.

RAVAGE, MARCUS ELI
    Five Men of Frankfort. 1929.
    Empress Innocence: the Life of Marie Louise. 1931.

ROTHSCHILD, RICHARD G.
    Jefferson, Lenin, Socrates. 1936.

SACHS, EMANIE
    The Terrible Siren: Victoria Woodhall. 1927.

SELDES, GEORGE
    Sawdust Caesar. 1935.

STONE, IRVING
    Dear Theo: Vincent Van Gogh. 1937.
    Life of Jack London. 1938.

UNTERMEYER, LOUIS
    Heinrich Heine. 1938.

WALDMAN, MILTON
    Sir Walter Raleigh. 1928.
    Elizabeth. 1933.
    Jean of Arc. 1935.
    Catherine de Medici and Her Children. 1936.

WERNER, M. R.
    Barnum. 1924.
    Brigham Young. 1925.
    Bryan. 1929.

YARMOLINSKY, AVRAHM
    Dostoievsky. 1924.
    Turgenev. 1926.

6. Books of Criticism and Belles-Lettres by Jewish Authors in America

BRUDNO, EZRA S.
    The Ghosts of Yesterday. 1935.
BURNSHAW, STANLEY A.
    Andre Spire and His Poetry. 1933.
COBLENTZ, STANTON A.
    The Literary Revolution. 1927.
DeCASSERES, BENJAMIN
    Mirrors of New York. 1925.
    Forty Imortals. 1925.
    The Superman in America. 1929
    The Muse of Lies. 1934.
DEUTSCH, BABETTE
    This Age. 1929.
    Portable Gold: Some Notes on Poetry and This Modern Poetry. 1935.
GOLDBERG, ISAAC
    A Study of Modern Satire. 1913.
    Studies in Spanish American Literature. 1922.
    Brazilian Literature. 1922.
    The Drama of Transition. 1922.
    Panorama. 1927.
    The Story of Gilbert and Sullivan. 1928.
    The Fine Art of Living. 1929.
    Tin Pan Alley. 1930.

CRITICISM AND BELLES-LETTRES

    The German Jew (with A. A. Myerson). 1933.
HELLMAN, GEORGE S.
    Later Essayists. 1921.
    The Way It Ended. 1921.
    Lanes of Memory. 1927.
JOSEPHSON, MATTHEW
    Portrait of the Artist as American. 1930.
    Nazi Culture. 1933.
KIRSTEIN, LINCOLN
    The Dance. 1935.
LAWSON, JOHN HOWARD
    Theory and Technique of Playwriting. 1936.
LEWISOHN, LUDWIG
    German Style. 1910.
    The Modern Drama. 1915.
    The Spirit of Modern German Literature. 1916.
    Poets of Modern France. 1918.
    The Drama and the Stage. 1922.
    The Creative Life. 1924.
    Cities and Men. 1927.
    Expression in America. 1932.
    Creative America. 1933.
    Permanent Horizon. 1934.
MORDELL, ALBERT
    The Shifting of Literary Values. 1912.
    Dante and Other Waning Classics. 1915.
    The Erotic Motive in Literature. 1919.
    The Literature of Ecstasy. 1921.
    Notorious Literary Attacks. 1926.
NATHAN, GEORGE JEAN
    Another Book on the Theatre. 1915.
    Bottoms Up. 1917.
    Mr. George Jean Nathan Presents. 1917.
    The Popular Theatre. 1918.
    Comedians All. 1919.
    The Theatre, the Drama, the Girls. 1921.
    The Critic and the Drama. 1922.

CRITICISM AND BELLES-LETTRES

    The World in Falseface. 1923.
    Materia Critica. 1924.
    The House of Satan. 1926.
    Art of the Night. 1928.
    Monk. 1929.
    Monks Are Monks. 1930.
    Testament of a Critic. 1931.
    Intimate Notebooks. 1932.
    Since Ibsen. 1933.
    Passing Judgments. 1935.
    Theatre of the Moment. 1936.
    Sociological Essays:
    Europe after 8:15. 1914 (with H. L. Mencken).
    A Book without a Title. 1918.
    The American Credo. 1920 (with H. L. Mencken).
    The Autobiography of an Attitude. 1925.
    Land of the Pilgrim's Pride. 1927.
    The New American Credo. 1927.

ROBACK, A. A.
    Jewish Influence in Modern Thought. 1929.
    Curiosities of Yiddish Literature. 1933.

ROSENFELD, PAUL
    Musical Portraits. 1920.
    Musical Chronicle, 1917-1923. 1923.
    Port of New York. 1924.
    Men Seen. 1925.
    Modern Tendencies in Music. 1927.
    By Way of Art. 1928.
    An Hour with American Music. 1929.
    Discoveries of a Music Critic. 1936.

SCHNEIDER, ISIDOR
    Proletarian Literature in the United States. 1935.

STRUNSKY, SIMEON
    The Impatient Observer and His Friends. 1911.
    Post-Impressions. 1914.
    Belshazzar Court. 1914.
    Sinbad and His Friends. 1921.

7. General Bibliography

ABRAHAMS, ISRAEL. A History of Jewish Literature. Phila., 1899. The Book of Delight and Other Papers. Phila., 1912. By-Paths in Hebraic Bookland. Phila., 1920.

ACKLAM, F. ELVA. Jewish Life in Modern Literature; a Bibliography. Madison, Wisconsin, 1930, 19-25.

BALDWIN, EDWARD C. Our Modern Debt to Israel. Boston, 1913. "The Jewish Genius in Literature," *Menorah Journal*, I, No. 3 (June, 1915), 164-172.

BIGELOW, POULTNEY. "My Friend the Jew," *The American Parade*, April, 1926, 43-48.

BLOCH, JOSHUA. Nazi-Germany and the Jews. An Annotated Bibliography. New York, American Jewish Committee, 1936.

BODENHEIM, MAXWELL. "Jewish Writers in America," *Menorah Journal*, VIII, No. 2 (April, 1922), 74-78.

BRITT, GEORGE. "Can Prejudice Survive Publicity?" *Opinion*, I (February 1, 1932), 6.

BROUN, HEYWOOD and BRITT, GEORGE. Christians Only. New York, Vanguard, 1931.

BROWN, JOHN MASON. Two on the Aisle. New York, W. W. Norton, 1938. Contains discussions of the following plays of Jewish dramatists: S. N. Behrman's *End of Summer* (142-145); Sidney Kingsley's *Men in White* (171-173); George S. Kaufman and Moss Hart's *You Can't Take It with You* (177-180); Elmer Rice's *We, The People* (204-208); George Sklar's *Stevedore* (211-

GENERAL BIBLIOGRAPHY

215); John Wexley's *They Shall Not Die* (211-212); Clifford Odets' *Waiting for Lefty* (215-217); *Awake and Sing* (217-219); *Golden Boy* (220-222); Marc Blitzstein's *The Cradle Will Rock* (224-226); Harold Rome and Charles Freedman's *Pins and Needles* (226-228); Julius J. and Philip Epstein's *And Stars Remain* (259-260); George S. Kaufman's *Of Thee I Sing* (282-286); *I'd Rather Be Right* (286-289).

COHEN, GEORGE. The Jews in the Making of America. Boston, Stratford, 1924.

COLEMAN, EDWARD D. The Bible in English Drama: An Annotated List of Plays Including Translations from Other Languages. New York, The New York Public Library, 1931. "The Jew in English Drama, An Annotated Bibliography," *Bulletin of the New York Public Library*, XLII (November, 1938), 827-850; XLII (December, 1938), 919-932; XLIII (January, 1939), 45-52.

COLEMAN, EDWARD D. "Jewish Prototypes in American and English *Romans* and *Drames à clef*," *Publications of the American Jewish Historical Society*, No. 35 (1934), 227-280. "Plays of Jewish Interest on the American Stage, 1752-1821," *Publications of the American Jewish Historical Society*, No. 33 (1934), 171-198.

CORBIN, JOHN. "Drama and the Jew," *Scribner's Magazine*, XCIII (May, 1933), 295-300.

DALY, CHARLES P. The Settlement of Jews in North America. New York, 1893.

DAVIDSON, MORRIS. "A Symposium on Hebraic Tendencies in Modern Art," *Opinion*, I (January 11, 1932), 10, 12.

DOBSEVAGE, I. GEORGE. "A Classified List of Standard Books in English on Jewish Subjects," *American Jewish Year Book*, XXV (1923), 213-214, 232-237.

FAGIN, N. BRYLLION. "Fannie Hurst," *The Reflex*, I (October, 1927), 109-114.

FRANK, FLORENCE KIPER. "The Jew as Jewish Artist," *Poetry*, XXII (1923), 209-12.

FRIEDMAN, HELEN MARIE. Suggestive Outline for the Study of English Translations of Yiddish Fiction, Drama, Poetry. Cleveland, 1931.

GENERAL BIBLIOGRAPHY

FRIEDUS, A. S. List of Dramas in the New York Public Library Relating to the Jews, and of Dramas in Hebrew, Judeo-Spanish, and Judeo-German; together with Essays on the Jewish Stage. New York, 1907.

FUCHS, JAMES. "Fiction and Fictions," *The Reflex*, I (September, 1927), 10-15. Discusses fiction of the Ghetto by Israel Zangwill, Abraham Cahan, and Samuel Ornitz.

GABRIEL, GILBERT W. "Are We Like That?" *Jewish Chronicle* (Newark, N. J.), XXV (May 12, 1933), 5. "The Jew in Falseface," *New Palestine*, XVI (1929), 279-280.

GOLDBERG, ISAAC. Major Noah: American Jewish Pioneer. Philadelphia, Jewish Publication Society, 1936.

GOLDSTEIN, FANNY. Recent Judaica: a List of Books of Jewish Interest Recently Added to the Library. Brief Reading Lists Nos. 45, 46. Boston, Boston Public Library, 1937, 1938.

HALPER, ALBERT. "Notes on Jewish-American Fiction," *Menorah Journal*, XVII (April-June, 1932), 61-69.

HAMILTON, CLAYTON. Seen on the Stage. New York, 1920. Chapter XXIV, "The Jewish Art Theatre," 176-183.

HAPGOOD, HUTCHINS. The Spirit of the Ghetto. New York, 1902.

HEARN, LAFCADIO. Occidental Gleanings. Edited by Albert Mordell. New York, 1925. "The Jew upon the Stage," 184-189.

THE JEWISH ENCYCLOPEDIA. Volumes I-XII. New York, 1905.

KANE, JOSEPH NATHAN. "The Jew on the Modern English Stage," *American Hebrew*, CVI (1919), 72, 101.

KARPELES, GUSTAV. Jewish Literature and Other Essays. Philadelphia, 1895.

KORNFELD, MURIEL G. "Drama and the Jew," *Hebrew Standard*, LXXVII (November 5, 1920), 4-6.

KRUTCH, JOSEPH WOOD. "The Random Satire of George S. Kaufman," *The Nation*, Vol. 137 (August 9, 1933), 156-158.

LANDA, MYER JACK. The Jew in Drama. London, P. S. King, 1926.

LANDMAN, ISAAC. "Jews and Present-day Dramatic Art," *Jewish Exponent*, XLVIII (November 20, 1908), 1.

LAZARON, MORRIS S. Common Ground. New York, Liveright, 1938.

GENERAL BIBLIOGRAPHY

LEISER, JOSEPH. "The Development of the Jew in the Drama," Review, IX (May, 1914), 11-21. Philadelphia.

LESSER, ALLEN. Weave a Wreath of Laurel. New York, Coven Press, 1938.

LEVIN, MEYER. "Maurice Schwartz," Opinion, I (May 23, 1932), 10-12.

LEVI, HARRY. Jewish Characters in Fiction. Philadelphia, The Jewish Chautauqua Society, 1911. 170-173.

LEWISOHN, LUDWIG. Expression in America. New York, 1932. Rebirth: A Book of Modern Jewish Thought. New York, 1936. Israel. New York, 1925. This People, New York, 1933. "On Jewish Literature," The Jewish Layman, XIII (February, 1939), 6-7, 10-11. "Jewish Literature in Europe," Opinion, I (February 29, 1932), 6-7.

LOGGINS, VERNON. I Hear America. Literature in the United States since 1900. New York, Crowell, 1937. Contains critical analyses of the work of Dorothy Parker, Robert Nathan and Fannie Hurst.

LYON, MABEL. "Some Recent Plays of Jewish Interest," Jewish Exponent, LVIII (October 17, 1913), 1-2. Philadelphia.

MANLY, JOHN M., and RICKERT, EDITH. Contemporary American Literature. Contains Bibliographies up to 1929 for the following American Jewish authors: Konrad Bercovici, Maxwell Bodenheim, John Cournos, Nathalia Crane, Babette Deutsch, Edna Ferber, Waldo Frank, Ben Hecht, Fannie Hurst, G. S. Kaufman, J. H. Lawson, Ludwig Lewisohn, Phillip Moeller, G. J. Nathan, Robert Nathan, James Oppenheim, Simeon Strunsky, Louis Untermeyer. New York, Harcourt, Brace, 1929.

MANTLE, BURNS. Contemporary American Playwrights. Contains discussions of the dramas of the following American Jewish dramatists: George S. Kaufman, Moss Hart (8-20); Sidney Kingsley (33-37); Morrie Ryskind, Ira Gershwin (46-48); Elmer Rice (54-61); S. N. Behrman (108-115); Clifford Odets (115-121); John Howard Lawson (152-154); Samson Raphaelson (155-157); John Wexley (164-165); Lillian Hellman (180-181); Victor Wolfson (181-182); Marc Blitzstein (184); Arthur Kober (186); Allen Boretz (186); Irwin Shaw (188); Leopold Atlas (189);

GENERAL BIBLIOGRAPHY

Rose Franken (190); Harry Segall (197); Laurence Gross (200); Beatrice Kaufman (201); Joseph M. Viertel (202-203); Gertrude Tonkonogy (207); Arthur Guiterman (217); Lawrence Langner (227-229); Bella and Samuel Spewack (230-231); Jules Eckert Goodman (234-235); Julius J. and Philip Epstein (239-240); Sid and Laura Perelman (240); Gilbert Seldes (245); Ben Hecht (247-248); Edwin Justus Mayer (250-251); Louis Weitzenkorn (251-252); Max Marcin (260); Edna Ferber (265); Fannie Hurst (270); Edgar Selwyn (280); Arthur Richman (283-284). New York, Dodd, Mead, 1938.

MANTLE, BURNS, and SHERWOOD, GARRISON P. *The Best Plays of 1909-1919.* New York, Dodd, Mead, 1933. Discussion with excerpts of Louis K. Anspacher's *The Unchastened Woman* (239-280).

MANTLE, BURNS. *The Best Plays of 1921-1922,* New York, Dodd, Mead, 1922. Discussions and abridgment of *Dulcy,* by George S. Kaufman and Marc Connolly, and *Ambush,* by Arthur Richman. *The Best Plays of 1922-1923.* Discussion and abridgment of *Merton of the Movies,* by George S. Kaufman and Edna Ferber. *The Best Plays of 1923-24.* Discussion and abridgment of *Beggar on Horseback,* by George S. Kaufman and Marc Connelly. *The Best Plays of 1924-1925.* Discussion and abridgment of *The Firebrand,* by Edwin Justus Mayer; *Dancing Mothers,* by Edgar Selwyn and Edmund Goulding; *Minick,* by George S. Kaufman and Edna Ferber. *The Best Plays of 1925-1926.* Discussion and abridgment of *The Butter and Egg Man,* by George S. Kaufman. *The Best Plays of 1927-1928.* Discussion and abridgment of George S. Kaufman's and Edna Ferber's *The Royal Family.* *The Best Plays of 1928-1929.* Discussion and abridgment of *Street Scene,* by Elmer Rice; *The Front Page,* by Ben Hecht and Charles MacArthur. *The Best Plays of 1929-1930.* Discussion and abridgment of *The Last Mile,* by John Wexley; *June Moon,* by George S. Kaufman and Ring Lardner. *The Best Plays of 1930-1931.* Discussion and abridgment of *Once in a Lifetime,* by George S. Kaufman and Moss Hart; *Five-Star Final,* by Louis Weitzenkorn. *The Best Plays of 1931-1932.* Discussion and abridgment of *Of Thee I Sing,* by George S. Kaufman and Morrie Ryskind; *The*

GENERAL BIBLIOGRAPHY

Left Bank, by Elmer Rice; *Another Language,* by Rose Franken; *Brief Moment,* by S. N. Behrman.

MELAMED, S. M. "Illusion and Reality," *The Reflex,* I (July 1927), 3-10. On Jewish interest in drama.

MELS, EDGAR. "The Jews as Portrayed in Stage Fiction," *Reform Advocate,* XXXV (1908), 218-221, 252-255.

MICHAUD, REGIS. The American Novel Today. Boston, Little, Brown, 1928. Discusses the following Jewish novelists: Waldo Frank, 13-16, 22, 254, 255-256; Ben Hecht, 271-274.

PATTEE, FRED LEWIS. A History of American Literature since 1870. New York, Century, 1915. Critical discussions of Emma Lazarus, 322, 336-338; Adah Isaacs Menken, 51; Horace Traubel, 165-185.

PHILIPSON, DAVID. The Jew in English Fiction. New York, Bloch, 1918.

ROSENBACH, A. S. W. "List of Jewish Books and Pamphlets by Jews or Relating to Them, Printed in the United States, from the Establishment of the Press in the Colonies until 1850," *Publications of the American Jewish Historical Society,* XXX (1926).

RUDENS, S. P. "The Evolution of Ben Hecht," *The Reflex,* I (July, 1927), 74-78.

SAMUEL, MAURICE. "Judaea Americana," *Opinion,* I (February 8, 1932), 6-7. (February 22), 8-10.

SCHNEIDER, REBECCA. Bibliography of Jewish Life in the Fiction of America and England. Albany, New York State Library School, 1916.

SCHWARZ, LEO W. A Golden Treasury of Jewish Literature. New York, Farrar & Rinehart, 1937. The Jewish Caravan. New York, Farrar & Rinehart, 1935.

SELDES, GILBERT. "Jewish Plays and Jew-Plays in New York," *Menorah Journal,* VIII (1922), 236-240.

SIMON, LEON. Aspects of Jewish Genius. New York, 1915.

SMERTENKO, JOHAN J. "Racial Genius and Art," *Opinion,* I (Jan. 25, 1932), 16.

SPARGO, JOHN. The Jew and American Ideals. New York, 1921.

SPITZ, LEON. "The Jewish Scene in the Days of Washington," *Opinion,* I (February 22, 1932), 12-13.

GENERAL BIBLIOGRAPHY

STERLING, ADA. The Jew and Civilization. Chapters VII and VIII. "The Jew in Literature." New York, Aetco, 1924.

SYRKIN, MARIE. "American Yiddish Poetry." *Reflex,* I (Sept. 1927), 106-110.

TRENT, WILLIAM P., ERSKINE, JOHN, SHERMAN, STUART P., and VAN DOREN, CARL. The Cambridge History of American Literature. New York, Putnams, 1917-1921. Critical references to the following American Jewish authors: Historical and Critical Bibliography of Yiddish Literature in America, Volume IV, 822-826; David Belasco, IV, 763-764; Charles Klein, IV, 769-770; Franklin P. Adams, III, 22; Louis K. Anspacher, III, 294; Mary Antin, III, 420; Abraham Cahan, IV, 600, 601, 605, 606, 607; J. N. Cardozo, IV, 591; Gustav Cohen, IV, 443; Lorenzo Da Ponte, IV, 449-50; Angelo Heilprin, III, 167; Charles Klein, III, 281, 286-7, 289, 293; Emma Lazarus, III, 47, 121-122; Martha Morton, III, 290; Elmer Rice, III, 295; Abraham Cahan, IV, 606-607; E. R. A. Seligman, III, 359; Louis K. Anspacher, III, 294.

UNTERMEYER, LOUIS. American Poetry since 1900. New York, Holt, 1920. Discusses the poetry of Maxwell Bodenheim, 169, 192, 197, 333-339; Alter Brody, 330-332; John Cournos, 308; Babette Deutsch, 387; Robert Nathan, 381; James Oppenheim, 264-275; Jean Starr Untermeyer, 227-233.

WAGNER, CHARLES A. "Song-Roots of Poetry," *Opinion,* II (Aug. 29, 1932), 11-12.

WARFEL, HARRY R. The American Mind; Selections from the Literature of the United States. New York, American Book Company, 1937. Contains selections from the writings of Emma Goldman, Anzia Yezierska, David Cohn, Louis D. Brandeis, and Horace M. Kallen.

WAXMAN, MEYER. A History of Jewish Literature. Vols. I-IV. New York, Bloch, 1930-1936.

FOOTNOTES

CHAPTER 1

[1] Reprinted by permission of *Atlantic Monthly*.

CHAPTER 2

[1] Reprinted by permission of Mr. George S. Kaufman.
[2] Reprinted by permission of Mr. George S. Kaufman and *The Nation*.
[3] "The Random Satire of George S. Kaufman," *The Nation*, August 9, 1933, pp. 156-8.

CHAPTER 4

[1] *New York World-Telegram*, March 19, 1935.
[2] *New York Daily Mirror*.
[3] The *New Republic*.
[4] *New York Daily Mirror*.

CHAPTER 10

[1] *Herald-Tribune* Books.
[2] Reprinted by permission of Robert Nathan.
[3] Reprinted by permission of Robert Nathan.
[4] Reprinted by permission of Robert Nathan.
[5] Reprinted by permission of Robert Nathan.
[6] Reprinted by permission of Robert Nathan.
[7] Reprinted by permission of Robert Nathan.
[8] Reprinted by permission of Robert Nathan.
[9] Reprinted by permission of Robert Nathan.
[10] Reprinted by permission of Robert Nathan.
[11] Reprinted by permission of Robert Nathan.
[12] Reprinted by permission of Robert Nathan and Alfred A. Knopf, Inc.
[13] Reprinted by permission of Robert Nathan and Alfred A. Knopf, Inc.

CHAPTER 12

[1] *American Literature Since 1870*, New York, 1915, p. 338.
[2] *Storm Beach*, New York, 1933, reprinted with permission of Houghton Mifflin.
[3] *American Literature Since 1870*, p. 337.
[4] *American Literature Since 1870*, p. 338.
[5] Allen Lesser, "La Belle Menken," *The Menorah Journal*, Spring 1937, p. 213.
[6] For a complete discussion of the origin and career of early American Jewish periodicals, see Bernard Postal, "The Early American Jewish Press," *The Reflex* (April, 1928), 68-77.

CHAPTER 13

[1] To, Publishers, 1932.
[2] *The Sea*, New York, 1924, p. ix.
[3] *The Sea*, p. ix.
[4] *Modern American and British Poetry*, New York, 1928, p. 46.
[5] Louis Untermeyer, *Modern American and British Poetry*, 1928, p. 235.
[6] *The Bookman*, LXVII (May, 1928), p. 302.

CHAPTER 14

[1] Lee M. Freedman, "Judah Monis," *American Jewish Historical Society Publications*, No. 22 (1914), pp. 1-24.
[2] Judah Monis, *The Truth*, Boston, 1722, p. iii.
[3] See Israel Abrahams, "Isaac Pinto's Prayer-Book," in *By-Paths in Hebraic Bookland*, Philadelphia, 1920, pp. 171-177. Compare with *The Jewish Encyclopedia*, Vol. X, p. 54.
[4] Morris Jastrow, Jr., "References to Jews in the Diary of Ezra Stiles," *A. J. H. S.*, X, pp. 6-36.
[5] Joseph Jacobs, "The Original of Scott's Rebecca," *A. J. H. S.*, XXII (1914), pp. 53-60; Gratz van Rensselaer in *Century Magazine*, 1880; *The Jewish Record*, Philadelphia, April 6, 1877. Cf. John Haynes Holmes, "*Ivanhoe* after a Century," *Opinion*, III (December, 1932), pp. 26-27.
[6] *Life of Henry Wadsworth Longfellow, With Extracts from his Journal and Correspondence*, Edited by Samuel Longfellow, Boston, 1891, II, 239.
[6a] Edward Wagenknecht, *Mark Twain, The Man and His Work*, New Haven, 1935, p. 237.
[7] For a complete study of the Jew in European drama, consult M. J. Landa, *The Jew in Drama*, London, 1928, and of the Jew in English Drama consult Edward Coleman in *Bulletin of the New York Public Library*, November, 1938, pp. 827-850 and later issues.
[8] Consult Herbert Friedenwald, "Jews Mentioned in the Journal of the Continental Congress," *A. J. H. S. Publications*, I, 65-89.

CHAPTER 15

[1] Edward D. Coleman, "Plays of Jewish Interest on the American Stage 1752-1821," *Publications of the American Jewish Historical Society*, No. 33, 1934, p. 198.

CHAPTER 18

[1] These lines were written before Toller's tragic suicide in New York, on May 22, 1939.

INDEX

Abbot, Abiel, 152
Abie's Irish Rose, 27, 166, 176
Adams, Franklin P., 16, 17, 128, 129, 140
Adding Machine, The, 26, 30, 31
Address on Democracy, 156
Adler, Jacob P., 43
Admetus, 120, 156
Aeschylus, 37
Alide, 121
Altar in the Fields, An, 92
American Beauty, 80
American Caravan, The, 130
American in the Making, An, 84
American Jewish Yearbook, 158
American Landscape, 25, 198
American Way, The, 10, 14, 24
Anderson, Maxwell, 4, 7, 15, 49, 51, 98, 117, 185
Another Language, 9, 11
Ansky, S., 176
Anspacher, Louis, 15
Anthony, Edward, 144
Antin, Mary, 119
Apassionata, 81, 86
Apocrypha, 156
Apple Cart, The, 53
Aristotle, 7
Arouse and Beware, 80
Arrowsmith, 88, 160, 179
As a Man Thinks, 88, 169, 174, 183

Asch, Nathan, 78
Asch, Sholem, 178, 187
As It Was Written, 83
Atkinson, Brooks, 15, 42, 189
Atlas, Leopold, 5
Auslander, Joseph, 10, 128, 145
Autumn, 95, 96, 97, 101, 107
Awake and Sing, 4, 7, 8, 33, 34, 35, 38, 41, 43, 44, 45, 114, 172, 173, 174, 176, 184

Babbitt, 17
Bankhead, Talullah, 21
Barbusse, Henri, 190
Barly Fields, The, 131
Barron, Samuel, 6
Bay Psalm Book, The, 149
Beach, John, 150
Beer, Morris Abel, 130, 145
Beerbohm, Max, 36
Beethoven, Ludwig van, 33, 37, 192
Before Verdun, 190
Beggar on Horseback, 10
Behrman, S.N., 1, 9, 15, 16, 51-67, 101, 189, 196
Bein, Alfred, 1, 5, 7
Benefield, Barry, 162
Benefit of the Doubt, The, 162
Bennett, Arnold, 25, 95
Bergson, Henri, 54
Berman, Henry, 87

239

INDEX

Bernstein, Herman, 84
Between Two Worlds, 25, 27
Beyond Life, 111
Beyond the Horizon, 3, 26
Beyond Woman, 92
Bibliography of Jewish Life in the Fiction of America and England, 163
Bicheno, J., 152
Birthright, 193
Bishop's Wife, The, 94, 96, 97, 102, 103, 104, 110
Bisno, Beatrice, 78
Black Pit, The, 7, 8, 28
Blitzstein, Marc, 6
Bodenheim, Maxwell, 78, 128, 133, 134, 135
Boudinot, Elias, 152
Boy in the Sun, The, 90
Boy Meets Girl, 9, 11, 73, 114
Brandes, Georg, 10
Bread Givers, The, 85
Brentano, Lowell, 78
Bride of Torozko, The, 195
Brief Moment, 10, 58
Brinig, Myron, 78, 92
Brody, Catherine, 78
Broken Necks, 115
Brothers, Richard, 152
Brown, Hypkin, 160
Brown, John Mason, 43
Browning, Robert, 173
Brudno, Ezra S., 5, 78, 86
Bury the Dead, 69, 189, 190
Butter and Egg Man, The, 14

CABELL, James Branch, 98, 110
Cahan, Abraham, 78, 84
Caliban in the Coal Mines, 130
Cardigan, 159
Case of Mr. Crump, The, 81
Case of Sergeant Grischa, The, 190
Cather, Willa, 163
Cedar Box, The, 131
Chambers, Robert W., 159
Chekhov, Anton, 37, 43, 46, 48
Children of the Tenements, 160

Children's Hour, The, 11
Chosen People, The, 88
Chute, The, 80
Cimmaron, 80
City Block, 82
Clear All Wires, 9, 74
Cobb, Humphrey, 188, 191
Cohen, Lester, 78
Cohen, Octavus Roy, 78
Colman, B., 150
Comedy, defined, 54
Company, The, 80
Comrade Yetta, 87
Concerning the Jews, 157
Connelly, Marc, 14, 17, 21, 102, 104, 176, 195
Corbin, John, 3, 10, 22
Counsellor-at-Law, 9, 25, 26, 90, 167, 168, 171, 174
Cournos, John, 78
Cradle Will Rock, The, 28
Crane, Nathalia, 128
Criminal Code, The, 12
Cumberland, Richard, 165, 173
Cycle of Manhattan, A, 90

DAHLBERG, Edward, 79
Days Without End, 4
Dead End, 2, 8, 191
Death and Birth of David Markand, 82
Deutsch, Babette, 128, 138, 139
Dewey, Thomas E., 181
Diamond Lens, The, 162
Dibdin, Charles, 166
Dickens, Charles, 126, 175, 176
Differences, 83
Dinner at Eight, 10, 21
Disraeli, 156, 180, 182
Doctor Addams, 92, 179
Doctor Rast, 88
Doctor's Dilemma, The, 115
Doll's House, A, 9, 21, 36
Dos Passos, John, 94, 161
Drake, Lawrence, 79, 92
Drama Critics' Circle, The, 172, 191
Dreiser, Theodore, 98, 195

240

INDEX

Dreyfus, Case, 171, 187
Dulcy, 10, 17, 18
Dumas, Alexander, *fils*, 30, 35

EASIEST *Way, The*, 15
Edrehi, Israel, 154
Edwards, Jonathan, 152
Ehrlich, Leonard, 79
Eili, Eili, 158
Eliot, John, 152
Elmer Gantry, 160
Emerson, R.W., 33, 156, 120
Enchanted Voyage, 97, 99, 100, 108, 110
Encyclopaedia Britannica, 37
End of Summer, 10, 57
Enemy of the People, An, 12, 36, 53, 117
Engelbrecht, H.C., 175
Erik Dorn, 81, 113, 115
Essay on Comedy, 54
Eternal Road, The, 197
Euripides, 6, 37
Europa, 178
Everyman, 6
Eyeless in Gaza, 178

FABULOUS *Invalid, The*, 24
Fagin, 175, 176, 182
Fancy's Sketch Book, 119
Fanny Herself, 56, 80
Farmer Bibbins, 160
Fat of the Land, The, 85
Fate, 156
Feinstein, Martin, 128
Ferber, Edna, 14, 21, 79, 86
Le Feu, 190
Fiddler in Barly, The, 96, 97, 98, 107, 108
Fineman, Irving, 79, 90, 179, 186
First Editions of American Authors, 122
First Lady, 24
First Legion, The, 185
Fleg, Edmond, 113
Forever Wilt Thou Love, 81
Foundry, The, 80
Fountains Opened, The, 150
Four Walls, 174

Frank, Waldo, 82, 92
Franken, Rose, 9, 11
Frederic, Harold, 160
Freedman, David, 79
Freud, Sigmund, 54
Friedman, Harold, 200
Friedman, Isaac Kahn, 85
From Polotsk to Boston, 84
Front Page, The, 9, 81
Fuchs, Daniel, 79, 91
Fugitive, The, 86

GALSWORTHY, John, 26, 30, 35, 36, 48, 179
Gargoyles, 115
Gentile Wife, The, 90, 174
Gentle People, The, 68
Gentlewoman, 169
Ghosts, 9, 36
Gilson, Etienne, 13
Glass, Montague, 87, 166
God of Might, 88
God's Angry Man, 80
Golden Boy, 4, 32, 36, 37, 47, 48
Golding, Louis, 176
Good Fellow, The, 22
Goodman, Kenneth Sawyer, 114
Gordin, I. J., 43
Gordon, William, 152
Gratz, Rebecca, 153, 159
Green Pastures, The, 102, 104
Guénée, Antoine, 152
Guiterman, Arthur, 128, 129, 140, 141

HALPER, Albert, 79
Hamlet, 8, 21, 36, 39, 164
Happy Hypocrite, The, 41
Hardy, Thomas, 25, 59, 96
Harland, Henry, 83
Hart, Moss, 14, 23
Haunch, Paunch, and Jowl, 168
Hauptmann, Gerhart, 7, 30, 35, 49
Having Wonderful Time, 176
Hearn, Lafcadio, 157
Harby, Isaac, 165
Hear, Ye Sons, 90, 186

INDEX

Heavenly Discourse, 104
Hecht, Ben, 9, 25, 76, 79, 81, 112-117
Hedda Gabler, 9, 36
Heenan, John Carmel, 124, 126
Heine, Heinrich, 10, 182
Helen of Troy, New York, 21
Hellman, Lillian, 11
Hemingway, Ernest, 161
Henry, O., 161, 162
Herrick, Robert, 163
Hersch, Virginia D., 79, 119
Hiawatha, 154
Hoffenstein, Samuel, 128, 130, 142
Holmes, John Haynes, 158, 191
Holmes, Oliver Wendell, 156
Homage to Blenholt, 91
Hook, Sidney, 10
Hooray for What, 200
Hopkins, Arthur, 5
Hotten, John Camden, 126
House of Mirth, The, 161
House of Rothschild, The, 183
Howard, Sidney, 51, 171
Humoresque, 119
Huneker, James, 158, 161
Hurst, Fannie, 79, 85, 119, 174, 175, 195
Huxley, Aldous, 178

IBSEN, 6, 9, 12, 21, 33, 36, 49, 53, 117
I Can Get It for You Wholesale, 97
I Can't Sleep, 45
Idiot's Delight, 191
I'd Rather Be Right, 15, 17, 21, 22, 24
If This Be Treason, 191
Imperial City, 25, 28, 31
Importance of Being Ernest, The, 56
Imported Bridegroom, The, 84
Infelicia, 122-125
In Memoriam, 128
International Brigade, The, 187
International Jew, The, 162
In the Gates of Israel, 84
Irving, Washington, 153, 119
Island Within, The, 90
Israel, 2, 171, 187
Israelite, The, 123, 126, 127

It Can't Happen Here, 160
It Is to Laugh, 174
Ivanhoe, 153, 159

JEW, *The*, 165
Jew and the Doctor, The, 166
Jew in Love, A, 113, 115
Jewish Cemetery at Newport, 153
Jew of Malta, The, 165
Jew upon the Stage, The, 157
Jews Without Money, 79
Joan and Peter, 95
John Marvel, Assistant, 161
Johnny Johnson, 191
Jonah, 93, 94, 95, 102, 103, 110
Journal of R. W. Emerson, 156
Judah, Samuel, B. H., 165
Judas Maccabaeus, 155
Jude the Obscure, 59
Juden, Die, 164
Judgment Day, 2, 15, 25, 44, 194
Judith at the Tent of Holofernes, 156
Jung, 5
June Moon, 10, 22
Justice, 26, 36

KANDEL, Aben, 79
Karigal, Haim Isaac, 152, 153
Kaufman, George S., 1, 9, 10, 11, 14, 15, 49, 53, 75, 119
Kelly, Myra, 159, 162
Kerr, Alfred, 10
Kingsley, Sidney, 1, 2, 5, 7, 8, 85, 169, 183, 190, 191
King Solomon and the Ants, 156
Kirstein, Lincoln, 79
Kishinef Pogrom, 158
Kober, Arthur, 176
Kotzebue, 23
Krutch, Joseph Wood, 23, 32, 54, 112
Kultur, 193

LANGDON, Samuel, 152
Lardner, Ring, 14, 16
Lassalles, Ferdinand, 157
Last Mile, The, 2, 168

242

INDEX

Lauren, S. K., 191
Lavery, Ernest, 185
Lawson, John Howard, 1, 6, 13, 91, 169, 171
Lazarus, Emma, 118, 120, 121, 123, 127, 156
Leave It to Me, 11, 74
Left Bank, The, 25, 28
Legend of Rabbi Ben Levi, 154
Leivick, Halper, 199
Lessing, Bruno, 79
Lessing, G. E., 164, 165, 173, 179, 182, 185
Let Freedom Ring, 79
Levi, David, 152
Levin, Meyer, 79, 85, 176
Levy, Melvin P., 79
Levy, Newman, 128, 141
Lewis, Sinclair, 17, 24, 63, 88, 98, 160, 179
Lewisohn, Ludwig, 2, 10, 79, 81, 90, 92, 171, 187, 189
Lieberman, Elias, 145
Life's Too Short, 170
Little Aliens, 159
Little Citizens, 159
Little Conscript, The, 86
Little Foxes, The, 11
Longfellow, H. W. 126, 152, 153, 154
Lopez, Abraham, 152
Lopez, Roderigo, 165
Love Is Like That, 54
Lowell, James Russell, 156
Loyalties, 179
Lummox, 86, 119

MacArthur, Charles, 9, 114
Macbeth, 6, 8, 36
Machinal, 26
Maibaum, Richard, 193
Maimonides, 179
Maltz, Albert, 5, 7, 12, 170, 189, 190
Mann, Thomas, 102
Man Who Forgot, The, 54
Marching Song, 170
Marlowe, Christopher, 165

Marx, Karl, 41
Mary of Scotland, 51
Masefield, John, 4
Masque of Kings, The, 51
Mather, Cotton, 150
Mather, Increase, 150, 158
Mather, Richard, 149
Maupassant, Guy de, 25
Maurice, Arthur B., 25
Mayer, Edwin J., 102
Mayer, Nathan, 83
McCarter, Margaret H., 159
Melting Pot, The, 176
Mencken, H. L., 24, 158
Mendelssohn, Moses, 166, 182
Menken, Adah Isaacs, 122, 123, 124, 125, 127, 155
Men in White, 8, 88, 169, 179, 183, 191
Men Must Fight, 191
Merchant of Venice, The, 165, 175, 182, 183
Merrily We Roll Along, 10, 23, 24, 169
Merry-Go-Round, 12
Merton of the Movies, 21
Meteor, 10
Midnight on the Desert, 178
Mielziner, Jo, 6
Millin, Sarah G., 11
Miss Swan Expects, 72, 76
Modern American Poetry, 133
Modern American Poets, 133
Moise, Penina, 118, 119, 120
Monis, Judah, 150
Moon Calf, 160
Mortara, Edgar, 124
Moscovitch, Maurice, 183
Mourning Becomes Electra, 3
Mrs. Peixada, 83
Muni, Paul, 168
Music at Evening, 94
My Uncle Florimond, 83

Nathan, George Jean, 32, 51
Nathan, Robert, 10, 79, 93-111, 130
Nathan Der Weise, 165, 173, 179, 182, 185

INDEX

Neighbors, 160
Newell, Robert Henry, 125
New Exodus, The, 160
New York in Fiction, 25
New Poetry, The, 133
Newport, Jewish Colony At, 152
Nichols, Anne, 166, 176
Nicholson, Kenyon, 53, 54
Nieto, Isaac, 152
Night's Work, A, 53
Noah, 102
Noah, Mordecai, M., 152, 165
Nobles, Milton, 15
No More Peace, 197
Norris, Frank, 91
Note on a Hebrew Funeral, 157
Nothing But the Truth, 150
Nyberg, Sidney, 79, 88

OBEY, Andre, 102
O'Brien, Fitz-James, 162
O'Casey, Sean, 30
Occident, The, 120
Occidental Gleanings, 157
Octopus, The, 91
Odets, 1, 4, 5, 6, 7, 15, 27, 32, 33-45, 49, 100, 114, 167, 172, 173, 174, 176, 197
Office, The, 80
Of Mice and Men, 100
Of Thee I Sing, 10, 18 quoted, 21, 22, 28
Of Time and the River, 177
Old Bunch, The, 85
Old Maid, The, 11
On Being a Jew, 104
Once in a Lifetime, 10, 22, 75, 169
O'Neill, Eugene, 3, 4, 6, 15, 26, 32
One More Spring, 94, 96, 97, 99, 108, 110

On Trial, 31
Oppenheim, James, 88, 128, 130, 132
Orchid, The, 96, 100, 108
Ornitz, Samuel, 79, 168
Over the Teacups, 157
PAGE, Thomas Nelson, 161

Painted Veils, 161
Palmer, John, 54
Paradise Lost, 4, 34, 38, 45, 46, 48, 49
Parker, Dorothy, 128, 143
Pater, Walter, 8, 112
Paths of Glory, 171, 172, 188, 191
Pattee, Fred Lewis, 118, 120, 122
Peace on Earth, 7, 28, 189, 190
Peep between Leaves of the Talmud, A 157
Pegler, Westbrook, 186
Peter, 160
Peter Kindred, 95, 96, 97
Petrified Forest, The, 51
Phillip, Adolph, 192
Phoenix, The, 155
Pichel, Irving, 14, 17
Pillars of Society, 36
Pinafore, 22
Pins and Needles, 28, 59, 200
Pinto, D. R. Yesurun, 151
Pinto, Isaac,, 151
Pit, The, 91
Playwrights Company, 51
Poems and Translations, 120, 121
Poems in Praise of Practically Nothing, 130
Poets of America, 123
Poppa, 74
Potash and Perlmutter, 87, 166
Poritzky, J. E., 2
Priestley, Joseph B., 15, 152, 178
Private Hicks, 13, 170
Private Life of Helen of Troy, The, 102
Prize Poems, 128
Prodigal Parents, The, 63
Professor at the Breakfast Table, The, 156
Professor Bernhardi, 160, 171, 172, 179
Professor Mamlock, 44, 160, 179, 180
Promised Land, The, 84
Puppet Master, The, 95, 99, 101, 106, 107

RABBI Ben Ezra, 173
Rabbi Ismael, 156

244

INDEX

Rahab, 82
Rain From Heaven, 10, 56, 189, 196
Ravage, M. E., 84
Rawson, Mrs. Susanna, 165
Read, Thomas B., 126
Reade, Charles, 126
Reade, Leslie, 44, 193
Recht, Charles, 79, 145
Red Damask, 91
Red Salute, 184
Reigen, 113
Reinhardt, Max, 2, 55, 197
Return of the Native, The, 59
Reunion in Vienna, 51
Reznikoff, Charles, 79
Ricardo, David, 189
Rice, Elmer, 1, 2, 9, 15, 25, 44, 49, 51, 90, 167, 168, 194, 198
Riis, Jacob, 160, 162
Rise of David Levinsky, The, 84, 90, 92
Road of Ages, 93, 94, 99, 100, 105, 106, 108
Road to Rome, The, 51, 102
Rocket to the Moon, 4, 47, 48
Rome, Harold J., 200
Rosenfeld, Paul, 90
Rossetti, Dante Gabriel, 122
Rossetti, William Michael, 122
Roth, Henry, 79
Roth, Samuel, 131
Rothschild, 124, 156, 174
Royal Family, The, 14
Ryskind, Morrie, 14

SACHS, Emanie, 79, 91
Sailors of Cattaro, 28
Salome of the Tenements, 85
Salvation of Israel, The, 152
Sam Dreben, Fighting Jew, 171
Sampter, Jessie, 118, 129, 145
Samuels, Maurice, 92
"Sandalphon," 154
Sandeman, Robert, 150, 152
Schneider, Isidor, 130
Schneider, Rebecca, 162
Schnitzler, Arthur, 25, 35, 113, 160, 171, 179

School for Prejudice, The, 166
Scott, Evelyn, 159
Scott, Sir Walter, 153, 159
Scoundrel, The, 76
Seaver, Edwin, 79
Second Man, The, 10, 52, 54
Seldes, Gilbert, 94
Selwyn, Edgar, 79
Shadow and Substance, 67
Shakespeare, 6, 8, 21, 36, 39, 48, 165, 175
Shatter'd Lamp, The, 44, 193
Shaw, Bernard, 3, 6, 26, 30, 33, 35, 49, 53, 104, 115
Shaw, Irwin, 68-72, 189
Sherwood, Robert E., 51, 191
Shoemaker's Holiday, A, 59
Shofar Blew at Sunset, The, 158
Shylock, 36, 165, 173, 175, 176, 180, 182, 183
Siegel, Eli, 128
Simpleton of the Unexpected Isles, The, 104
Singer, I. J., 176
Sing out the News, 200
Sklar, George, 1, 7, 12, 189, 190
Slaves in Algiers, 165
Slesinger, Tess, 79, 81
Smith, F. Hopkinson, 160
Some Thoughts on Christianity, 150
Songs of a Semite, 121
Spagnoletto, The, 121
Spewack, Bella and Samuel, 9, 11, 17, 29, 43, 73-77, 114, 173, 174, 176
Spitzer, Marion, 79
Spoon River Anthology, 33, 38
Spring Song, 9, 11, 29, 43, 74, 173, 174, 176
Stage Door, 24, 80
Star in the West, 152
Steel, 15
Stehelin, J. P., 154
Stephen Escott, 81
Stern, G. B., 11
Stevedore, 7, 8, 28
Stiles, Ezra, 153
Stone, Charles Stuart, 122

INDEX

Stone, Irving, 79
Stone, L. C., 79
Storm Beach, 119, 120
Strange Interlude, 3, 15
Street Scene, 9, 25, 26, 28, 31, 49, 167
Subway, The, 26
Success Story, 13, 33, 91, 171
Sun Also Rises, The, 161
Susannah and the Elders, 102
Symphony of Six Million, 86

TALES *of Chicago Streets,* 115
Tales of a Wayside Inn, 154
Talmud, The, 172
Temptation of Anthony, The, 130
Ten Million Ghosts, 190, 191
Tether, The, 86
Theatre Union, 27
There is Another Heaven, 94, 102, 104
They Shall Not Die, 12, 168
They Who Knock at Our Gates, 84
Thomas, Augustus, 88, 169, 179, 183
Three-Cornered Moon, 11
Three Discourses, 150
Three Soldiers, 161
Three Waltzes, 169
Till the Day I Die, 4, 6, 34, 38, 44, 45, 197
Toller, Ernst, 2, 35, 55, 187, 197
Tonkonogy, Gertrude, 11
To Quito and Back, 81, 114, 115
To the Ladies, 10, 21
Traditions of the Jews, The, 154
Treatise on the Gods, 158
Turkey in the Straw, 80
Twain, Mark, 157
Two Black Sheep, 162

UNCHASTENED *Woman, The,* 15
Union Square, 80
Unpossessed, The, 81
Untermeyer, Louis, 128, 129, 130, 131, 133, quoted, 136, 137, 146
Up Bayou Dubac, 162
Upstream, 189

VALLEY *Forge,* 4, 51
Vanity and Some Sables, 162
Variations, 158

WAGNER, Charles, 128
Waiting for Lefty, 4, 9, 12, 27, 35, 36, 41, 43, 49, 114, 167, 176, 197
Waltz in Goose Step, 197
Wards of Liberty, 159
War Goes On, The, 187
War Song, The, 74
Wasserman, Jakob, 5
Water Carrier, The, 176
Wave, The, 159
Weachter, Theodore, 193
Weavers, The, 7
Wood, Clement, 123
Weidman, Jerome, 79, 91
Wellman, Rita, 90
Werfel, Franz, 2, 35
We, The People, 9, 26, 27, 30, 31, 167, 195
Wexley, John, 1, 2, 12, 15, 168
Whitman, Walt, 122, 125
Whittier, John, 156
Who Is Who, 199
Whole Truth, The, 150
Wilde, Oscar, 36, 56, 123
Willard, Samuel, 150
Wine of Choice, 10, 57
Winslow, Thyra, S. 79
Winterset, 7, 72, 172, 185
Wit and the Unconscious, 54
Witness to Our Lord, A, 150
Wise, Isaac, M., 123
Witte Arrives, 88
Wolf, Friedrich, 44, 160, 179, 197
Wolfe, Thomas, 177, 178
Wood, Charles, E. S., 104
Woodcutter's House, The, 96, 97, 107
Worshippers, 87
Wylie, I. A. R., 162

YEKL, 84
Yellow Jack, 171, 172

246

INDEX

Yezierska, Anzia, 79, 85, 119, 176
Yoke of the Torah, The, 83
Yoshe Kalb, 176
You Can't Take It with You, 10, 15, 22, 24
Young, Stark, 32, 39, 100
Youth Grows Old, 131

ZANGWILL, Israel, 175
Zola, 187
Zugsmith, Leane, 79
Zukofsky, Louis, 128
Zweig, Arnold, 190
Zweig, Stefan, 2